How to Buil

Sci-Fi Model Spacecraft

RICHARD MARMO

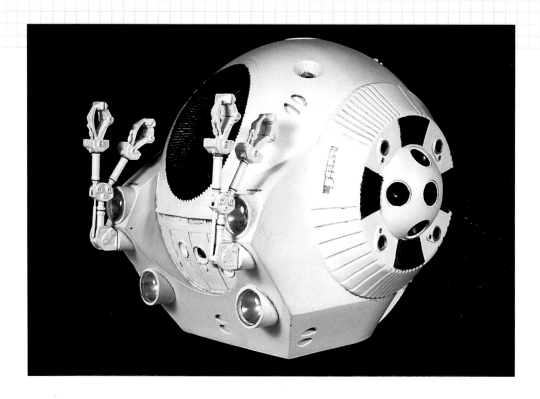

specialtypress
PUBLISHERS AND WHOLESALERS

Published by

Specialty Press Publishers and Wholesalers
39966 Grand Avenue
North Branch, MN 55056
United States of America
(651) 277-1400 / (800) 895-4585
http://www.specialtypress.com

Distributed in the UK and Europe by

Midland Publishing
4 Watling Drive
Hinckley LE10 3EY, England
Tel: 01455 233 747 Fax: 01455 233 737
http://www.midlandcountiessuperstore.com

ISBN 1-58007-064-7

Front Cover: *The Star Wars universe is full of interesting spacecraft – two of the lesser-known ones are the Empire's TIE Bomber and the Rebel Alliance B-wing. They may not have had much screen time, but both ships are available in kit form. Here they're shown duking it out in front of galactic nebula NGC 3603 (see Page 4 for more info on this Hubble Space Telescope image). (Ship photos by author, background courtesy NASA, photo montage by Dennis R. Jenkins)*

Back Cover, Upper Left: *Sci-fi Models aren't just Star Wars and Star Trek though, as shown by the diverse grouping on the back cover. Here, Solvaset is being used to snug down the decals on Glencoe's Lunar Lander kit.*

Back Cover, Upper Right: *This finished Monogram kit of the Space Taxi is a prime example of how we thought space travel was going to be in 1959. Reality is a lot different, isn't it?*

Back Cover, Lower Left: *The author applying a final clear coat to the B-wing's graphics*

Back Cover, Lower Right: *A Klingon Bird of Prey perched atop a Vulcan landscape diorama.*

Title Page: *One of the more interesting and intricate resin kits on the market is of the space pod from 2001: A Space Odyssey. A complete build-up of this kit is shown in Chapter 7, where you'll learn some advanced techniques for working with resin kits.*

How to Build
Sci-Fi Model Spacecraft

TABLE OF CONTENTS

What has this got to do with science fiction? Well, nothing. But it gives us a chance to describe the image used on the cover. In this stunning picture of the giant galactic nebula NGC 3603, the crisp resolution of NASA's Hubble Space Telescope captures various stages of the life cycle of stars in one single view. To the upper right of center is the evolved blue supergiant called Sher 25. The star has a unique circumstellar ring of glowing gas that is a galactic twin to the famous ring around the supernova 1987A. The grayish-bluish color of the ring and the bipolar outflows (blobs to the upper right and lower left of the star) indicates the presence of processed (chemically enriched) material. Near the center of the view is a so-called starburst cluster dominated by young, hot, Wolf-Rayet stars and early O-type stars. A torrent of ionizing radiation and fast stellar winds from these massive stars has blown a large cavity around the cluster. To the lower left of the cluster are two compact, tadpole-shaped emission nebulae. Similar structures were found by Hubble in Orion, and have been interpreted as gas and dust evaporation from possibly protoplanetary disks (proplyds). The "proplyds" in NGC 3603 are 5 to 10 times larger in size and correspondingly also more massive. This single view nicely illustrates the entire stellar life cycle of stars, starting with the Bok globules and giant gaseous pillars, followed by circumstellar disks, and progressing to evolved massive stars in the young starburst cluster. The blue supergiant with its ring and bipolar outflow marks the end of the life cycle. This true-color picture was taken on March 5, 1999 with the Wide Field Planetary Camera 2. (NASA)

How to Build Sci-Fi Model Spacecraft

How to Build
Sci-Fi Model
Spacecraft

DEDICATION AND AUTHOR'S BIO

DEDICATION

This one's for Tony Weddel, one of the best aviation artists you'll ever hope to find. With that said, every other category of art he's ever done is just as good. Doubt me? Then check out his editorial ink sketch in Chapter 1 and his dramatic UFO print in Chapter 4. Am I partial to his work? You bet! But I think you'll agree my opinion is justified.

AUTHOR'S BIO

I was born December 10, 1942, in Memphis, Tennessee. I've spent most of my life in Texas, including 8 1/2 years in El Paso and since 1961 in Ft. Worth. During 1943-1944, I lived a few months in Jackson Heights, New York — literally a couple of blocks from La Guardia Airport. My mother loved aircraft and would take me down to watch the planes take off. I suppose that's when aviation got in my blood, and it's never left. A love for aviation segued quite naturally into aerospace and then science fiction/fantasy. Why not? Regardless of the subject, everything moved through air and/or space.

I also began reading at a very early age, coming up on the classic sci-

ence-fiction writers such as Isaac Asimov, Arthur C. Clarke, Poul Anderson, Phillip K. Dick, Robert A. Heinlein, James Blish, A.E. Van Vogt, H.G. Wells, Jules Verne, and all the rest of the great science-fiction masters. Combine that with classic horror and science-fiction movies of the 1940s and 1950s, radio drama (yes, they used to have dramatic programming on radio), and with such early

TV programs as *Tom Corbett Space Cadet*, *Rocky Jones Space Ranger*, the original *Twilight Zone*, and *Science Fiction Theatre*, I couldn't have avoided developing a love for science fiction if I'd wanted to.

Thanks to bad health as a child, my parents started buying me model kits when I was around six or seven to keep me occupied and to give me something to do besides read. It started with stick and tissue, rubber-band-powered models, then the early Aurora plastic kits, and I was hooked. 1967 saw me begin making a living (or trying to) as a freelance writer/professional model builder. This came about as the result of my being encouraged by my parents, getting progressively deeper in the hobby (including building models of just about any subject), becoming a founding member of the International Plastic Modelers' Society/USA (IPMS/USA #2), and discovering that I had a talent for writing and communication. I've been at it ever since, and can't imagine doing anything else.

I'm single, and I share my home with a 1/2 German Shepherd, 1/2 Collie dog named Max. I adopted him when he was a year old, and he was already named, so don't blame that on me!

How to Build
Sci-Fi Model Spacecraft

Ask someone to define science fiction and you'll get almost as many answers as there are people. If nothing else, that proves that most people don't understand the genre.

Science fiction, oversimplified in the extreme, is the projection of any given situation to its logical or extreme conclusion by asking a simple two-word question. What if? What if we could go to the Moon? What if Mars was populated? What if the Earth was hollow? What if robots had souls? The possibilities are endless. Politics, science, population control, euthanasia as government policy (Isaac Asimov tackled that question in his novel *Pebble In The Sky*), aliens hunting humans (the movie *Predator*), and so on. Time travel and manipulation of the space-time continuum is another aspect. Biology out of control is another.

Some would say that *Star Wars* and *Star Trek* are science fiction, though *Star Wars* is actually space opera.

Others would point to the stories written by Jules Verne. Then there's the *John Carter of Mars* series (romance/adventure in a science fiction setting) that was written by Edgar Rice Burroughs. Contrast that concept with his hollow- or inner-Earth books. *Dracula* by Bram Stoker, *Frankenstein* by Mary Shelly, and the *Lord of the Rings* series by Tolkien each fall into the horror/monster/fantasy area. Believe it or not, *Gulliver's Travels* qualifies as science fiction or science fantasy, even though it was a rather biting satire of English society during Jonathan Swift's lifetime.

War of the Worlds, by H.G. Wells, sent the entire U.S. into a panic when it was performed as a series of news bulletins on radio in 1939. Martians had invaded us! UFOs/flying saucers moved to the forefront in 1947 as the result of a flying saucer crash outside of Roswell, New Mexico. Originally acknowledged by authorities as an extraterrestrial spacecraft, it was later explained away as a weather balloon. That event created separate camps of believers and debunkers, leaving a mystery that continues to this day.

Hard-core science fiction takes known events and/or technology and projects it to its ultimate conclusion. *Lucifer's Hammer*, for example, was a

If you can find it, this kit of the Adamski UFO produced by now defunct UFO Technologies is one of the finest quality resin kits I've ever seen.

novel that dealt with the impact of a large meteor on Earth. The same basic theme appeared in the films *Armageddon* and *Deep Impact*. And we're all familiar with *2001: A Space Odyssey*.

Science fiction (along with fantasy and horror sub-categories) has been a part of cinema since the days of silent movies. *Nosferatu* was probably the first movie version of *Dracula*. There are movies on vampires, monsters such as *Frankenstein*, and on and on. Early television brought such wonders as *Buck Rogers*, *Tom Corbett Space Cadet*, *Rocky Jones Space Ranger*, and others.

Science Fiction Theatre and the classic *Twilight Zone* captured the hearts and minds of millions. Series of more recent vintage include *Star Trek*, *Star Trek: The Next Generation*, *Star Trek: Voyager*, *Deep Space 9*, *Space: Above and Beyond*, *Battlestar Galactica*, *Babylon 5*, *The X-Files*, and more.

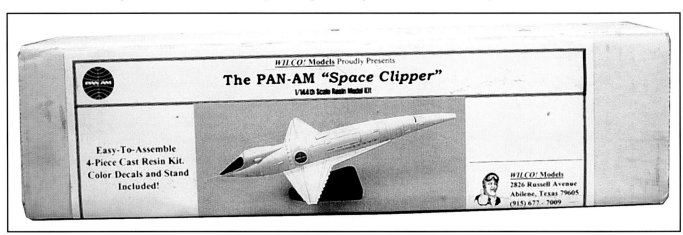

Wilco! Models offers a number of excellent science-fiction resin kits, such as this Pan American "Space Clipper" from 2001: A Space Odyssey.

Remember the movie Destination Moon *and the Spaceship* Luna? *An offering from Wilco! Models enable you to have one of your own.*

In case you're thinking that there hasn't been a lot of schlock mixed in, guess again. For every good book, comic book, film, or TV show that fell into the science fiction category, there were many — most likely dozens of— others that ranged from so-so to unintentionally funny to downright ridiculous. Probably the apex of ridiculous/hysterically funny 'science-fiction' films was *Attack of the Killer Tomatoes*. These 'creatures' were giant, people-size tomatoes that rolled in hot pursuit of their victims, finally gobbling them up with a loud "Gulp!" How the actors got through their scenes with a straight face is beyond me!

Science fiction has had its ups and downs, in part because many people erroneously think of it as strictly imagination with no basis in reality. Others simply don't bother — or are afraid — to open their minds to possibilities that may exist beyond their immediate vicinity. However, if you keep an open mind and enjoy asking 'what if?' you'll find science fiction in all of its forms to be richly rewarding and intellectually stimulating.

When it comes to building science-fiction models, the possibilities are equally wide-ranging. Everything from the serious to the humorous is grist for the modeler. If you wish, you can concentrate on replicating equipment, figures, or settings from TV shows or films. How about a collection of UFO designs, though most would have to be scratch-built? The possibilities are nearly endless.

That, in turn, leads to a problem when trying to determine the focus of a book on science-fiction modeling. If I'd

tried to cover every sub-category, a thousand pages wouldn't have been enough. So, after much thought, I finally decided to limit this book to spacecraft and vehicles. Even that required me to establish some strict boundaries. For instance, you won't find any mention of the *Seaview* or Nemo's *Nautilus* in these pages. Vehicles they are, but they're limited to water operation. There are also quite a number of surface vehicles (science-fiction versions of armored vehicles) but they're not here either — except for one.

Because of the popularity of such TV series as the original *Star Trek* and its numerous spin-offs, *Babylon 5*, the five *Star Wars* films (with one more to come as of this writing), and such classics as *2001: A Space Odyssey*, I decided to concentrate on spaceships and vehicles. Essentially, this book is devoted to craft that move through space. After that explanation, some of you may wonder why I've included a model of H.G. Wells's Martian War Machine and the armored personnel carrier (APC) from the movie *Aliens*, but it's perfectly logical if you stop to think about it.

The Martian War Machine is a hybrid in a sense, being a cross between an aircraft and a tank. While not a spacecraft, it *does* operate in the air and

is capable of protecting its occupant in space, making it a vehicle/semi-spaceship. Besides, if you've ever seen the 1957 movie *The War of the Worlds*, there's something mesmerizing about that beast floating over the landscape, destroying everything in its path.

As for the *Aliens* APC, it was transported to the planet's surface by a spacecraft's shuttle for use by the troops to make their initial incursion. Despite some futurists' opinion to the contrary, there will always be a place for wheeled, armored vehicles in combat.

However, nothing that you've just read means anything *if you can't successfully build a model of that science-fiction subject you're lusting over*. That, in a nutshell, is the sole purpose of this book; to present a variety of construction projects in a way that will allow you to acquire or improve the skills needed to produce models that you can be proud of.

Whether a kit is manufactured in resin, styrene, vacuform, or multimedia, two things are required to create a quality model: constant improvement of your model-building skills, and patience. This book is intended to help improve your skills. Patience is entirely up to you.

Now turn the page. We've got a lot of building to do.

Styrene-kit manufacturers have produced quite a number of science-fiction kits. One of the later kits from AMT was Anakin's Podracer from Star Wars: Episode I.

Decades ago, Aurora produced a kit of the Space Coupe that was straight out of the Dick Tracy comic strip. Polar Lights has considerately repopped the kit. If you never bought one of the originals or didn't know it existed, now you can.

It's not just recent TV shows that have spawned spaceship kits. The Eagle I from Space: 1999 was kitted by MPC/Fundimensions.

CHAPTER 1

How to Build Sci-Fi Model Spacecraft

TOOLS, PAINT, AND GLUE

Whether your models are kits, kit-based, or scratch-built, there's one great truism that you'll have to deal with. Namely, that you can't build anything with only your teeth and toenails! Like it or not, you're going to have to have a certain amount of equipment. How much you'll need depends on you and the model you're building. There are, however, certain basic items that you simply cannot do without.

So, what tools are you going to need? First and foremost: knife handles, a selection of replacement blades, sprue cutters, a couple of tweezers, and scissors. Other essentials are cement and paint.

KNIVES

I'll grant you that a knife is a knife, but that's not always true where the modeler is concerned. I knew a modeler who whittled a nuclear submarine out of a pair of 2 x 4s with nothing more than a pocketknife, but most of us aren't going to get very far trying to build a model with a jackknife, switchblade, or mini-Bowie. What you want is a hobby knife with replaceable blades. X-Acto is, of course, the best-known manufacturer, to the point that X-Acto has become a synonym for "hobby knife."

Mascot, Excel, and Testors (along with many other manufacturers) all offer their own. Some handles have a smooth surface; others are ribbed or knurled on the surface to provide a better grip. Then there's the question of shape. Most are cylindrical, which allows them to easily roll off your bench and wind up sticking point first in areas where you *really* don't want them. That problem has been addressed by some manufacturers with the creation of triangular or octagonal handles. Others add an odd-shaped butt-cap.

And if you want something that absolutely *won't* roll, take a look at the flat scalpel handles that are offered.

While the good old #1 handle with #11 blade is the standard (regardless of brand), be aware that there's also #2 and #3 handles. The #2 is used for the larger, wider blades while #3 is designed for saw blades and gouges. You'll also find two different sizes of

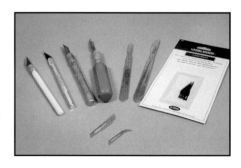

Here's a mixed bag of knives, scalpels, and replacement blades from Excel, X-Acto, and Testors. Left to right, the picture shows a plastic-handled #1; standard metal #1, #2, and #3; two sizes of scalpels; and a package of #11 replacement blades. In the foreground are a couple of different scalpel blade styles.

scalpel handles, again depending on the particular blade being used.

Since knife handles aren't particularly useful without blades, spend some time at the hobby shop or in the pages of a hobby tool catalog browsing through the blade selection. Besides the #11 blade, which you'll use more than any other, add a selection of other blade styles to your toolbox. Start with a couple or three that you think you'll use, and then add others as your experience grows. The same comments apply to scalpel blades, which include some truly odd-looking curved and hooked styles.

Most hobby blades (such as the #11) come in packs of multiple blades. For example, Testors markets them in a blister pack with 5 blades to a card. Other companies put 'em in tubes as well. Some, such as Excel, offer larger quantities for those who need or want to buy them in bulk — up to 100 in a single box.

Just as there's more than one kind or size of handle, there's more than one kind of blade — and I don't mean size or shape. Most blades are made from carbon steel, with the quality varying. This results in some blades that dull faster than others. You'll also find that the blades can be sharpened again if you wish. Considering the low cost of replacement blades, why bother?

One other type of blade (available from Excel) deserves mention here. It's made of stainless steel. They cost a little more, but they also last a lot longer, particularly the tip. If you do a lot of detail cutting where the sharpness of the tip is important to you, it wouldn't hurt to keep one of your spare handles (You *do* have more than one, don't you?) loaded with a #11 stainless steel blade.

What kind of hobby knife should you have? At least one #1 handle w/#11 blade. Beyond that, it's whatever works for you. It also wouldn't hurt to keep a box of Band-Aids on hand. Knives, by their very nature, are *sharp* (I know, I'm stating the obvious.), and it's an absolute certainty that you'll wind up drawing blood (yours) from time to time. Of course, the safety police insist on warning you that you could get hurt, so be sure to push the knife *away* from you at all times. Nice idea — but impractical. That method won't cut you, but it also eliminates the control that's needed for delicate model building. Just be careful, use common sense, and keep the Band-Aids handy.

Sprue Cutters

Sprue cutters are nothing more than a variation on small diagonal cutters. They're designed for the express purpose of achieving a close, clean cut

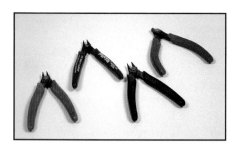

Many companies offer sprue cutters. The three shown here are from Xuron, X-Acto, and Testors. On the far right is a pair of hard wire cutters offered by Xuron. They make short work of smaller diameter music wire, instead of the wire making short work of your diagonal cutters.

when removing kit parts from the sprue, and they do an excellent job. It's quite possible to remove a part so cleanly that you'll need nothing more than a couple of swipes with fine sandpaper to eliminate the last vestige of sprue from it.

Excel, Xuron, and Testors are three of the better-known companies that produce quality sprue cutters.

Tweezers/Scissors

Tweezers exist in more shapes and sizes than you think. There are the ordinary eyebrow tweezers that reside in every medicine cabinet and have been swiped – um-m-m, borrowed — by every model builder who's ever lived, frequently at serious risk of life and limb from the ire of their original owners.

However, browse through hobby shops and a variety of catalogs and you

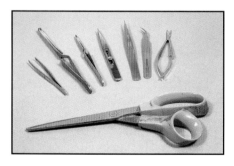

Six different styles of tweezers barely scratch the surface of what's available to choose from. On the right is a nifty pair of squeeze-handled scissors (squissors) that'll get you into tight spots on decal sheets. And never forget the familiar conventional scissors.

find out how extensive your choices are. Conventional tweezers of varying lengths, cross-action tweezers that can double as clamps, bent-tip tweezers, and more. Some have blunt, square tips, others are tapered to a sharp point and designed to pick up items so small that they border on invisible (human hairs and cat hairs, for example). High-dollar tweezers designed for the electronics industry are probably capable of grabbing an individual dust mote — if you could see it!

Along with a selection of tweezers, you also need to include at least one pair of scissors so you'll have a way to cut decal sheets. As to what size, this is a case of whatever works for you. Some modelers can literally perform magic with a standard size pair of Fiskars that you find in fabric centers. Others want the smallest pair they can find so they don't interfere with their vision.

Other Tools

Knives, sprue cutters, and tweezers are not the only tools you'll wind up using, just the ones you'll use most often. What additional tools will wind up on your bench will be the result of your specific requirements. It's a certainty that a variety of clamps will accumulate, and these can be anything from wooden spring-type clothespins to office-supply clips. Rubber bands are invaluable. If you plan on building wood display bases or Plexiglas dust covers, the larger specialized clamps intended for woodworkers will be needed.

If it'll hold it 'til it dries — it's a clamp. Clothespins, rubber bands, woodworking clamps, and office-supply spring clamps are just a few of the methods I've used over the years.

Will you be creating dioramas that contain complete or partial walls of buildings? Then you'll want a few squares to keep the walls truly vertical. They're also handy when it comes to getting a true right angle when the wall turns a corner. And they're essential while cutting lumber for a wood base or frame.

Squares come in all sizes, including some so small you can barely pick them up. Materials vary as well, though most are metal. If you look closely at the photo, you'll see three squares, though the one on the left is nearly invisible. It's made from clear plastic, while the others use conventional metal.

Another important item, unless you're planning on using your Mk. I eyeball computer for everything, is a way to measure dimensions. This can be anything from a regular 12-inch ruler to a set of digital calipers. Me? I happen to be very partial to a six-inch steel scale with tenths- and hundredths-of-an-inch divisions. The short length makes it very easy to get into restricted areas and the decimal divisions allow precise calculations. When I need even more accuracy, or to measure something round, like tubing, I couldn't do without my dial calipers.

One other thing that you will find to be nearly a constant companion is sandpaper. Regardless of the material — plastic, resin, wood, or whatever —

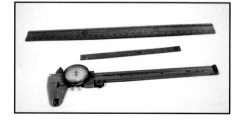

Bottom to top are my favorite dial calipers, six-inch scale calibrated in 10ths and 100ths, and an ordinary 12-inch ruler.

you'll wind up with a healthy selection of sandpaper. Experience and the specific project you're working on will determine the particular grits that you'll need. I try to keep a variety on hand so that I don't have to run down to the hardware store at the last minute.

Finally, there are the power tools. These range all the way from the Dremel MultiPro that's a virtual necessity, to small bench-top machinists' lathes. And, if your interests lie in the very large (meaning six- or eight-foot) spacecraft models, fancy wood bases, sophisticated display cases to house your collection, or even the construction of a room addition to your house for use as a shop, consider full-blown multi-purpose tools such as the Shopsmith Mk. V.

VISION AIDS

It's great to have all these specialized tools sitting expectantly next to a high dollar, multi-media kit that you're all excited to dig into. However, if you can't *see* what you're working on, all is for naught. Depending on your subject of choice, a particular kit may have parts or details that you can barely see with the naked eye, never mind being able to handle or paint. Unless you have the eyesight of an eagle, you're going to need some kind of magnifier.

All kinds of bench-top lamps are available that are designed around magnifying lenses. They work, and if you like 'em, that's fine. But they have a tendency to be a little cumbersome and, depending on the particular model, they can get in the way. Headband magnifiers are, in my opinion, a far better way to go. Again, there are a wide variety of styles available, and they all work. I happen to be especially partial to the tried 'n' true Opti-Visor. It has a wide range of lenses available, it's comfortable, it can be easily used over eyeglasses, and it's eco-

nomically priced. While it took a few decades, I've worn one out and am now working on my second one!

Do you *have* to choose an Opti-Visor? Not at all. There are plenty of choices, with everyone trying to build a better mousetrap, so to speak. You can even get slightly simplified surgical-quality magnifiers that carry a price tag of several hundred dollars! It's simply a matter of what you and your wallet prefer.

ADHESIVES

CEMENT

You'd think that glue is glue, but that's not so. And because science-fiction models have a habit of showing up in a variety of materials (frequently all in the same kit, making it a true multi-media product), you can't just pick up a single bottle of cement and expect it to work on everything. Let's do a quick

A selection of sandpaper ranging from 100 grit to Crocus Cloth is essential.

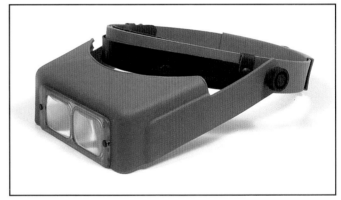

If you can't see it, you can't build it. This Opti-Visor solves that problem quite handily. Wear glasses? No problem. It works over them as well.

Some power tools are a luxury, but this Dremel MultiPro Model 395 variable-speed tool with one of their diamond-coated cutting wheels is an absolute necessity.

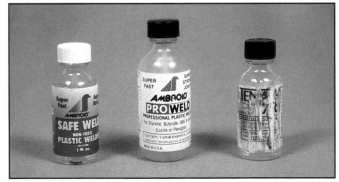

Here are three types of liquid cement for styrene kits. On the left is Ambroid's Safe Weld non-toxic cement, which has a citrus odor and works quite well. Then there's their standard Ambroid ProWeld (my personal favorite), and a bottle of Tenax 7R.

rundown on what glues/cements work where.

Styrene

Except for the snap-together variety, a plastic kit will never be anything more than a collection of loose parts without some way to hold them together. So what do you use? Since we're joining plastic to plastic, it's fairly obvious that some kind of plastic cement will be called for. However, there's more than one kind of plastic cement. Visit your friendly hobby shop and you'll find this out in short order.

Tube cement, such as that made by Revell and Testors (among others), is thickened plastic cement. Packaged in a squeeze tube, it's generally easy to handle, stays where you put it, and has a relatively quick drying time. Liquid cement, frequently referred to as plastic welder, approximates the consistency of water, and is marketed under such names as Weld-On #3, Micro-Weld, Tenax-7R, and Ambroid ProWeld, to mention only a few. It's usually packaged in one- or two-ounce bottles. Testors also offers very good liquid cement that seems to combine features of both tube and liquid.

While tube cement is applied by simply running the nozzle along the part's edge where you want the glue, liquid cement requires a totally different and — to my mind — more effective approach. In order to properly use liquid cement, parts to be joined are held in contact with each other, the cement being applied to the seam with a brush or draftsman's ruling pen. Doing so permits the cement to flow along the joint through capillary action, also resulting in a very rapid drying time.

The reason for the differences between the two cement types lies in the way they work. Tube cement acts as an adhesive joining two separate parts. Liquid cement, or welder, works by dissolving the surface of each plastic part, permitting the surfaces to intermingle and form a 'welded' bond. In effect, the two parts become one.

Which kind should you use? That will be strictly up to you. I've used 'em all, from the old Revell "S" Type in the 1950s, to the latest liquid welders. They all have their strong points, though I no longer use anything but liquid for styrene construction, and am *very* fond of Ambroid ProWeld.

MIXED MEDIA

There are a couple of other types of cements you need to be familiar with if you're going to tackle conversions or garage kits made from resin: cyanoacrylates and epoxies.

Mixed-media kits combine parts made from more than one kind of material. For example, styrene, resin, and photo-etch brass may all appear in the same kit and need to be glued to each other. Plain old styrene cement won't do the job. For that, you need something different.

Cyanoacrylates

Cyanoacrylates, familiar to most people as 'superglues' and frequently referred to by modelers as CAs, cure in 10 to 45 seconds and are invaluable for installing parts that fit at odd angles or must be held under tension until the cement sets. They also do a superb job of gluing your fingers together!

CAs used to be available only one way — water thin. Because the stuff ran literally everywhere and people

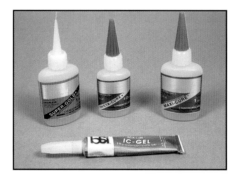

When working with non-styrene parts, you can't do without cyanoacrylates. Four different formulas from Bob Smith Industries are seen here, including a tube of their fabulous IC-GEL.

tried to use it like normal cement, more than a few things wound up being cemented together that shouldn't have been. Hospital emergency rooms can tell fascinating war stories about anatomical combinations created with CA that were previously thought to be physically impossible. Be that as it may, today there are so many formulations from thin to super-thick that you need a program to keep them straight. Bob Smith Industries offers a line of CA that I am *extremely* partial to. There are also spray-on accelerators to speed things up even more — as if we needed to. With the right combination of products, it's even possible to build up fillets, fairings, and contours.

Incidentally, many modelers today are even using CAs as their only cement for assembling styrene kits. Not a choice I'd make, but if it works for you, there's no reason not to.

EPOXIES

Epoxies are a two-part adhesive that when combined, create the final product through chemical reaction. Depending on the particular formula, cure time runs from 5 minutes to 20 minutes or more.

Just like CAs, epoxies are available in a wide variety of formulas. Everything from syrup consistency liquid to putty sticks and ribbons. Each has their uses; it's up to the model builder to determine which is best for a particular need.

Regardless of the variety in question — and whether liquid or solid in form — all epoxy is comprised of a resin and catalyst (or hardener) that are mixed together to form the final product. Once the two parts are thoroughly mixed (or kneaded, in the case of epoxy putty), it's simply a matter of getting it

Epoxies have their place as well. While most take the form of two-part honey-consistency liquid, others, such as Milliput, are formed into strips of putty that are kneaded together for activation.

About the only lacquers most modelers will ever use are clear coats, available in both spray cans and bottles for airbrushing.

PAINT

Whenever you build models, regardless of the material involved, you eventually come to the question of replicating a realistic finish. When it comes to plastic models, and, yes, resin is a form of plastic, one absolute statement can be made. Unless a component is intended to be clear, paint everything. Attempts have been made to mold plastic in realistic colors so that no painting is necessary. Nice idea, but no cigar. Some manufacturers have created pre-*finished* mixed-media kits, meaning the parts have been pre-*paint-*

Enamel paints have been produced under just about every label imaginable. From left to right are bottles of Model Master, Humbrol, Floquil, JMH Combat Colors (test marketed but never produced), Testors, and Pactra. In the background are cans of Model Master and Floquil thinner.

ed for you at the factory. That's a horse of a different color. I've seen pre-finished die-cast car/truck kits that were so well done that you couldn't tell the plastic parts from the metal — and everything looked like painted metal.

However, for kits such as those in this book, regardless of how economical or expensive the kits are, you'll obtain the best results if you paint everything except the clear parts. Besides enabling you to eliminate any last vestige of seams, there's a far more important reason — realism. Plastic, regardless of color, has a slightly translucent surface. This means that light is reflected from a thousandths-of-an-inch or less below the model's surface. A painted surface prevents that, resulting in the proper solid, or 'hard,' appearance that's so important to a realistic finish.

There are basically three types of paints that modelers will deal with: lacquers, enamels, and acrylics. If you're the adventurous sort, there are also Urethanes, Epoxies, Water Colors, and Artist's Oils to name only a few. Most of them you'll never go near unless you have a very specific requirement. Artist's Oils are a special case. Many modelers use them to obtain certain types of weathering effects. They're particularly popular among many whose passion is the building and painting of figures.

LACQUERS

As far as most denizens of the model world are concerned, their exposure to lacquer probably is limited to lacquer clear coats such as Model Master Gloss, Semi-Gloss, and Flat Lacquer Overcoats. There's still a fairly extensive line of lacquer colors available in spray cans that are familiar to the automotive modelers.

ENAMELS

Enamel paints, if you're over 30, are what we all grew up with. They're petroleum or solvent based and require a compatible thinner made from petroleum distillates. In other words — the real stuff. Model Master offers an extensive line, much of it being marketed by Fed Standard numbers for the benefit of the aerospace enthusiasts. Then there's a variety of primary and automotive colors under the Testors label, and a wide range of railroad colors from Floquil. England makes a contribution with a line of enamels from Humbrol. Some of these brands have been around for decades. As a matter of fact, I was using the little square bottles of Testors in the late 1950s (at the incredibly high price of 10 cents per bottle). Believe it or not, I still have some that I bought in the 1960s, *and the stuff is still perfectly good!*

ACRYLICS

While acrylics for modelers can be traced all the way back to Poly-S, they've only recently (in the last decade or so) developed a widespread following. Part of the reason their popularity has increased is the fact that they're non-toxic, have little if any odor, and can be thinned and/or cleaned up with water.

That's all well and good, but some of them are so thin that they're difficult to hand brush. When you do need to thin them, some thin with water, while others require alcohol or the manufacturer's special thinner. Most clean up with water. You do want to make sure you don't let the stuff dry in your airbrush, because once it's dry, you almost have to sandblast it to remove it.

Is this to say that acrylic paints are not a good choice? Not at all. There's a place for all types: lacquer, enamel, *and* acrylic. It's simply a matter of learning which type will produce the best results for your needs.

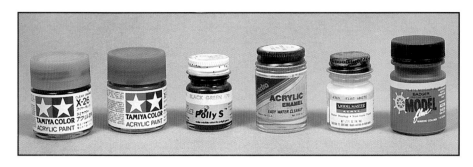

More and more modelers are moving to acrylics, and the choices are equally wide ranging. Again from the left, Tamiya, Polly-S (now replaced with Polly Scale), Pactra Acrylic, Model Master Acrylic, and Badger, to name only a few.

compressors that can run to as much as one to two thousand dollars.

What I've just said doesn't mean that you have to spend a fortune. You can get a nice basic airbrush set, complete with canned air, for as little as $30. Then you simply climb up the ladder as your skills increase.

WHAT ABOUT YOUR LUNGS?

With liquid cement, CA, epoxy, enamel, and lacquer paint; if you're beginning to think your workbench is taking on all the appearances of a mad scientist's laboratory, you're not far off. Then there's sanding dust from plastic and resin components.

PAINT APPLICATION METHODS

Paint doesn't do your model a lick of good if it just sits in the bottle, which means you have to have a way to apply it. Generally speaking, there are three.

SPRAY CAN

First and simplest is the good ol' spray can. The method works and it really isn't a bad choice for monochrome schemes. Even multi-color schemes can be done with spray cans if you're willing to do a lot of masking. Rattlecans are particularly useful when it comes to priming a model or applying clear coats.

PAINT BRUSH

Next up is a method that's been around essentially unchanged for cen-

turies — the paintbrush. No matter your preferred method of painting, you won't be able to avoid the use of a conventional brush. Fine details can't be done any other way. For the most part, you'll find the sizes from 2 or 3 on down to around 15/0 or 25/0 to be the most useful.

AIRBRUSH

As your experience grows, you'll find yourself eventually moving up to what has become a virtual fixture in model building — the airbrush. Airbrushes are delightful tools that range all the way from very low cost designs that are little more than controlled spray cans, to extremely sophisticated tools with a price tag in the hundreds of dollars. The air sources are equally wide ranging. On the low end is canned air and adapters for inner tubes. At the opposite extreme are

And then there are airbrushes. From bottom to top: a basic single-action Aztek A270, a double-action Aztek A470, a double-action Rich AB-100, a double-action Badger Model 175 Crescendo, a double-action Badger Model 360, and a top of the line double-action Badger Sotar 20/20.

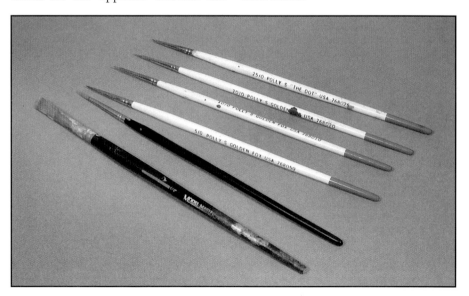

If you have agreed to disagree with conventional brushes and you don't have an airbrush, excellent work can be done with spray cans — with practice. Rattlecans are also frequently the best way to shoot primer or solid base colors. Brands range all the way from Krylon to Model Master, Bondo, and more.

Bottled paint requires paintbrushes. You'll probably wind up with the range of sizes seen here, but the specific model you're working on will control your choice.

However, all it takes is a little common sense and reasonable precautions to build models without endangering your health.

Granted, you can build models in a closed room that's filled with so much floating dust and paint vapor that you need a flashlight to cut through the fog, but it sure ain't smart. If nothing else, a spark at the wrong time can set off a

Airbrushes need air, which generally means a compressor of some sort. This Aztek AC200 is reasonably priced, reliable, and it comes with a pressure regulator and a water trap. It will serve the needs of most modelers for years.

dust explosion, moving your model building activities to the other side of the pearly gates! Even if you avoid that event, spend a few years inhaling those kinds of particles, and you're liable to learn more about emphysema than you ever wanted to know.

When it comes to the fumes and vapors emitted by paints and glue (even if you can't smell it), some decent ventilation will solve most of the problems. If you're sitting close to a window, open it. Install an exhaust fan. Invest in a spray booth.

Sanding dust can be handled with a particle or dust mask that you can find at your local Home Depot or neighborhood hardware store. Read the labels, because some will protect against smaller particles than others. As long as you don't insist on inhaling deeply while your face is three inches above a cloud of dust, just about any of them will offer good protection.

Some modelers, and our friendly safety police, would have you wearing a double-element respirator, safety goggles, full face shield *over* the gog-

From left to right are hardware variety particle masks, a surgical mask, and a double-element respirator.

gles, hearing protectors, a protective apron, and elbow length gloves before you even open the box, never mind actually start building the model. Aside from the fact that we'd wind up looking like a worker in a NASA clean room, that's more than a little overkill!

Ordinary, everyday precautions will keep you out of trouble and still allow you to participate in the joys and pleasures of model building. That's the approach I've taken for the last 50+ years and I still have my lungs.

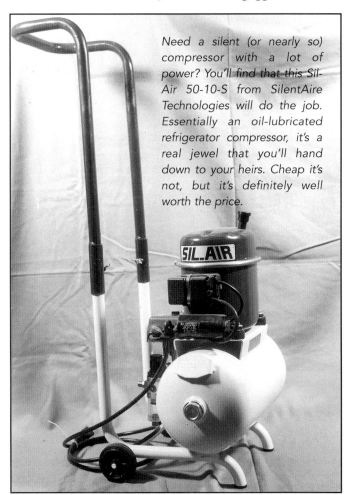

Need a silent (or nearly so) compressor with a lot of power? You'll find that this Sil-Air 50-10-S from SilentAire Technologies will do the job. Essentially an oil-lubricated refrigerator compressor, it's a real jewel that you'll hand down to your heirs. Cheap it's not, but it's definitely well worth the price.

The pen of Tony Weddel depicts what we model builders would look like if we followed all the recommendations of the safety police! This is model building?

CHAPTER 2

How to Build Sci-Fi Model Spacecraft

STYRENE KITS

Prior to the early/mid 1970s, just about all science fiction/fantasy/ spacecraft kits were produced from injected styrene plastic. Several factors were involved. Tooling costs were relatively cheap (the tools were even made in the U.S.) and the raw material for plastic — oil — was practically being given away. Doubt me? Consider, then, that gasoline was selling for 19 to 27 *cents* per gallon. Moderate size kits were being priced at $.79 - $.98 cents each, and large, fairly complex kits wore price tags of $6.98 - $9.98.

But, as so frequently happens, things change. By the mid 1990s, we'd all reached the point of considering $20+ for an AMT Enterprise kit to be very reasonable. Granted, the increase in oil was a major contributor, but so was tooling costs. They were rising so precipitously that manufacturers began going overseas for their tooling. And let's not forget the truly exorbitant license fees being demanded by the film

studios so you could have the privilege of producing a model. Then there was the cottage industry.

Thanks to the one-man, part-time companies, vacuform and urethane resin kits, along with conversions and detail components, have given the science fiction enthusiast the ability to create models that would have been impossible just a few years ago. But these types of products are labor intensive, which translates into expensive. Now you see spacecraft kits offered by cottage industry companies that frequently carry prices of $60 to $200 and up — sometimes *way* up.

Before you panic, keep in mind that you can still find repops of old kits at very reasonable prices. Also, if you're willing to have a little patience, you can find companies that buy up never-built kit collections and offer them at decent prices. It's also possible to find some very good buys on E-Bay. Remember, just because the prices of some kits are bid up into the strato-

sphere doesn't mean you have to match them. There are plenty of good kits with faded or damaged boxes (or no boxes at all) that can be had for a very economical price. After all, if you're planning on building the kit, what's the point is spending all that extra money for an original box in perfect condition? It's your choice.

Since there are so many injection science-fiction kits out there (with a good portion stashed in your closet, garage, or basement), let's run through the construction of a couple or three injected styrene kits built straight out of the box. If you haven't done that much model building, or it's been a few years, or you're entirely new to the hobby, it'll lay the groundwork for the chapters to come.

GLENCOE LUNAR LANDER

No, this is not the Apollo 11 Lunar Module. Originally produced by Lindberg in the 1950s and repopped by

Glencoe some years ago, it's an example of what we thought a lunar lander was going to look like — before Sputnik rather rudely awakened us.

If you're wondering why this lander looks so spindly and fragile, it's because it was intended to be built in Earth's orbit. As a result, it would never be subjected to more than 1/6 of Earth's normal gravity on the Moon. However, dreams are free but reality is a harsh mistress. Since the model is stated to be 1/96th scale and stands 10 inches tall, a moment with a calculator tells you the real thing would have topped out at a spectacular 80 feet! Certainly not the most practical spacecraft idea we've ever had.

In spite of its apparent fragility, dreamers naively imagined a single-stage ship carrying large quantities of fuel in a pair of spheres and the crew compartment mounted above that. Of course, science-fiction films and books have made considerable use of just such designs.

Here's the old Lindberg kit in its latest incarnation as a Glencoe Model.

But enough background. This particular kit is an excellent choice for anyone just beginning to get their feet wet in model building. You can even do most of the painting with a spray can. That said, let's get started.

THE MODEL

With the possible exception of the Lindberg Flying Saucer, which has all of 10 parts plus stand and doesn't need painting because it's molded from glow-in-the-dark plastic, this Lunar Lander is about as basic as you want to get. Its 39 parts and decal sheet make it sound more complicated than it really is. As I said earlier, the stated scale is

1/96th of the actual size, and you'll even find three miniscule spacesuit-wearing figures that can be mounted on the base to put things in perspective.

References? There aren't any. Follow the kit's painting guide or use your imagination. Just keep in mind that common sense and logic will (or should) keep you away from totally impractical schemes. To show you what I mean, we'll be using a combination of kit instructions and logical imagination in this project.

CONSTRUCTION

This kit's pretty basic, meaning you could follow the instructions exactly and not have any problems. However, a brief detour here and there can make things even easier. I began with the first two steps, building up the crew compartment and main fuel tanks. Speaking of detours, step one is where I took the first one. Unless you're planning on not painting the model or eradicating the joints, *do not* install the clear ports on the crew compartment (parts number 22). We'll get around to those at the very end. Incidentally, you can go ahead and assemble the parts in step four, clamp where needed, and then set them aside for now. Being styrene, any good styrene (or plastic) cement will do just fine, but I fell back on my old favorite,

Ambroid ProWeld. As with all liquid cements (or welders), all you have to do is hold the parts together and run a brush or ruling pen down the seam, allowing the cement to flow into the joint, then clamp where necessary and leave 'em to dry.

There are those who would have you believe that you can touch the tip of a liquid cement applicator to one point on a seam and the cement will then run all the way around the joint by capillary action. Well, yes and no. Capillary action is a fact of life, so *if* the seam is the result of a perfect fit and *if* the joint isn't too long, then the technique will work. Have a rough or loose joint? A really long seam? Then don't be afraid to use as much as you need, in some cases just flat out slopping it on, and don't worry about the single point application method. Remember, whatever cement method you use is determined by one thing: that it does the job for you. In fact, that statement applies to *any* aspect of model building. Everyone develops their own way of doing things. What works for one won't work for another. I've said this so many times that I can hear it in my dreams, but it bears repeating: Just because I do it a certain way doesn't mean that *you* have to take the same approach. My method of building a model is just one way of doing the job, *not* the only way.

So, back to the Lunar Lander. With the cement dry, it's time to eliminate the seams. What? You weren't going to? You'd better rethink that, because that's one thing that separates an assembled kit from a realistic model — that and the elimination of parting lines.

SEAMS AND PARTING LINES

Seams are self-explanatory, essentially the raised ridges that result from the slightly softened plastic squeezing out of the glue joint and hardening. To create a realistic model, those ridges have to be removed, smoothed down to the model's surface so that the joint becomes invisible.

Parting lines are first cousins to seams, but they're produced during the manufacturing process instead of by you gluing parts together. Styrene kits are created by injecting molten styrene plastic (thus the name injected styrene) into steel, aluminum, or copper molds that contain cavities the shape of the desired parts. Once the plastic cools, you have to have a way to get the parts out of the mold. Obviously, the molds must have been made in two parts and then clamped together. The parts are removed by reversing the process and separating the molds.

When you pull the sprue and its attached parts from the mold, look closely and you'll find very fine, raised ridges of plastic where the molds were joined. Depending on the design of the parts and quality of the mold, the parting lines can be virtually invisible to the naked eye — until covered with a coat of paint. In order to produce a quality model, both the seams *and* parting lines must be eliminated.

SCRAPING

There are several companies that market seam scrapers. They work quite well, so it's just a matter of experimentation to see which one is most comfortable for you. I don't use 'em. Nothing wrong with them, it's just that they didn't exist 20 or 30 years ago and I solved the problem with what was available at the time. As far as I'm concerned, an Excel knife with #11 blade works just fine.

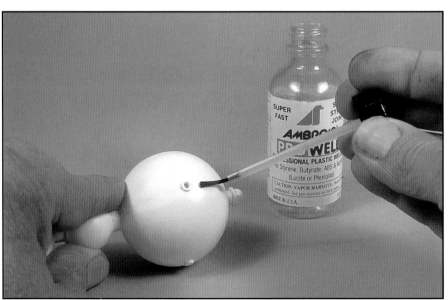

Hold the parts together, brush on some Ambroid ProWeld, then squeeze and hold or clamp 'til dry. The brush is built into the bottle cap, but some modelers prefer to use a regular paintbrush or a draftsman's ruling pen.

The worst of the dried seam can be scraped down with a knife blade.

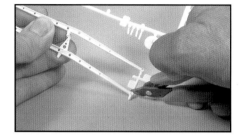

Other one-piece parts such as the frames, legs, antennas, etc., can be removed from their sprue.

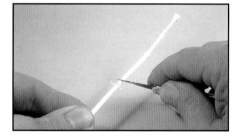

A sharp blade or scraper makes quick work of those fine parting lines.

All you do is keep the blade perpendicular to the seam and scrape until you're almost down to the surface. The method is very similar to using a woodworker's drawshave. As you near the model's surface, slow down and start paying close attention. If you're working on a curved surface, make sure that you match the contours so that you don't put a flat edge where it shouldn't be.

Keep in mind the fact that you're not going to achieve a finished, invisible seam by only scraping the seam. For that, you'll need sandpaper.

SANDPAPER

If, after you've recovered from the shock of that statement, you had thought sandpaper was the last thing

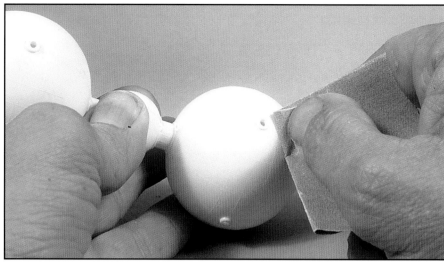

Some fine sandpaper and a little patience will blend the seams into the contours of a curved surface so that they're completely invisible.

on Earth you'd use on a plastic or resin model, think again. It's just as essential on those materials as it is on wood.

Sandpaper, of course, comes in many grits, or levels of roughness. The smaller the number, the rougher the sandpaper. Conversely, the higher the number, the finer, or smoother, it is. For example, 50 grit will take the point off a nail, while 600 grit or higher can be used wet to polish clear plastic. Most modelers wind up with a selection from 100-600, though some will add a sheet of crocus cloth to the mix. Crocus Cloth is high-grit sandpaper, dull red in color, which can be used wet or dry for final polishing.

BACK TO THE MODEL

From this point on, it's pretty much by the numbers — with a couple of exceptions. For example, go ahead and install the exhaust plate as called for in step three, but don't add the exhaust bells. You'll also find installation of those four small rods, which are actually the feed tubes that transport fuel from the tank to the exhaust bells, is a lot easier with the aid of a pair of tweezers.

The oxygen tank and the rectangular housing that mounts inside two of the frame legs can be added now. However, leave the two antennae and the hydrogen tank (parts 9 and 10) off. They'll only get in your way.

Per the instructions, install the frame legs, and then add the two square

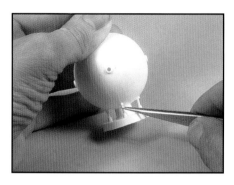

Xuron makes a great set of tapered tweezers that are a big help in installing the fuel transport tubes that run from the fuel tank to the exhaust plate.

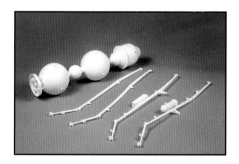

Here the crew module/fuel tanks subassembly and the frames/legs are about to be joined.

braces. Use light rubber bands, string, tape, or whatever else works to keep everything in position until the cement dries. If all else fails, turn on the TV and watch a program while clamping it in your hand!

When it's good and dry, add the two antennae (but not the hydrogen tank), and you're ready to prime.

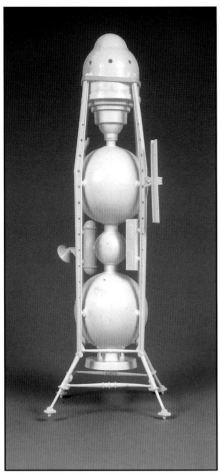

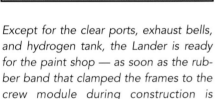

The first step is to apply two or three coats of your favorite primer. Fix any flaws that show up, shoot it again, and it's time for the base color.

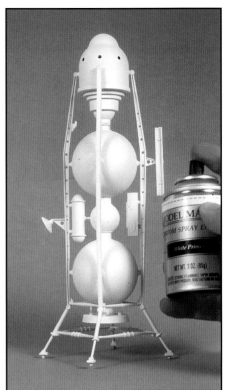

Painting the Lander is simplicity itself. A good, even coat of Model Master White Primer (or Model Master Flat White — same difference) is all it takes.

Except for the clear ports, exhaust bells, and hydrogen tank, the Lander is ready for the paint shop — as soon as the rubber band that clamped the frames to the crew module during construction is removed.

PRIMER

When it comes to styrene, just about any good lacquer or enamel-based primer will do the job. Testors offers a gray primer in their Model Master line that's excellent. Prefer Floquil? They have one that'll do just as well. If you want to get your primer from the auto supply store, try the one I used — Bondo Easy Finish Primer.

Regardless of the primer you use, there's a more basic question that only you can answer; are you going to prime in the first place and, if so, how are you going to prime. "Wait a minute!" you say. "Isn't priming priming?" Well — maybe.

Believe it or not, there are more than a few long-time modelers who *never* use a prime coat and wind up with beautiful models. Still others go so far as to actually mask off the immediate area around the seams and prime *only* the seam. Me? I've always primed the whole thing on the premise that it's the only way you're going to be able to eliminate all seams and wind up with a smooth, uniform base for your final finish. Call me crazy, but I think it's the best way to go.

Anyway, I shot several light coats of Bondo Easy Finish Primer from a rattlecan, checking between coats to make sure I was getting the results I wanted. If I found a flaw, I did a little more light sanding and shot another coat. Sounds like I used a lot of paint, but light coats prevent heavy buildup. Be sure to spray the base as well. Remember, practice and experience will solve a lot of your problems.

PAINT

First of all, the entire model got a coat of Testors Model Master White Primer (Model Master Flat White works just as well). You should actually give it several light coats, allowing each coat to dry long enough for you to be able to handle it. Because you're spraying light coats (and white over gray), it'll take several coats to get an opaque finish. Leave the base in gray primer.

At this point, you have a nice, uniform, flat white spaceship — which is about as realistic as a cartoon. You still need to do detail painting and decaling. Decals, if you haven't learned yet, don't take kindly to being applied over flat paint. The obvious solution is to spray the entire thing with a clear gloss, but then you'd be just as unrealistic at the other end of the scale. So what's the answer? It happens that Model Master (from Testors) offers a Semi-Gloss Lacquer Overcoat that's perfect for the job. A few coats of that from a spray can and I had a spaceship ready for detailing and decaling.

Do keep in mind that, as an alternative, you can spray a solid coat of clear gloss, apply the decals and then use semi-gloss or flat clear for a final topcoat. In fact, many situations require exactly that approach. It all depends on the particular subject, the result you're after and, quite frequently, the quality of the particular decals.

DECISIONS! DECISIONS!

Remember when I said that we were going to combine kit instructions and logical imagination? Now's the time for it. The first one of these I built many years ago was an original Lindberg kit. The color scheme was overall flat white. Glencoe's repop features a cover depicting an all-silver ship with black exhaust bells and translucent red portholes. The instructions, however, describe a fairly complicated scheme. The main fuel tanks and crew compartment are white, and the frame legs, leg braces, and antennas are silver. The exhaust plate and feed tubes are bronze, the exhaust bells and hydrogen tank are red, and the oxygen tank is green. In a word — no. My early Lindberg kit was probably closer to a realistic scheme, though it lacked proper detailing.

What I settled on was an overall semi-gloss white ship. I did paint the little round hydrogen tank semi-gloss red, while leaving that delicate mounting frame white. Once that was dry, I could install it in its proper position. The oxygen cylinder that is mounted to the inside of one of the frame legs gets a coat of semi-gloss green and the exhaust bells (that are molded from clear styrene) were painted flat black and installed. A thin copper line is painted down the inside of the long antenna, while the other antenna gets a coppery wash. With that done, all that remains are the decals.

DECALS

The decals and their placement are pretty well called out in the instructions. I would suggest, however, that

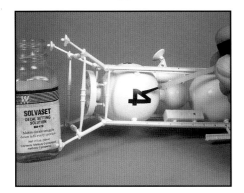

A light application of Solvaset allows decals to look like they were painted on.

you use either the number 4 as shown in the instructions, or the number 1, but *not* the combination of 41 as provided on the decal sheet — they just don't look right. By the way, take a close look at the Lunar Lander insignia that goes on the upper main tank. It shows a bare human foot just about to crush a lunar mountain!

Decal application really isn't that difficult, but you do need to do certain things. Since decals don't like flat paint (under a microscope, the stuff looks like a collection of hills and valleys), you have to do something to smooth out the paint surface. That something is a gloss (or semi-gloss) clear finish as mentioned earlier.

When combined with a decal-setting solution such as Solvaset, the decal snuggles right down over the raised detail and into all the nooks and crannies, looking for all the world like it was painted on. Once the decals were on and dry, a final coat of semi-gloss sealed everything and I was ready for the final details.

Oops! I knew I was going to make a mistake. The exhaust bells were painted flat black and installed before the decals were added. They were now semi-gloss black. No problem. A couple of minutes with a paintbrush and they were flat black again.

THE LITTLE STUFF

Remember those portholes I hadn't installed? Now's the time. Test fit each one and enlarge the holes that they go in *very gently* with the tip of a #11 blade used as a reamer. Don't get over-enthusiastic. If the fit is a little tight, it won't take much to loosen things up.

When you're satisfied with the fit, install the portholes with either white glue such as Elmer's or Bob Smith Industries Super-Gold + cyanoacrylate. This particular CA doesn't fog clear styrene.

All that remains is to mount the ship to the base, paint the three figures wearing spacesuits flat white, cement them to the base in whatever location you prefer and, believe it or not, you're done. Now you have another spaceship for your display case, or your first one if you're just getting into this hobby.

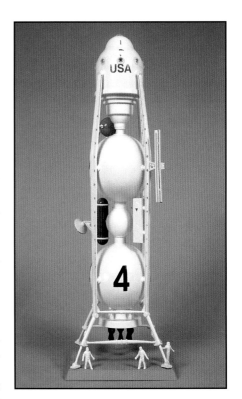

Here is the finished Lunar Lander in all its glory. Note the spacesuit-wearing figures on the base that help provide a sense of scale. There's quite a difference between what we thought Lunar Landers would look like and the reality of Apollo 11, *isn't there?*

This one (the markings are different and the base is black) was built in the 1970s from an original Lindberg kit.

MONOGRAM SPACE TAXI

During the late 1950s, Monogram produced a number of kits of spacecraft designed by Willy Ley. For those who don't know, Willy Ley was a German and a contemporary of Werner von Braun. Ley came up with a number of spacecraft designs that were supposed to reflect the future of American space flight. Four of his designs were released as Willy Ley Space Models kits by Monogram. At least two of them wound up as preliminary concepts for our current space shuttle. One, however, was interesting but never came close to reality. That one was the so-called Space Taxi.

Anyway, the kit was released in 1959, vanished a few years later, and was repopped by Revell-Monogram in 1996 as part of their limited edition Monogram Classics line. As you would expect, it's unavailable again.

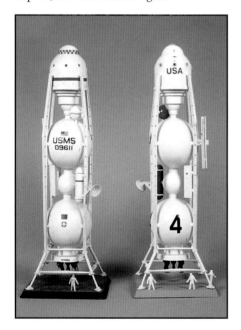

If I hadn't told you, you'd never know these finished models were produced by two manufacturers, separated by some 25-30 years! After all, the parts came out of the same mold.

In any event, the kit makes for a rather fascinating model with its open passenger cages (the passengers would be wearing spacesuits), enclosed cargo bay, and pressurized "driver's compartment." It's also the kind of model that can't — or shouldn't — be built according to the instructions.

ANALYSIS

This kit, and hundreds, if not thousands, of others of all kinds over the last few decades, is a perfect example of why you need to at least glance at the instructions before you toss 'em aside and start building it your way. According to the instructions, you're supposed to install the wire lifelines as well as paint and install the "driver" on the deck section first. Then, with the wires in the way and the painted driver to protect, you finally get around to starting construction. Well, there's a better way.

If you dry fit the hull halves and the deck, you find out that the 'driver' can be installed at a much later date. And, if you get creative, so can the lifeline wires. The same comments can apply to several other components, including the portholes and driver's windshield. By the time we're done, you'll have a quality model, you'll have developed new skills, and you'll have virtually ignored the instructions in the process. In other words, you're becoming a model builder.

STARTING POINT

Since I had no intention of installing the driver first, I held the hull halves together and made sure the driver could be fitted into position at a later date. Then the driver was put aside for the time being, the deck was installed in the left hull half (the one with the hatch opening), and all interior surfaces were sprayed with gray primer. Note that this includes the inner surfaces of the airlock

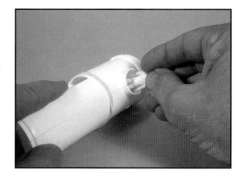

To make life a little easier, I checked the fit of the driver to see if he could be installed later.

bulkheads and the operating hatch.

Operating hatch? It happens that this kit was produced in a time period where many models featured "realistic operating parts." Far too many weren't "realistic" because of molding limitations, while others were on the delicate side. They would operate for a while, and then the hinges would break. The Space Taxi's working cargo hatch's hinges had a relatively sloppy fit, and while it fit the opening rather well, you had to tolerate a fairly prominent button molded onto the hatch that would allow you to open it. This provided excellent "play value," as they say these days, but it isn't what you'd want for a realistic model. Unless you like that kind of thing, leave the hatch off for the time being.

I also did not install the glass for the three portholes. The parts are nicely done and fit quite well, but I didn't want to deal with the problem of masking them. An alternative method that I use occasionally would work here.

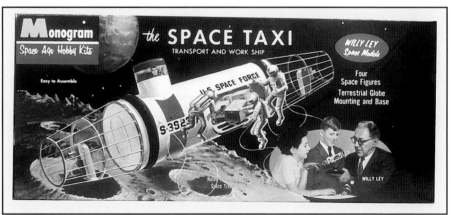

We were supposed to use this Space Taxi (!) to move around between ships and space stations in orbit. At least that's how we saw it in the 1950s when this kit was first introduced. It appeared again as a limited edition in the late 1990s.

CONSTRUCTION

After hand brushing the cargo net detail with Model Master FS 34087 Olive Drab, the hulls were joined, strapped with rubber bands (they could also be held together with spring clamps or whatever else works), and left to dry. The airlock bulkheads came next, and then all the seams were worked down to my satisfaction.

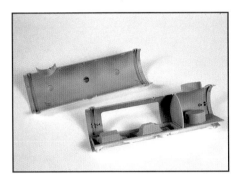

I installed the interior parts (less the driver) and sprayed a coat of gray primer. The ports would be added later from the outside, as would the support wires for the spacemen.

Each of the passenger cages is made in two sections: front and rear. You're supposed to build up the cages, complete with passenger and thrusters, and then add the completed units to each end of the Taxi. It can be done that way, but then you'll have problems with the seams where the cages join the Taxi. Instead, I mounted the rear half of each cage to the Taxi first. After cleaning up the seams, wadded up paper towel was stuffed in the hatch opening and into the portholes. Then

The two halves are glued together, and then clamped 'til dry. Feel free to use rubber bands, spring clamps, or anything else that works. Notice that the cargo hasn't been installed either.

I masked off the raised ribs at each end of the Taxi, and then used my Aztek A470 to spray Floquil Engine Black.

the Taxi, along with the separate front cages and outer surface of the cargo hatch, was shot with primer. Once dry, I sprayed an overall coat of Testors Model Master Flat White from a can.

The raised ribs at each end of the Taxi are masked and sprayed Model Master FS 37038 Flat Black. While I used an airbrush, a rattlecan will work quite well in this case, as long as you do sufficient masking to protect against overspray.

Once you've removed the tape, spray the exterior with Testors Semi-Gloss Clear, then set the Taxi aside and build up and install the thrusters in the front cage sections. If you're going to have a passenger, paint him to your satisfaction and install in one of the rear cage sections. Make sure you have a secure installation, because the figure will be inaccessible once the front cage is added. Install the front cages and it'll be decal time.

DECALS

Decals are decals, at least where the waterslide variety are concerned. Depending on the manufacturer and whether or not they're kit-provided or offered as aftermarket sheets, they can be thick or thin, brittle or flexible, and

so on. Some respond well to the very mild decal-setting solutions while others require heavy-duty solvents such as Solvaset. Then there are decals that will practically curdle on the paper if you so much as open a bottle of setting solution in the same room! About the only thing they have in common is that you dip them in water, wait a few seconds to a minute or two, and then slide (hence the name "waterslide") them onto the model's surface. So how do you know what works with what? That nasty little critter called experience. Just get in there and do it. Believe me, I've ruined my share of decals over the years.

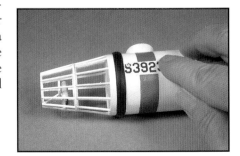

Decals are positioned and then snuggled down with your favorite decal setting solution. In this case, the black numbers and red band are all part of a single decal. A clear carrier film connects them.

Once in a while, the decal's carrier (the clear backing) will yellow on you, the result being that it won't disappear on the model's surface after it dries. Check out the photos of my Space Taxi and you'll see that's what happened to my kit's decals. Most of the time it's a factor of age (I'd had that kit for about 5 years), but basically it's just something that can happen. I have other decal sheets that have been sitting in a box for the last 30 years and they're as clear as the day they were printed.

Anyway, I used the decals as they came to show you what aged decals look like on a model. Everyone has their own method, but there's generally two ways to eliminate that yellowed backing. One is to simply tape the sheet (face out) to a window and leave it there for a few days. The sunlight usually bleaches the yellow out, leaving you with a clear carrier film. Or, if you have a steady hand and the nerve that goes with it, use a brand new #11 blade to cut around the letters, numbers, and/or designs and remove the surplus carrier.

Keep in mind that this trick only works *after* the decal has been applied, treated with setting solution, allowed to dry until the letters/numbers/ designs have dried sufficiently to regain their correct form (but have *not* dried enough to prevent removal of the carrier from the model's surface). When the treated decals have reached this stage, you can trim around the designs/letters and then carefully remove the surplus film. It's nowhere near as hard as it sounds, but it does take practice.

FINAL STEPS

After removing all the masking, which in this case means pulling all the wadded up paper towels and tape strips out of the interior, I installed the door permanently in an open position. The top hatch was painted red, while the driver and the two "floating" spacemen were painted more or less according to the instructions.

The driver was finally cemented in place, followed by the driver's window and the top hatch. By this time I was running out of parts, so I knew there wasn't much left to do. Just the portholes, display base, and umbilical lines.

Portholes

If you remember, I didn't install the plastic portholes at the beginning of this project, mainly to avoid the problem of masking. Those of you who prefer doing things the hard way can still install the clear plastic portholes by tapping the tip of a new knife blade into the back surface, then installing them through the open cargo hatch. It *can* be done, and I've taken that approach myself on various models when I've had to. But why do it when there's no need?

Instead, I used Testors Clear Parts Cement & Window Maker. This stuff is essentially a high-tensile variation on white glue, and similar products are available from other manufacturers. You can also get the same results with plain old white craft glue, but as long as the Testors product is around, there's no need to. Using the nozzle of the bottle, or a paintbrush loaded with the cement, you simply swirl the goop around the edges of the opening, simultaneously moving toward the center and pulling out at the same time. As they say, it's all in the wrist, and if you've never tried this technique before, it'll take a little practice to get it right. If you mess up, just wipe the

stuff off with a wet finger and try it again. Once you get the opening filled, position the opening so that it's horizontal (to prevent the liquid from slumping to one side before it's dry) and leave it alone until it becomes clear.

Do keep in mind that while the method works great for the Space Taxi portholes, small windows, and similar items, there is a practical limit. This entire technique is based on the physics of surface tension. If the opening is too large to fill completely with a single coat, it won't work.

The Base

The base is comprised of three parts: a clear, inverted cone; a small replica of the Earth; and a clear swivel ball that fits into a socket on the bottom of the Taxi. Build up the Earth model (it has two parts), paint it a medium blue, and then pick out the continents with various shades of greens, browns, and sand tones until you're satisfied with the results. If you want to really get fancy, try painting a swirling pattern of clouds over the entire planet. Cement the finished Earth model onto the clear base. Then all that remained was to snap the ball mount into the bottom of the Taxi — I

The technique is truly "all in the wrist," but Testors Clear Parts Cement & Window Maker is a great way to create small transparent areas and simplify masking problems.

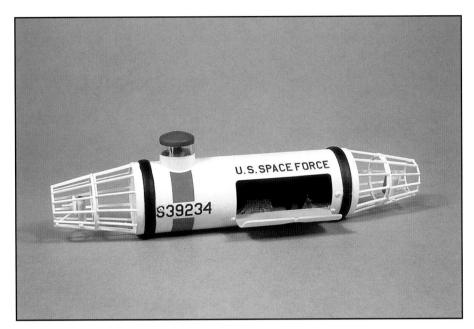

A wide variety of cylindrical objects can be used to bend soft wire into the desired shape. Anything from paint bottles to drill bit shanks are fair game. All that matters is that it's the correct diameter you need.

At this point, the Space Taxi is complete except for the installation of the spacewalkers and the mounting of the finished Taxi on its base.

thought. My first attempt resulted in exactly one comment: Uh-oh! In order to avoid having to protect all these extraneous parts during construction, I blithely ignored the fact that the mounting ball was *supposed* to be installed at that time. Now what?

Actually, the answer was pretty simple. All I did was use a knife to ream out the diameter of the mount opening in the bottom of the Taxi (a little bit at a time) until I had a tight fit for the mounting ball. In other words, test fit, test fit, test fit. Did it actually seat all the way into the molded socket the way it was supposed to? No. But the tight friction fit I attained still allowed the Taxi model to be positioned at will and no one would be the wiser — until they read this paragraph. Now the finger extending down from the mounting ball is press fitted into the top of the Earth sphere, and the Space Taxi is completely done except for the addition of a couple of spacewalkers.

Spacewalkers

If the Space Taxi concept itself doesn't tell you how far away from reality we were during the late 1950s, the spacesuit designs used on the spacewalking figures ought to do it. They combine flexible arm and leg sections with hardened torso, knee, and elbow shells. What's worse, the helmets are opaque spheres with a narrow slot for vision. Finally, the helmets are painted different colors for ease of identification.

In any event, I sprayed the two space-walking figures with a shot of Testors White Primer, and then went back over the dried paint with a brush and some slightly tinted white. You're not looking for a big color difference, just enough to settle into the recesses and avoid a toy-like monotone appearance. I painted one figure's helmet flat red, while flat aluminum (silver would work as well) took care of the visor slots. The oxygen tanks on their backs got a coat of Model Master FS 14187 Willow Green.

With that done, all that remained was to shape the umbilicals and mount everything to the Taxi. You get two lengths of semi-soft wire to use as umbilicals. They'll do the job very nicely, once you figure out how to bend nice, smooth curves into them that simulate the way they would appear in zero gravity. A natural inclination is to bend them with your hands. Don't. No matter how careful you are, you'll create miniscule kinks or angles that would definitely be out of place in Earth's orbit. Once you stop to think about it, there's a very simple solution.

Find yourself a series of round objects with various diameters. They can be literally anything, but I wound up using a bottle of Model Master paint, a cylindrical knife handle, and the shank of a 7/32-inch diameter drill bit. By shifting back and forth from one diameter to another, it took only a minute or two to get the configuration I wanted.

Once I had the umbilicals shaped, one end was cemented into the back of each figure (you'll find a mounting hole near the top of the oxygen tanks) with a dab of IC-GEL. Then the other end of each umbilical was inserted into their mounting holes on the side of the Taxi. Again, IC-GEL was used, but instead of trying to hold the figures in midair while the CA cured, I positioned the figures (one at a time) and added a very small drop of Insta-Set accelerator to immediately snap the CA.

And with that, a fascinating but totally impractical spacecraft design from the 1950s was ready to join my collection. The Space Taxi is proof positive that things frequently don't turn out the way we think they will.

Once the wire is formed to your satisfaction, add the spacewalkers, plug the combination into the Taxi, and you're finished.

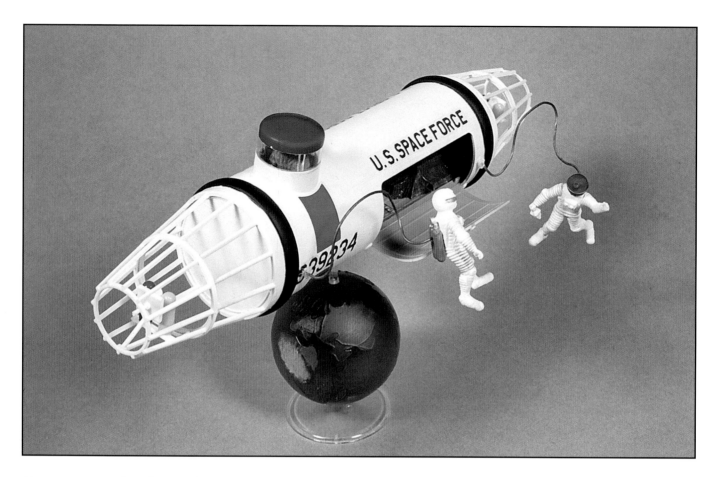

Here you can see how forming the wire around smooth radiuses helps create the illusion of zero gravity in the finished model. Orientation of the astronauts is important here – they shouldn't look like they're standing on the same plane.

Considering that this kit dates back to 1959, it builds into a very nice model indeed, even straight from the box.

Thanks to the popularity of Babylon 5, Revell-Monogram gave us a 1/72nd scale kit of the Starfury Mk. I.

STARFURY MK. I

Those of you (and I'm one) who consider *Babylon 5* to be one of the best, if not *the* best, science fiction series ever to hit television will need no introduction to the Starfury Mk. I. For the rest of you, a brief description:

More accurately known as the SA-23E Mitchell-Hyundyne Starfury, the ship is a single seat, cross-wing fighter. The pilot is "seated" in a standing position to minimize the effects of high g-forces. Thrusters are positioned for maximum maneuverability. The ship is not only capable of reversing course in mid-flight, it can also fly backwards.

CONSTRUCTION

Both upper and lower wings require installation of inner wing panels, which result in seams that have to be filled. Depending on how tightly your kit's panels fit, you may be able to do the job with Super Gold + gap filling CA. I opted for Model Master Red Putty and applied it with a spatula blade. That blade, incidentally, is part of a five blade spatula set manufactured by Hobby Stuff and is designed to fit a standard #1 knife handle. The variety of shapes and sizes allow excellent control over putty application.

Once the seams were filled and sanded to my satisfaction, I digressed from the instructions and added the fuselage to the *top* wing first, instead of the bottom.

Test fitting had shown that it'd be far easier to clean up the lower wing/fuselage seam with both wings installed than would be the upper. I know it sounds like I'm flogging a dead horse, but test fitting is one of the best friends a model builder can have. Also, by installing the top wing first, the instructions would have you trap a tab on the top of the cockpit bucket under the leading edge of the top center section. Instead, I decided to leave the cockpit bucket until later. Are you worried about the top tab? We'll cut it off at the proper time.

ACCURIZING YOUR KIT

On the off chance that some of you have never heard the term, accurizing is nothing more than the process of changing or correcting a model so that it more accurately represents the prototype subject in question. Next, we will accurize our Starfury's guns. The kit's guns simply don't match available references.

Keep in mind that accurizing this model is entirely relative. They did build a full-size cockpit module for filming, but most of the flight scenes in the various episodes are CGIs (computer generated image), meaning that fine details can vary from image to image. As a result, whatever corrections you make will be accurate *only for that one specific CGI*, though

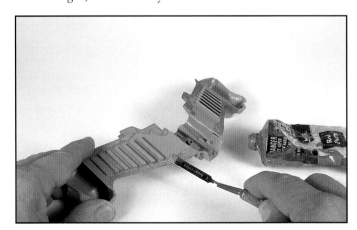

Model Master Red Putty is one of several ways to fill seams. Here I'm using a narrow spatula blade from Hobby Stuff to apply the putty.

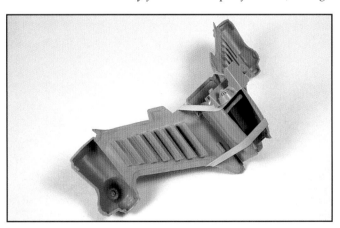

Contrary to the instructions, I mounted the fuselage to the upper wing first. In this case, a rubber band makes the perfect clamp.

it will be pretty darn close for the others.

With that said, rebuilding the guns really isn't that difficult. All you need are three different sizes of brass tubing (check your local hobby shop), a knife, a razor saw, a drill, and some patience. For the Starfury, I used .125-, .155-, and .190-inch diameter K&B tubing. Before you cut the plastic barrels off of the gun body, measure the barrel's overall length, and then add another .125 inch or so to allow for seating in the hole you'll be drilling.

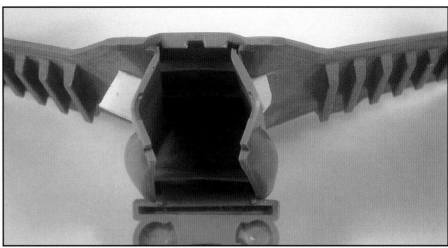

Both upper guns and filler blocks are in place. The right hand has been trimmed to shape with the other one waiting its turn.

Starting at the upper right and moving to the lower left, each successive stage in the gun accurizing can be seen. The process looks a lot more complicated than it really is, and it goes a long way towards improving the look of the finished model.

The longest piece of tubing forms the actual barrel and is cut from .125-inch diameter. By the way, tubing is best cut with a Dremel MultiPro and a diamond cutting wheel. Lacking that, a fine tooth razor saw will do the job. As for the socket drilled into the gun body, I used a hand-held pin vise.

The largest diameter tubing (.190 inch) that forms the step-up section of the barrel was cut to length, and then a piece of .155-inch diameter tubing was cut to act as an invisible spacer between the two sections. Now slip the .155-inch section *into* the .190-inch section, aligning the front edges. Add a little water consistency CA to bond the two together. The resulting combination is then slipped over the main barrel and positioned so that the front edge is about .050 inch back from the barrel's muzzle. Follow with a little more CA and then mount the back end of the

assembly in the socket you previously drilled in the gun body. Finally, repeat three more times to finish accurizing your Starfury's guns.

Even though the guns are built, there's still a little more work to do. If you mount the guns per the instructions, you wind up with a nice little gap between the gun body and fuselage that doesn't exist on the real ship. Also, the gun body has a hollow in it to simplify mold design. You don't have to worry about covering the long opening in the side of the gun body because it won't be visible. However, you do need to cut a piece of sheet styrene to cover the back of the gun body. Finally and most importantly, you need to cut a couple of fillers for that gap between the guns and fuselage.

All that's needed for this job is a couple of small pieces of .020-inch thick sheet styrene. Cut 'em more or less to shape, then cement them in place. By the way, you'll also want to cut the gun mounting tabs off the underside of the top wing. Once the fillers have dried hard, start whittling them down with a new #11 blade, checking frequently with the guns for proper fit. When you're satisfied with the fit, go ahead and install the top pair of guns — but not the bottom. We'll get to those in a while.

Add the Lower Wing

Lower wing is next, and this is where you'll have to spend a little more time on seam work. The left side

After adding the bottom wing, a thin bead of Super Gold + CA was used to fill wing/fuselage seam.

wing/fuselage seam fits well enough that it can easily be handled with Super Gold +. However, it's a little different story on the right side.

I suppose because I've gotten used to working with the stuff, the obvious solution to the larger gap on the right side was Super Gold +. That's what I used and it worked quite well. But if you haven't learned to build up fillets over larger gaps with CA and the idea of trying it on this seam leaves you a little queasy, stick in a narrow piece of styrene strip as a filler and then add the CA. Either method works.

Panel Lines Go, Panel Lines Come

All too frequently, in the process of scraping and sanding seams, panel line detail tends to disappear. Then comes the question of how to restore them. Recessed detail is easily handled by running over them with a scriber so that you deepen what's left and renew their prominence. If you've managed to eradicate them completely, a straight edge or metal pattern guide (even plastic for that matter) can be used with the scriber to scribe them over again. You're still cutting into the surface.

Raised detail is something else. As I keep saying, everyone has their own methods, but one of the easier ways is to score over the vanished panel line with a sharp #11 blade. Use a straight edge and a lot of care to keep the tip from wandering. The knife blade cuts into the surface, forcing two small ridges of plastic to rise *above* the surface, one on each side of the blade. When you shoot a coat of primer or paint, the scored groove left by the blade fills in and the result is a restored, raised panel line. Like everything else in model building — and I keep harping on — it *does* take practice to get it right.

When you're left with the problem of restoring raised lines on a tapered, curved surface such as the Starfury's engine pods, straightedges and other guides won't do you much good. Here, it's strictly experience and a steady hand. Holding your tongue just right might not hurt either!

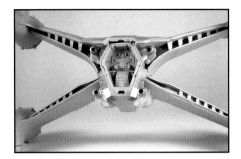

All four guns and the cockpit tub have been installed in this view. As with the upper guns, filler blocks are also being added to the lower guns.

The Other Guns

Lower guns go in next, and you'll notice that you can't do it the kit's way and have a realistic appearance. A spacer/brace needs to be added right at the front of the cockpit, spanning the gap between the cockpit wall and the gun body. Don't forget to trim them down to the correct contours after they've dried sufficiently.

Finish the Construction

The rest of the construction is pretty much straightforward. Thrusters and vanes are by the book. Only the cockpit bucket will take a little extra work.

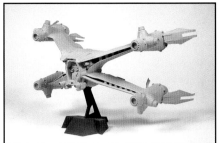

At this point, the Starfury lacks only cockpit detailing, a pilot, and a canopy. It has been primed and all remaining flaws have been corrected.

Remember that I said the upper tab on the bucket would be removed at the proper time? Well, now's the time. Cut it off, smooth the top edge down and you'll find the cockpit bucket will slip right into position.

Before dealing with the pilot and canopy, the entire model got a shot of primer. Seams were then checked for flaws, rough spots, etc., and cleaned up in the normal manner. Then a final coat of primer was applied.

COCKPIT DETAIL, PILOT, AND CANOPY

You can spend as much or as little time on the cockpit detail as you wish. Details vary from episode to episode and the same can be said for photos found on websites. Simply put, it's pretty much your choice. From what I've been able to find, basic interior color can be anything from a greenish color to various shades of grays. Then there are a variety of warning placards not provided on the decal sheet that add a little color to the interior. By the time you add the pilot and the canopy, quite a bit of the detail isn't visible anyway. Finally, a Starfury in flight has a red glow (safety lights) in the cockpit. If you want to replicate that appearance, overspray the cockpit interior with some Tamiya X-27 Clear Red. Alternatively, spray the *inside* of the canopy. The result is the same.

You can say the same for the pilots. Depending on whether you want a standard Earth Force pilot or one assigned to Black Omega will control your choice of a lighter or darker gray. In all cases, the faceplate is gloss black. Just don't use the face decal that's pro-

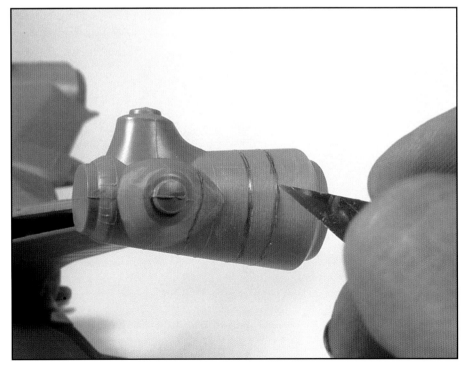

Raised panel lines can be restored by scoring them with a sharp knife blade and then spraying a coat of primer over them.

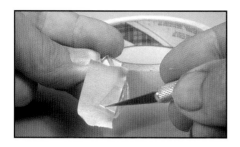

Thanks to the raised frames, masking the canopy requires nothing more than a few pieces of Scotch Drafting Tape, a sharp #11 blade, and about two minutes.

vided because it'll never fit properly.

While all of that was drying, I masked the canopy. Since it has very prominent raised ribs, masking with Scotch Drafting Tape is a very easy project.

Install the pilot, add the canopy, and you're ready to paint. Incidentally, I'd suggest you use either Ambroid ProWeld or BSI Super Gold + to install the canopy. There's nothing near the canopy edges to cause the ProWeld to run where it shouldn't, so normal precautions will keep you out of the trouble. Prefer using CA? Super Gold + is a version of CA that will not fog clear canopies.

Now Paint It

One of the toughest things about finishing a Starfury is figuring out what scheme to put it in. And then there's the question of personal markings. The instructions alone give you six different schemes. If that's not bad enough, ten minutes on the internet will get you at least 15 to 20 more, some of which incorporate extremely detailed "nose art" that's based on World War II fighter nose art!

Then there's the problem with the kit-provided decals. Various construction articles I've read relate serious problems with getting the decals to follow all the surface contours. That's corroborated by a note in the instructions that the decals aren't compatible with decal setting solution. Apparently it's the adhesive that causes all the problems, which leaves you with the choice of creating your own custom decals, painting all markings directly on the model, or picking a generic scheme using minimal markings. If you're still relatively new to model building, the generic scheme is probably the best way to go, so that's what I opted for here.

Basic Color

Except for the Black Omega squadron (whose ships should actually be flat black and not anthracite gray metallic), the instructions indicate that all Starfurys are overall Light Sea Gray. Well, that's pretty much open to interpretation. Some kind of gray, certainly, but exactly what shade is up to you. Other excellent choices are FS 36320 Light Ghost Gray and FS 36375 Dark Ghost Gray. You can also use one color as your base and the other to add a little definition to some of the panels. Don't forget that Starfurys will show quite a bit of weathering/battle damage, some more than others. In other words, within certain limits, you have an awful lot of latitude.

I wound up spraying an overall coat of Model Master FS 36375 Dark Ghost Gray — or at least I was going to until one of those magical "Oops!" factors kicked in. My Starfury had been primed with a rattlecan of Bondo 720 Light Gray Easy Finish Primer. When I started to airbrush Dark Ghost Gray on it, I couldn't see the Ghost Gray! It turns out the Bondo Primer is a dead match for Dark Ghost Gray. Thanks to that fortuitous turn of events, I could move directly the detailing stage.

Details and Thrusters

A generic Starfury doesn't have that much color detail to it. There are three intake recesses along the outer leading edge of each wing that are specified as anthracite gray metallic. You'll also find a small rectangular recess (exhaust vent?) at the rear end of a fairing on the top of each wing that gets the same treatment. I wound up using Floquil Gun Metal because it has a slightly bluish cast to it. All this detailing was done by hand with a 20/0 Polly S brush.

Despite the fact that you're not supposed to be able to do it (the stuff is pre-thinned for airbrush application and lacquer to boot), I hand brushed all of the thrusters with Model Master Metalizer Titanium Buffing Metalizer and didn't bother to do any buffing. Not only did it give me a good starting point for eventual weathering of the thrusters, it goes to show that just

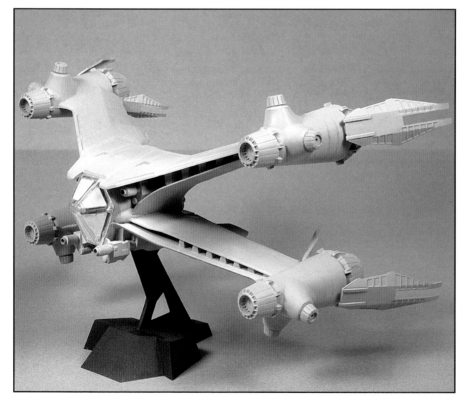

I installed the masked canopy after detailing the cockpit to suit me and adding the pilot.

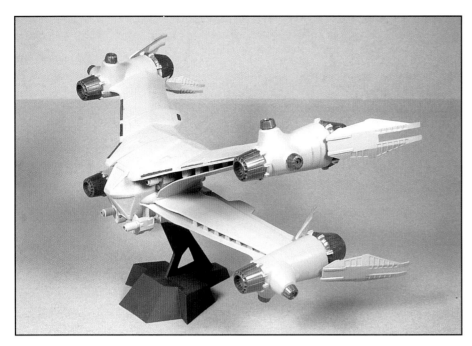

A pristine (and unrealistic) Starfury awaits decals and weathering.

because something is designed for a specific use doesn't mean you can't use it a different way.

Once the paint was dry, which wasn't long where the Titanium was concerned, an overall coat of Floquil Crystal-Clear had it ready for the decals.

DECALS

Decal application turned out to be an interesting experience. Due to the problems I mentioned earlier that other modelers had reported, I had gone so far as to select a standard or generic set of markings as a result (no nose art). If you're thinking I was more than a little wary at this stage, you're right. Turns out that I didn't need to be. Application of all the decals went without a hitch. In fact, I didn't even encounter any of the milkiness or surplus adhesive that the instructions warned about.

Now, despite what I just said, there are two caveats. First, I used absolutely *no* decal set or decal solvent. I wasn't about to risk botching the job at this late date. All of my decals snuggled down satisfactorily without any, but consider all were relatively small with only a raised panel line or two to deal with. If your curiosity gets the better of you, slap one you're not going to use on a scrap model and do some experimenting.

Secondly, if you opt for one of the large nose art decals, be prepared for trouble. If you can't use decal solvent, you most likely will have a problem getting it to lay down over all the contours. One way around that is to cut small slits in strategic areas with a new knife blade. Another way is to apply a thin layer of white glue over the area first, and then add the wet decal. The white glue will help pull it down. You may also find that both white glue and a slit here and there will be necessary. In other words, play it by ear.

Finally, after the decals had dried, I shot the Starfury with a coat of Model Master Semi-Gloss Clear Lacquer, stripped the masking off the canopy, and was ready to wallow in the dirt for the final step. Weathering.

WEATHERING

Weathering techniques used on models of combat vehicles is pretty much the same when it comes to the basics. The trick is in determining just *how* dirty and beat up a particular vehicle should be. For example, the Starfury in this chapter and the B-Wing in the next chapter have seen more than a little wear and tear. It shows, too, and there are perfectly valid reasons for it. Some craft look like they just left the factory, no matter how many missions they've been on. In real life, you have to consider such factors as availability of maintenance facilities, attitude of the ground crew, whether you're on the defense or offense, and even the political atmosphere of the particular group/nation whose flag you're operating under. In science fiction, you have the ability in many cases to determine all those factors in your own mind in order to justify the amount of weathering you've decided to use.

But I digress. Back to the Starfury at hand. Since Starfurys were often in

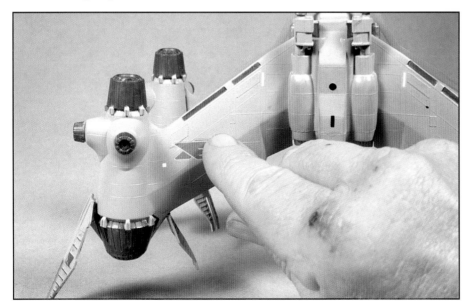

The smaller decals went on with no trouble. By the way, some modelers and most decal manufacturers warn against never, ever touching a wet decal with your fingers. Obviously that's another "rule" that depends on what works for you.

constant combat, the idea was to keep 'em fighting and never mind what they looked like. As a result, an operational Starfury is likely to look pretty darn grungy.

Also, no matter how well a machine is built, you're going to have seams, joints, hoses, couplings, hinges, and many other small points that are either going to leak different fluids or act as a collection point for grime and grit. Constant expansion/contraction of components from the extreme temperatures of space doesn't help matters either. Finally, since the Starfury was designed for maximum maneuverability (literally being able to turn on the proverbial dime), weathering patterns can move in any direction. What's the upshot of all this rambling? I pretty much rely on the combination of two different techniques (as needed) to create the various leaks, streaks, stains, and misting that would likely be found on well-used combat spacecraft. Matter of fact, I've become quite fond of it to the point that you'll find it showing up now and again in subsequent chapters.

Minor leaks, small streaks, semi-visible stains, and similar effects utilize dry-brushing methods. It's not difficult once you get the nerve to try it, although it looks like you're just making a mess at first glance.

More prominent streaking, stains, scorching from thruster blasts, and general misting are done by airbrushing Model Master Clear Black Transparent Window Tint. Airbrushing the Tint isn't the problem, but you can't just open a bottle of paint and pour it in the airbrush cup. It's only available in spray cans, so you'll have to squirt some into a cup to

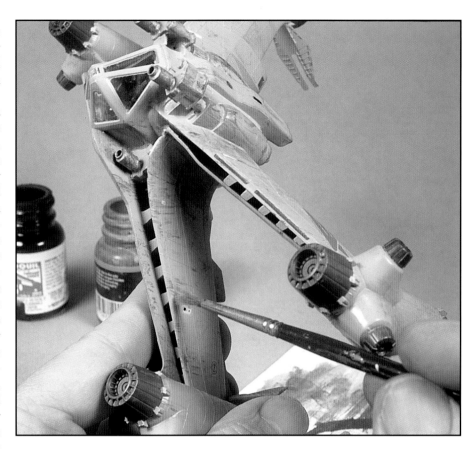

Miniscule streaks of hydraulic fluid or grime are stroked back from the leading edges of the wings. Note the light staining around and behind the guns as well. Incidentally, after the decals were applied, the model got a coat of semi-gloss, and the masking was removed from the canopy before weathering began.

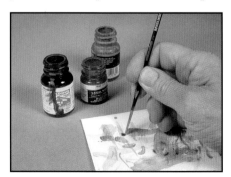

Bottles of Floquil Engine Black, Model Master Rust, dirty thinner, and a scruffy brush were used for the dry-brush stage of the Starfury.

All of the dry brushing has been completed at this point.

Final streaking with Transparent Black Window Tint is underway here.

obtain a liquid for your airbrush. See the B-Wing weathering section in Chapter 3 for specific directions on both techniques.

Because of the extremely long taper needle it possesses, I used my Rich AB-100 to do the final weathering on both the B-Wing and Starfury. The exact pattern of streaking, as well as its intensity, will depend on the effect you're after. However, in the case of the Starfury and its turn-on-a-dime thruster design, you want to be sure to indicate the scorching/staining deposited on the ship's skin from firing of the braking and maneuvering thrusters. Remember that when the braking thrusters are fired, the ship will still be moving forward for a second or two before reversing course or slow-

Finished at last, this Starfury becomes yet another defender of Babylon 5. Compare this weathered, used, and realistic view to the "pristine" shot on Page 33.

ing. As a result, the thruster's exhaust will actually flow back over the end of the wing even though the thruster's energy was directed *ahead* of the ship. This is the kind of information you need to keep in mind when striving for realistic patterns.

NOTHING LEFT

Nothing left except the stand. It's a simple two-piece affair that's quickly glued together and sprayed flat black. Now it is ready to have the finished Starfury mounted on it.

Notice that skin scorching from the various thrusters is not uniform — nor should it be. Areas near the most frequently used thrusters will show the most scorching. That will be determined by what kind of dogfights the ship has been in.

3

How to Build Sci-Fi Model Spacecraft

WORKING WITH RESIN:
LITTLE KNOWN *STAR WARS* SHIPS

O nce you get away from the main line *Star Trek/Star Wars* and the occasional UFO or movie-based spacecraft and start casting your eye on lesser-known subjects, you quickly move away from styrene kits. While there are exceptions, most of the more, ahem, unusual subjects are produced by the aftermarket, also known as 'garage' companies. The name is appropriate, because more often than not, these kits are limited edition efforts and are frequently manufactured in the company owner's home workshop that's located in, you guessed it, his garage. Many of the companies also tend to be one-man operations that actually qualify as a paying hobby. Whether it's a labor of love or a full-time business, this is where you find the exotic kits that you wish someone would make.

Urethane resin is a two-part liquid plastic that combines chemically (catalyzes) by exothermic reaction (the release of heat) to create a solid materi-al. The combined liquid can be poured (before it 'kicks' or begins to catalyze), usually by hand, into flexible silicon rubber (called RTV for 'room temperature vulcanizing') molds. While the molds, being flexible, allow for the inclusion of high relief detail, it's a labor-intensive process. The quality of a particular kit is totally dependent on the skill of the pattern maker, how the pattern is broken down for the mold, the quality of the final mold, the skill of the person pouring the resin, the weather (humidity), and Murphy's Law (anything that can go wrong will go wrong, at the worst possible moment).

Despite that just-described gauntlet that potential resin kits have to run, there are a plethora of resin kits out there to satisfy our lust for models of little known or unusual spacecraft and vehicles. For example, if you can't get enough of *Star Wars* but are beginning to tire of X-Wings and Tie Fighters, Scale Model Technologies (SMT) has a couple of offerings that we'll build in

this chapter. Specifically, the Rebel B-Wing Attack Fighter and the Empire's TIE Bomber. Both are resin kits and both are to 1/48th scale. Or at least that's what the box says. The B-Wing scales out to 1/41.5th, assuming you accept the stated size for the real ship as being 16.9 meters tall. That's determined by multiplying 39.37 (the number of inches in a meter) x 16.9 (the height of the real B-Wing) and dividing by 16 (the height of the model in inches) to get 41.5 (which you read as 1/41.5th scale) to get the scale of the model.

B-WING ATTACK FIGHTER

The majority of resin kits are not intended for the beginning modeler, and these SMT offerings are *no* exception. That is not to say that there are no resin kits suitable for the less experienced. Manufacturers of styrene plastic kits are even beginning to include resin detail parts in their products. However, if you've never tackled a resin kit and

you're anxious to add a B-Wing to your collection of spacecraft — wait just a cotton pickin' minute!

First, get your hands on a couple of simple resin kits. Subject doesn't matter. What you want is a relatively simple kit with no more than 10 or 15 parts that is also economically priced. Read through the resin projects in this book to become familiar with the techniques and then practice them on those simple kits.

Good things come in plain packages. The B-Wing from Scale Model Technologies is an example of that.

Got a couple of finished resin kits under your belt? Feeling better about working with resin? Good! Now let's tackle the B-Wing.

The B-Wing was one of the more unusual *Star Wars* designs and was only seen on-screen briefly in *Return Of the Jedi*. Heavily armed with Ion and laser cannons, it incorporated a totally unique design that placed the cockpit module at one end of the primary wing. As a result, the cockpit remained stationary while the rest of the ship rotated around it. Beyond that, there was a pair of folding wings (called S-Foils) that could be positioned perpendicular to the main wing, or anywhere in between. Since the S-Foils and the main wing each carried Ion- and/or laser-cannon batteries, considerable firepower could be concentrated into a single cone of fire, depending on how the S-Foils were positioned.

Standard weapons configuration would find an Ion cannon on each S-Foil, with the main wing gun pod mounting an Ion cannon, a laser cannon, and an emission-type proton-torpedo launcher. Two auto-blasters would also be mounted in the nose of the cockpit.

However, you want to keep in mind the fact that the weapons' hard points utilized a modular design. Ergo, weapons configuration could be changed in only a few hours time.

GETTING STARTED

As I said, resin kit quality varies all over the scale, sometimes even copy to copy from the same manufacturer. Case in point is this B-Wing. I've read various reviews on this kit that included complaints on such things as panel

While not a small model, all of these parts manage to fit into that one box. Honest.

lines that didn't line up. As it happened, I didn't have any trouble of that sort, or any surface pinholes either.

That kind of problem is something you simply have to learn to correct. The cause can be laid right at the feet of those flexible rubber molds used to create such beautiful detail. Because they *are* flexible, you'd be amazed at how easy it is for mold halves to slip out of alignment. Start doing your own resin casting and you'll see what I mean.

Construction began with a knife-and-sandpaper session to clean up whatever flash existed. Though you'll find the occasional exception, flash is pretty much a fact of life when it comes to resin kits. Much of it simply flakes off when you rub your hand over it, though some requires a light touch with a knife and/or sandpaper. Sometimes you run into a situation that takes both sandpaper *and* elbow grease.

In my particular B-Wing kit, most of the parts were spin cast, the idea being for the parts to be hollow. Not only does this make the finished model

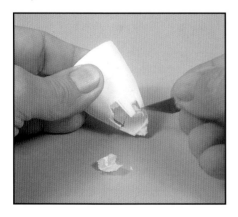

Take whatever time is needed to clean up whatever flash you can find. There will be flash; how much flash depends on your particular kit.

lighter, it also makes it easier for those of you with a penchant for lighting to be creative. Properly done, spin casting results in hollow parts with a sturdy wall thickness. My kit had irregular hollow areas and an occasional wall that was literally paper-thin. I didn't break through any of the skin, but would've had I not been paying close attention. It really didn't cause me a problem, aside from the fact that it prevented me from pinning any parts together.

Instructions are something else again. As with so many resin kits, they leave a lot to be desired. You get eight illustrated steps, a photo of the finished model and some brief construction advice packed onto both sides of two 8 1/2 x 11-inch sheets of paper. They raise at least as many questions as they answer. You'll need to study them in concert with a close examination of the parts before you tackle the kit. Keep in mind that if you are an experienced resin kit builder, you'll probably trash the instructions and build the kit your way.

Now, in fairness to SMT, they are aware of the problems I've mentioned. By the time you read this, the thin walls should be history. In fact, the resin main wing will have been supplanted by vacuformed halves that are replete with wire mesh inserts for the leading-edge grilles. The instructions should be improved as well. Incidentally, never hesitate to contact the manufacturer of any kit with constructive criticism. That's the only way they can improve. Also, if you have any really bad or unusable parts, most companies are only too happy to provide free replacements.

ENGINE POD

Intake vanes are slipped into the engine pod from the back. Once they're correctly aligned, I cut a long extension tube for my bottle of Super Gold + and ran a bead of CA around the interior seam.

That was followed with the two sections of rear decking. In this case, the illustrations in step two are a very clear aid to proper alignment. Note that I will not install the engine nozzles until after the model is completed and painted.

Installing the intake vanes in the engine pod is a piece of cake, if you cut a long extension tube for your bottle of CA.

MAIN WING

The two halves of the main wing are long, thin, and partially hollow. They also have a tendency to warp, which means you'll need to straighten them out. Since you have to heat resin parts first, most modelers use either a hair dryer or hold the part under hot running water. Either one works, but I take a third approach — a heat gun.

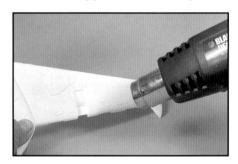

While using a heat gun on warped parts, be sure to keep the gun moving so no one spot gets too hot.

Whatever method you use, keep the heat moving over a wide area rather than concentrating it at a single point. Once the resin begins to soften (meaning it's warm enough to give or flex, not sag or take your thumbprint) you can straighten it out or gently bend it back into its correct configuration.

Now for the next problem: holding it in position until it cools. One way is to open the door to your refrigerator's freezer and simply hold the part (including your hand) inside for 30 or 40 seconds until the resin takes a set. Or do what I did on the B-Wing. Set each half down on a flat surface and put a weight on it until it cools. Since my B-Wing had such a thin skin in some areas, I found that an empty coffee cup was more than enough weight.

Here I weighted the wing half down with a coffee mug 'til the part cooled. You can get the same result in many other ways.

Turns out that the two halves weren't identical, so I aligned the front and bottom edges, ran a bead of the thinner Super Gold down the front seam, added a couple of temporary clamps and gave it a shot of InstaSet accelerator.

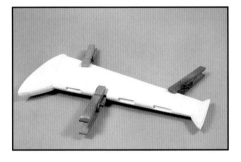

The main wing halves have been glued together and clamped. Wooden clothes pins were all I needed in this case. If you have one of the earlier kits, be careful not to crack that thin skin.

Now that the two halves weren't going to move, Super Gold was continued all the way around, followed by InstaSet. Seams were sanded before the CA got too hard. Model Master Red Putty was then applied where needed to even out any steps and sanded when dry.

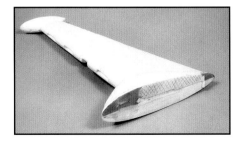

I used a combination of sheet styrene and putty to eliminate the uneven step in the main wing's top surface.

On the top end of the main wing, it was necessary to come up some .015 inch in one area to even out the step. Rather than use putty for all of it, I built up a shim of sheet styrene and then blended the putty into the shim.

S-FOIL MOUNT

If I had my druthers, I'd have pinned the S-Foil hub to the top of the main wing. Since I couldn't, I resorted to another Bob Smith Industries product, IC-GEL. This stuff is a gel formula, which allows you to use it like ordinary tube glue — aside from the fact that it'll set in 10-15 seconds, just like any other CA. Unlike other gel CAs that you've seen, it comes in a large 3/4-oz tube at a very reasonable cost. It will last you for two years if you keep it out of the heat. It also has something most CAs don't — a degree of sheer strength.

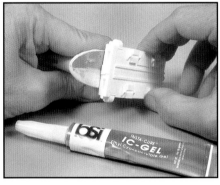

When I was unable to pin the S-Foil mount/main wing joint, I resorted to IC-GEL.

After identifying the correct location for the S-Foil hub, I applied a layer of IC-GEL, added the hub, waited for it to cure, and then moved on.

ENGINE POD/COLLAR ASSEMBLY MOUNT

Again using IC-GEL, the engine pod was mounted to the S-Foil hub. Don't overlook the fact that there's a top and bottom to the engine pod. You'll find a long mounting bar on the bottom and a short one on top. They fit into raised rib outlines on the adjacent parts. After the engine pod was installed, it was followed by the collar-assembly mount, and I was beginning to have a spaceship on my hands.

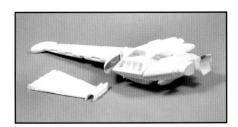

Real progress at last! The engine pod and collar assembly has been added to the main wing/S-Foil mount. Also, those delicate little Ion cannon housings are in on the tips of the S-Foils (you can only see one in this shot).

At the same time, I added the wingtip housings for the Ion cannon to the S-Foils. While nicely done, the housings are extremely thin and need to be handled like eggshells. By the time you add the guns, though, they'll be plenty sturdy.

GUN RECONSTRUCTION

All of the gun barrels had to be replaced, a common problem with resin. Long, thin resin cylinders have a habit of warping, and straightening them doesn't do a lot of good. If you manage to heat and cool them so that they're straight, just placing them near a warm table lamp will likely warp them again. And the thinner the cylinder (barrel), the worse the problem. A better solution is to simply replace them. And it ain't that hard.

The process is essentially similar to the method used in accurizing the Starfury guns: cut out the barrels and then replace each with new barrels built up from brass tubing. What *is* different

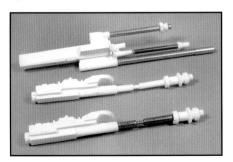

From bottom to top: A rebuilt Ion cannon, an original Ion cannon with a warped barrel, and a rebuilt main gun battery. Brass tubing and an abrasive cut-off wheel (and patience, of course) make rebuilding the guns an easy job.

about the B-Wing guns is that I retained the resin recoil rings/barrel muzzles, meaning that they will have to be installed on the new brass barrels. Note that not all the rings/muzzles are identical. The S-Foil cannons and one cannon on the main battery have both recoil rings and muzzles. You'll have to carefully drill out the bore on these resin muzzles. Another main battery cannon has recoil rings that are positioned back from the end of the brass barrel. Drill all the way through the rings, then slide over the barrel to the correct position and CA. Finally, the last member of the main battery has a step-up muzzle extension that is easily reproduced with a piece of brass tubing.

I did have to scratch-build one thing — the targeting sensors that mount on the gun bodies. Though mine were missing from the kit, scratching them up was simplicity itself. Their location is clearly indicated in the instructions (be aware that the sensors are handed), so all I did was cut four thin slices of 1/8-inch diameter Evergreen tubing, install them with CA, and then add a drop of CA to the front. This not only seals the hole, but slightly domes it as well.

Again, SMT is working to improve the guns as well. Instead of one-piece guns, newer kits will provide the main end and front detail of the laser cannons as resin castings that are then combined with kit-provided plastic pipe (tubing). You can still use brass tubing in the manner that I did, but either method should be quite satisfactory.

GUN INSTALLATION

Installation of the rebuilt guns is relatively easy, though the main battery housing could be a bit challenging for the less experienced. I installed the S-Foil Ion cannon by first gluing (with IC-GEL) the front, inboard side of the cannon body to the cannon housing. Again, the targeting sensors are handed, so make sure each cannon's targeting sensor is on the *outboard* side.

Now add a little more CA to the outboard side of the cannon body, and gently press the outside of the housing into position and shoot with Insta-Set. Flip the foil upside down, add a little CA to the cannon body's top rib where

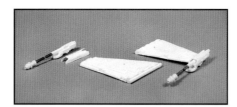

On your right is an S-Foil completely assembled and ready for installation. To the left is an S-Foil, cannon housing, and rebuilt cannon just waiting to be joined.

it butts against the housing, follow with Insta-Set, and you're done. Repeat for the other S-Foil. Do take your time to test fit as much as necessary so that both S-Foil gun installations are properly aligned.

With a wall thickness of about .030 inch, assembly of the main battery housing is just a little tricky. The kit's drawings clearly show how everything aligns, but you're on your own after that. There's a rib mount on both the top and bottom of the gun body that is designed to span the housing's centerline. So, after aligning the gun's position fore and aft, I CA'd the top edge of the housing half onto the rib, leaving half the rib thickness free.

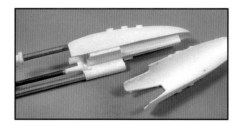

Joining those eggshell-thin housing halves around the main battery is one of the trickier aspects of this model. Patience! Patience! Patience! It wouldn't hurt to hold your tongue just right, either.

Then I repeated the process on the bottom rib. I repeated the whole sequence for the other half of the housing, which resulted in a gun/housing unit that was joined only along the top and bottom ribs. The remaining part of the housing seam was still loose and not all that well aligned.

From this point on, I started at one end, aligned a short section of seam, held them in position with my fingers using sufficient pressure for the edges to be in contact, applied some CA, and then followed with a shot of Insta-Set.

Then I moved to the next open section, repeated the process and so on until the entire seam had been joined.

Finally, before the CA had attained its final hardness, I went back over the

Apparently I did something right, because the finished unit is ready for installation. And I didn't even CA any of my skin to the surface in the process!

seam with sandpaper to smooth everything down. It sounds a heckuva lot more complicated than it really is. Tedious? Yes, but the method works quite well. About the only thing you really have to be careful of is to keep your fingers away from the CA.

Finally, the completed main battery was installed at the bottom of the main wing. Normally, you'd think that the seam on the gun pod would match the seam on the wing. In an injected styrene kit, yes —but not necessarily where resin is concerned. What matters is that the end result *looks* right, which means that you take your time.

You're also going to rely heavily on your Mk. I eyeball computer and whatever references you can find. In this case, the drawing in step 7 of the instructions will be a huge help.

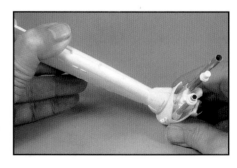

Finally, the main gun battery is installed on the bottom of the main wing. Be aware that you probably won't be able to match centerline to centerline and have it properly aligned. Keep your Mk. I eyeball computer handy.

COCKPIT/COLLAR ASSEMBLY

The collar assembly, including the cockpit, is the stable part of the ship that the rest rotates around. I built up the assembly, less cockpit module, and installed the result on the collar-assembly mount. With that, the main part of the B-Wing was complete, but there were still a few other details and the cockpit to go.

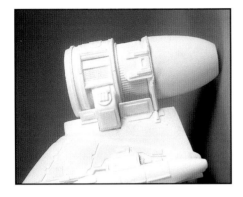

The collar assembly (minus the cockpit module) goes on next.

OTHER THINGS

When you build a B-Wing, particularly one the size of this beaut, you are going to have one major problem that absolutely *must* be solved. Namely, just how in the galaxy are you going to set this thing down in a display case? For that matter, how can you even paint it? The B-Wing doesn't have any landing gear, and when it shows up in a video game's hanger deck, it appears to be floating on an anti-gravity field. As they say — 'the difficult we do immediately, the impossible takes a little longer.' It turns out this problem isn't even all that difficult if you apply a little thought.

I drilled a 1/8-inch diameter hole in the back of the S-Foil mounting plate when I reached a point where I had to have some way to set this thing down.

Fortunately, the S-Foil hub is a solid casting and the back of it has a flat face. All I did was drill a 1/8-inch diameter hole into the center of the rear face to a depth of an inch-and-a-half or two. This would allow me to shove in a piece of 1/8-inch diameter music wire. A couple of inches behind the ship, I bent about a 110-degree angle and then cut the wire at a point two or three inches below the bottom of the main wing. Then I drilled a hole in a piece of pine board that will serve as a temporary base, stuck in the vertical wire leg, and there you have it. Now I could prime and/or paint the model without anything touching it. We'll replace the board with a proper display base later on.

CANOPY

The B-Wing canopy was originally cast clear resin. It is acceptable, but nowhere near as clear as vacuform plastic would be. It's now been replaced with a much better vacuform canopy. If you've never dabbled with vacuform kits or components, you'll find out that they're just a little different. To begin with, they're flimsier (relatively speaking) than styrene or resin kits. It's not uncommon to have to design in reinforcing bulkheads or other types of bracing. Also, because the plastic is so thin (anywhere from .010 to .080 inch), joining edges can present a problem similar to the resin main battery housing on this kit. If you are getting the idea that vacuform kit construction is, uh, unique, you're right. But despite its uniqueness when compared to styrene or resin, there are plenty of times you have to deal with it for certain details, because nothing else will do. Though vacuform products run the gamut from small detail parts to complete kits that are both complex and intimidating. Most modelers become familiar with vacuforming as a result of one single part — canopies.

Many modelers vacuform a duplicate of a kit's stock canopy in order to get a thinner and (frequently) clearer canopy. Others prefer to buy a commercially available vacuform canopy for the same purpose, but avoiding the need for their own vacuform machine. No matter how they get one, they're still left with the problem of how to trim and install the little beast.

As far as this vacuform canopy is concerned, here's how to tackle it. Vacuform parts have a surplus piece of plastic attached to the bottom of each component that has to be removed. This is the result of the vacuforming process where a sheet of softened plastic is placed over the pattern and a vacuum applied to pull the soft plastic tightly against the pattern. Put the end of a vacuum-cleaner hose against your skin and then turn the vacuum on. Your skin is drawn into the vacuum hose in the same manner as that softened plastic against a pattern. In fact, many garage kit makers use shop-grade or industrial strength vacuum cleaners to produce their parts. And is there a serious model builder alive who hasn't heard of, or used, the old Mattel Vacuform?

Anyway, either cut or trim around the canopy to release it from its carrier sheet. Just be sure to cut outside the edges, because it's a lot easier to remove more plastic than to replace it, especially where clear canopies are concerned. Either a knife or small scissors will do in this case.

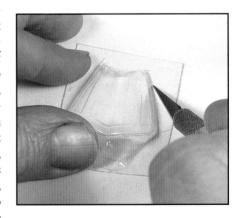

Scoring around the outside of the vacuformed canopy is the best way to remove it from its backing sheet. Now it's a matter of cut and try until it fits.

From here on, it's cut and try. Take your time and trim down the edges to their final size. Do keep in mind that some vacuform parts can be either slightly larger or smaller than they need to be in order to fit properly. It's going to be up to you as a model builder to make the appropriate adjustments. Fortunately, getting the canopy to fit on the B-Wing is fairly easy. Now set it to one side.

COCKPIT

Considering its minimal screen time and the fact that filming (or studio) models don't have interiors unless they're needed, there's no way to create a truly accurate cockpit. In other words, it's ad-lib time. After watching some of the *Star Wars* episodes several times, I settled on an overall Model Master FS 36440 Flat Gull Gray for an interior color, even including the pilot's seat. I would say ejection seat, but since the pilot isn't wearing a pressure suit there's little point in ejecting into airless space.

The instrument panel shroud was painted Model Master FS 37038 Flat Black and the various buttons and raised panel details were a mix of black, red, green, yellow, and silver. The pilot got an orange suit, black boots, and white helmet. Once dry, he was mounted in the seat and installed in the cockpit.

This is the finished cockpit module, complete with pilot, mounted to the front end of the collar assembly. Since no interior shots were ever seen of the inside, you can detail it to whatever level you wish, and no one can say you're wrong. When you add the canopy, your cockpit is done.

WHAT GLUE FOR THE CANOPY?

A lot of modelers have trouble installing clear parts, especially canopies. If they're using liquid cements, they can foul the inside of a tight-fitting canopy through capillary action. Tube glues can squeeze out in places you don't want them to, and most CAs can fog clear parts while curing. As a result, the use of white glue (Elmer's, etc.) is rather widely recommended for safe installation of clear parts. Quite a number, if not the majority, of model builders tend to swear by white glue for clear parts. Me? I pretty much swear *at* it! This is due mainly to the fact that white glue forms a weak joint. I prefer to fair in the canopy/fuselage joint and do my masking *after* installing the canopy. The weakness of white glue makes it difficult to impossible to indulge that preference.

Now don't get the notion that I eschew white glue entirely. I use it whenever and wherever it'll do the job. It's just that I don't consider canopy attachment to be a proper use when there's a better way. That way is Bob Smith Industries Super Gold + CA.

Granted, most CAs *will* fog clear parts, especially if you can't get air ventilation into the area. BSI Super Gold + is, however, a horse of a different color. The label states specifically that it won't frost (fog) clear plastic, and it lives up to its billing.

Super Gold + is a gap-filling formula, so all you have to do is run a bead around the edge of the canopy opening and carefully install the canopy. You may find it easier to attach one edge first and then work your way around. Once you're used to working with CA, you'll find that you can correct small cavities/flaws and even build up contours when something doesn't match up right.

Once I was satisfied with the installation, I masked the glass and then mounted the completed cockpit module on the collar assembly. Oh, before I forget it, be sure to paint the front of the collar gray to match the cockpit interior. There's no aft bulkhead in the cockpit module, so the collar assembly face functions as one. Also scrape the paint out of the groove that the cockpit will glue into. Since the

entire ship is designed to rotate around the cockpit, it's possible to install the cockpit in any position. However, if you pick any position other than the main wing being vertical, it will affect the way you mount it on a base.

PRIMER/PAINT

Everyone has their own ideas on how to get a realistic paint job on a model. Some work, some don't, even though their creators *think* they do. Be that as it may, if it makes you happy, it's right, unless you're building for contests or a client. Regardless, you need to keep one thing in mind: Every preceding layer of color affects every successive layer of color. As a result, the final color applied to a model (the color everyone who views the model will see) is affected by all that has gone before, from the primer out.

Since spacecraft are made from metal (or some other exotic material that we have yet to discover), the surface is going to have a "hard" appearance. Ergo, I have reached the point (with much prodding from Tony Weddel) that I apply a base color of silver or aluminum (bare metal in other

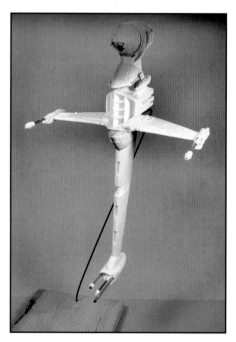

At long last, the B-Wing is completely built and ready for painting. Note that the cockpit area has already been primed during installation of the canopy. As soon as I prime the rest of the ship, it will be ready for its final colors.

words) over the primer before dealing with the final paint. This approach results in a hard metallic appearance that enhances a model's realism.

So, once I had a primered B-Wing that I was happy with, the entire ship was airbrushed with Floquil Old Silver. Keep in mind that there are many different kinds of silver available, from flat aluminum to bright silver to lacquer metalizers. Each has a different look when dry, and once you're familiar with the variety, they can enable you to make very subtle adjustments to the tone of your final color.

As for the final color, instructions specify an overall pale gray with a medium blue-gray on the ends of the wings and the guns. A photo of the finished model contradicts this somewhat by showing the medium blue-gray only on the end of the lower wing and guns. When you check the movie, *Return of the Jedi*, you'll find the B-Wing only appears clearly for about seven seconds, and your only view is the rear, since they're moving away from you in preparation for an attack on the Death Star. In those frames, the medium blue-gray appears to be on the lower wing/gun pod and on the outer third of the S-Foils — but *not* on the foil-mounted guns.

On the other hand, photos of the studio model that I found on the Internet show a B-Wing that's almost a white-gray overall with a very light blue-gray on the ends of all three wings, including the guns. The same color is used on the exhaust nozzles, intake, and panels on the side of the engine nacelle. What to do? What to do?

DEFINING THE PROBLEM

As I touched on briefly in chapter two while building the Starfury, determining the proper color for a spacecraft model that appeared in a film is tricky at best. For one thing, you have to decide whether to represent the model as it appears in the film or match the actual studio model. The two are not necessarily the same due to the changing lighting conditions used during filming and the specific effect a director is striving for.

Secondly, the various "technical manuals" that we all scarf up so that we can build a truly accurate replica are created after the fact. Colors specified in their pages may or may not be the same as the studio model or what you see in the film.

Films cause a third problem, where ships and vehicles are created strictly as CGIs (computer generated image), a practice that's becoming more and more common. CGIs exist only as digital files. Since those files can be altered at will, you can have three ships of the identical type where each one displays a slightly different color tone, markings, or details. It's enough to make you wonder if you even stand a chance of creating an exact replica. And the short answer, with occasional exceptions, is probably not.

THE SOLUTION

Given all the variables involved, it may come as no surprise that the solution is *your* executive decision. First, decide if you want to create a collection of studio models or representations of the real spacecraft. In either case, the method will be the same. Only the colors and details will change.

If studio models are your thing, you'll be tracking down and analyzing as many photos of the actual model (or models) as you can find. Then it's simply a question of which one you want to replicate. Remember, there may be as many as a half dozen or more filming models of the same ship in various sizes, no two of which will look the same.

Do you prefer, as I do, to create models of the real ships in the finished film? Then besides interpreting photos, you'll also be staring at two-second film clips or slightly fuzzy freeze frames until you're cross-eyed, then trying to reconcile all the differences you'll spot. Eventually you'll settle on a specific combination of colors/markings and get around to finishing the model.

Just in case you think I'm being a little cavalier regarding the colors and markings of science-fiction models, keep a couple of things in mind. First and foremost, you're building models for enjoyment, relaxation, and fun — unless you build as a business. Even then, if you're not enjoying it, you're in the wrong business. Beyond that, there's a humongous difference between a spacecraft that exists only in your mind and/or on film and an exact replica of the space shuttle Columbia built as a memorial to its last heroic crew and their final mission.

BACK TO THE B-WING

So, after wading through the process just described, and successfully uncrossing my eyes, I settled on a very light overall gray, but not the white-gray of the studio model. My intent was to match the B-Wing's on-screen appearance.

I started mixing the light gray with equal parts Model Master FS 36622 Camouflage Gray and Model Master FS 37875 Flat White. It turned out that it was too gray, so I added another part of Flat White, and another, and another. By the time I got the shade I wanted, the ratio was somewhere around seven or eight to one. If you're thinking that's the hard way to get light gray, you're right. In this case it didn't matter because I needed quite a bit of paint, due to the B-Wing's large size. You'd probably find it easier to add a little Camouflage Gray to a lot of Flat White.

At any rate, I sprayed the entire B-Wing light gray, then masked off and sprayed medium blue-gray on the ends of all three wings, including all of the guns. There are also four tapered blue-

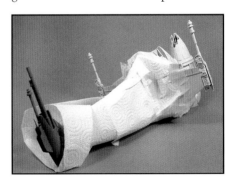

After spraying an overall, custom-mixed light gray color, it was time to mask off the ends of the wings, S-Foils, and guns to be sprayed Model Master Blue Gray. Due to this thing's configuration, I masked and sprayed the bottom of the main wing first. Then the rest of the model was masked and the S-Foil tips were sprayed. Notice the extensive use of paper towels. Not only does it save on tape, it reduces the risk of the tape pulling paint loose.

gray panels on the rear cone of the crew module. Rather than mixing a color, I used Model Master U.S. Navy Blue Gray. The recessed tip of the rear cone should also be Blue Gray. Once that was dry, the model got a couple of coats of Floquil Crystal Cote so I could add the decals.

DECALS

As it turned out, the decals were missing from my kit, but they were quickly replaced by SMT. Do keep in mind that the kit's decals provide only the orange discs and small canopy markings. However, the SMT website lists four different sets of nose art you can order that are designed to fit each side of the main wing. I opted for the one called Dragon, but other sheets are titled Angel, Stars, and Teeth. Incidentally, you do need to be aware that Angel is a full nude, particularly if you have young children or a personal aversion to the subject.

Most decals today are printed as individual designs on the backing paper with the clear carrier barely extending beyond the design. This eliminates the need to cut as close to each design as possible. Not so in this case. Once the designs were printed, the entire backing sheet received a coat of Testors Clear Flat Lacquer. While the resulting decals are very thin and yet reasonably sturdy, you are left with one chore. Namely, each design will have to be closely trimmed in order to minimize the amount of clear carrier.

Having done that, I started my decal session by applying the orange discs on the top of the S-Foils. That was the easy part. What takes a little time and patience is the dragon. Trimming

Nose art sheet or not, you'll have to trim the designs as closely as reasonable to get rid of the extraneous clear film.

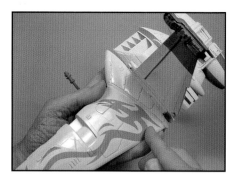

Use care when positioning the decals, especially the nose art. While they're not particularly fragile, you can still tear them. Once in place, blot out the surplus water, add Solvaset or similar, and let 'em dry.

around that convoluted dragon to the extent possible left me with a long, narrow design that would take a little bit of TLC to position without tearing. Again, the designs release so quickly that by the time you've dipped them in water and pulled them out, they're ready to slide off.

Once the dragon is in position, I blotted up the excess surface water and then began to squeegee out the water trapped under the decal in order to get the decal in full contact with the model's surface. Some modelers use a paper towel or tissue to do the job. I've been at this so long that my finger suffices. Just like giving a fingerprint, all I do is roll my finger from side to side, gently driving the water out from under the decal. And gently is the name of the game. Press too hard and you'll wind up with the decal applied to your finger! Also be sure the decal doesn't shift or wrinkle in the process. Finally, brush on some Solvaset or other decal solution and let the decal dry. Oh, yeah, don't forget the rescue arrow that goes directly in front of the windscreen.

DETAILS, DETAILS, DETAILS

Using a 1/4-inch chisel-tip bristle brush, I brush painted the remaining details. The same Model Master Blue Gray already used on the wings/gun pods was selected for the Cooling System Intake, Shield Generator, Hyperdrive Monitor, and the Microaxial Navigation Sensor that's located on the leading edge of the main wing. And don't overlook the raised panels, which I'm assuming are additional armor plat-

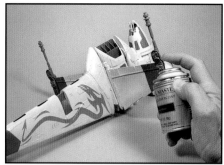

After final detailing with a conventional brush and Model Master Blue Gray paint, but before unmasking the canopy, the entire ship gets a shot of Model Master Semi-Gloss Clear Lacquer.

ing for the cockpit. They're also Blue Gray. Three small, rectangular recesses in the leading edge of the main wing were painted Model Master FS 36118 Gunship Gray. When all the paint had dried, the entire ship got a coat of Model Master Semi-Gloss Lacquer.

EXHAUST NOZZLES

At first glance, the B-Wing appears to be a four-engine ship. After all, it has four exhaust nozzles. Well, looks can be deceiving on occasion. In actual fact, the B-Wing is powered by a *single* Quadex Kryromaster engine. The four nozzles can be individually adjusted, a feature that presumably allows for greater maneuverability. In any event, I had left the nozzles off until the model was nearly complete. Now my attention turned to them.

SMT cast these parts as solid pieces with nicely recessed openings. Though they beg to be drilled out, they work quite well as they are. A little judicious shading will make the exhaust openings look deeper than they are. At any rate, I drilled a small hole in the butt end of each nozzle and mounted them on toothpicks for painting. Primer comes first, of course, followed by Model Master Metalizer Steel. Then a light dusting of Model Master Metalizer Titanium on the outside, a heavier shot inside the nozzle throat, and it was time to figure out the installation.

While there are no locators on either the engine housing or nozzles to aid in their installation, it really isn't all that hard. There are four U-shaped scallops spaced around the rear of the

Just prior to installation, the exhaust nozzles are sprayed with a mix of Model Master Steel and Titanium Metalizers. It's amazing what you can do with clothespins and toothpicks to hold these things for painting, isn't it?

engine housing. Each of the nozzles should be centered in the cutouts when viewed from the side. Additionally, each pair of nozzles should align vertically and horizontally when viewed from the back. Do you have their positions pretty well set in your mind? Now go ahead and install them.

UNMASKING THE CANOPY

The time has come to unmask the canopy. However, don't just stick your knife blade under the tape and pull it up. Between the paint and multiple layers of clear coat, try that and you'll find paint chipping around the edges like crazy. Avoid the problem by scoring around the edge of the tape *before* you

I've just unmasked the canopy. Everything worked as planned and the vacuformed canopy allows a much better and more realistic view of the cockpit than the original cast clear resin version did.

try to strip it. Be sure to put a new blade in the knife first so that you can use minimal pressure. *Now* get the point of the knife under one corner of the tape and gently pull it up.

THE LAST FINAL DETAILS — HONEST

Rather than leave the guns the same Blue Gray as the wingtips and gun housings, I painted them all Model Master Steel. There's a pair of autoblasters in the nose of the cockpit module and they get a coat of Model Master Steel as well. Keep in mind that various brands of Steel aren't identical. That can work to your advantage by allowing you to get just the right tone you're looking for. If none of them seem right to you, try adding a drop or two of Model Master Gun Metal to the mix.

Here I'm in the process of painting the ribbed Gyrostabilization sections that are found on the cockpit/collar assembly.

The last thing left to do is to paint the two ribbed Gyrostabiliztion sections on the cockpit module. They need to be a dark metallic color. One way to replicate it is to simply paint it with Floquil or Model Master Gun Metal. Another is Model Master Metalizer Titanium. Of course, Metalizer is a lacquer thinned to airbrush consistency. Though intended for airbrushing only, it *can* be brushed

on. I'm used to it, so that's what I did. If the idea of hand brushing thin lacquer over enamel makes you uncomfortable, then use one of the enamel Gun Metals. Remember, whatever works for you is the right method.

USE YOUR WEATHER EYE

Unlike Empire vehicles, Rebel ships were anything but clean. When you're outmanned, outgunned, with nothing but right on your side, there's precious little time for any kind of spit and polish, never mind the time it takes to wash, wax, and/or properly repair battle damage and weathering. Even repairs were frequently held together with chewing gum and baling wire. What mattered was that they were operational.

Working under that premise, I got down and dirty. Besides my old standby bottle of dirty thinner, I made up a couple of others. A little bit of Model Master Airbrush Thinner was poured into a pair of 35-mm film canisters. Then I took a fairly worn chisel-tip brush (anything reasonably ragged will work), dipped it into a bottle of Floquil Grime, swirled the brush around in some of the thinner, stroked the brush on scrap paper to remove most of the paint, and then started dry-brushing the B-Wing. The same method was used with a bottle of Model Master Rust and another container of clean thinner, dry-brushing different areas. Keep in mind that the S-Foils are hinged on the real ship, so you'll have wear and hydraulic leaks in that area. You'll also have streaks created by charred debris that the ship flies through and on and on.

When you get a little too heavy with your weathering applications, you can fade out the color or adjust the streaking by swiping quickly with your finger.

It won't take long before you find yourself falling into a rhythm. You'll also wind up blending the various colors and dirty thinner. Also, don't overlook the fact that if you happen to put a streak on too heavily, you can fade it out, or even alter its shape, by simply wiping over it with your finger. Be quick, though, because you have to do it before it begins to dry. You've got maybe three or four seconds to do it. Last but not least, if you *still* think some or all of the weathering is too heavy, let it dry. You'll find that all of the weathering effects will fade slightly, improving their realism.

Finally, I shot some Model Master Clear Transparent Black Window Tint into a 35-mm film can. This was necessary because the Window Tint is available only in a spray can. To use it (or any other aerosol paint) in your airbrush, you first have to transfer the liquid into an open container. You do this by holding the container (35-mm film

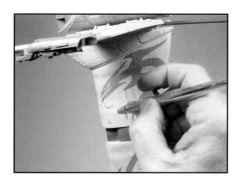

Finally, I finished up with some additional streaking and fading by shooting Model Master Clear Transparent Black Window Tint thru my Rich AB-100 airbrush.

can, bottle, paper cup, or whatever) at about a 45-degree angle. Then direct the spray nozzle at the container's far wall and spray. The paint will hit the surface, condense, and run down the wall into the bottom of the container. Now pour the liquid paint into your airbrush and have at it. By the way, if you've never

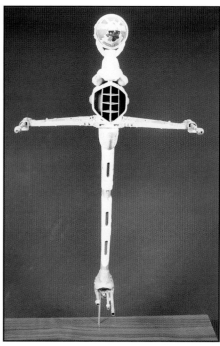

Here is a shot looking down the business end of a B-Wing. Not exactly what you want to see if you're the enemy.

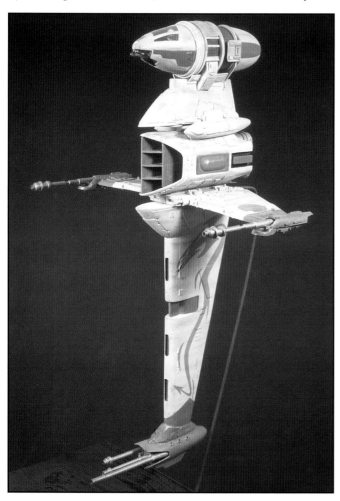

From a 3/4 left front, it's easy to see how rebuilding the resin guns with brass tubing improves the B-Wing's final appearance.

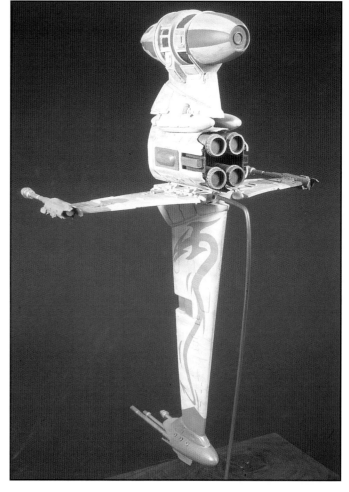

This 3/4 rear view is similar to what you see in Return Of The Jedi. Note the four exhaust pipes driven by a single engine.

tried this trick before, it can be quite messy until you get the hang of it.

From this point on, it's simply a matter of streaking and misting the Transparent Black Window Tint until you get the results you want. It also helps to use an airbrush with a tip capable of spraying extremely fine lines. While I can get the results I want with just about any airbrush, I switched over to my Rich AB-100 because it has an extremely long taper needle. The longer the taper, the finer and smaller the area you can spray with greater ease.

Keep in mind that the transparent tint will build up slowly while allowing the underlying color to show through. It also had a tendency to fade slightly as it dries, so if you think you've been a little heavy handed, it could wind up being exactly what you're looking for.

WHAT ABOUT A BASE?

Early on, I had already worked up a temporary base that combined a large piece of wood with a 1/8-inch diameter music wire support rod. The support rod would be retained (no choice), but now it was time to come up with a proper base. It'd still be wood, but the question was what configuration. Due to the B-Wing's size (16 inches tall) and the fact that it is supported by a slightly flexible metal rod, you could have a serious tip-over problem.

You can be as fancy or as simple as you want, as long as it's large enough to avoid the tip-over risk. I ended up with a 14 1/2 x 7 1/4-inch piece of 3/4-inch thick walnut, mainly because that's what I had left from building other bases. The fact that I would've had to buy a six or eight foot long board to make my base a few inches longer had something to do with it as well. Occasionally you just have to work with what's on hand.

All I did was sand my base and clearcoat it with Deft Semi-Gloss Clear Wood Finish (it took about 1/2 a spray can before I was happy with the results). Then I measured in 1 inch from a long side and 7 1/4 inch from one end and drilled a 1/8-inch diameter hole through the base. Because of the way my music wire support rod was bent, my hole was drilled on about a five-degree slant.

Finally, I removed the support rod from the B-Wing *and* its temporary base, squirted some Super Gold + into both holes, reinserted the rod, and quickly made final adjustments before the CA snapped. It worked like a charm.

TIE BOMBER

The TIE Bomber m*akes its only screen appearance in The Empire Strikes Back.* Blink and you'll miss it because they (there are two of them) get a tremendous fifteen seconds of exposure. If you've seen the movie, you know the scene. After the *Millennium Falcon* dives into a large opening in an asteroid (turns out they wound up in the stomach of a large beast) to escape the Empire's forces, a pair of TIE Bombers skim the surface of the asteroid dropping concussion bombs. Thanks to SMT, we can finally have a TIE Bomber of our own without resorting to scratch-building.

Everything comes in a relatively small box with a rather unique wraparound label on it.

FIRST, FIND A TIE FIGHTER

The TIE Bomber is one of those kits that use major components from other kits to complete the model; at least at the time I wrote this book. SMT plans to include both wings in future kits. Those of you with the earlier kits will have to track down one of the old Darth Vader Tie Fighter kits from MPC. Since it's no longer on the

market or in production, you'll need to deal with companies that resell old kits. Still, it's not that much of a problem. I found mine after a couple of hours searching classified ads in FineScale Modeler and one phone call. Price? $18.00 plus shipping.

Well, almost everything comes in the box. You still have to track down a Darth Vader Tie Fighter kit to swipe the wings from.

CONSTRUCTION

In contrast to the B-Wing, there are no soft or thin spots from faulty spin casting. Everything is crisp and the amount of flash is quite acceptable. Only four parts required replacement and I scratch-built duplicates instead of contacting SMT. When we get to that point, you'll understand why. And since the TIE Bomber displayed no markings in the film, there are no decals to deal with. My only real problem was with the instructions, which were poor at best and lousy at worst. Of course, that problem is being addressed by SMT, even as I write this.

After spending a couple of hours with the instructions and a headache, I began by installing the front of the bomb-bay hull to the bomb-bay hull (the shorter of the two cylindrical castings). There are eight rectangular recesses around the perimeter of the front casting. Be sure that you orient the part so that two of the recesses are level right-to-left and in line with the holes in the sides of the hull when viewed from the front. Instructions tell you to align each recess with one of the hull's panel lines. That's all well and good, but you'll have to try different positions to see where the best alignment occurs.

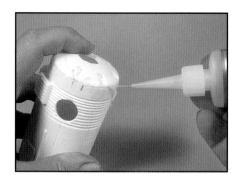

Actual construction began by joining the bomb bay front to the bomb bay hull. Be sure that the front is oriented correctly.

Why am I beating you over the head about this? Because when the hull is completed, the large holes in its sides will slip over the axis shaft and butt against a center box. If alignment of those recesses (as well as certain other parts) is noticeably off, the finished model will never look real, no matter how hard you try.

Latches

Now for a little tedium. There are eight small T-shape fittings (actually latches) that allow the front to be removed for bomb loading. Once you've cleaned up the flash, they're mounted around the perimeter of the hull, each one in line with a recess and positioned so that the cross-arm of the T straddles the seam between the bay front and bay hull. But first you have to sand the back of each latch so that it matches the curvature of the hull. SMT suggests finding a piece of 2-inch diameter tubing, wrapping a piece of sandpaper around it, and then sanding the back of the latches until they match the curve.

That little T-shaped latch between my thumb and forefinger is being sanded to a proper contour before installation. There are eight of these things, and you'll probably lose a little skin in the process.

Well, the technique is correct, but there's no point looking for a 2-inch tube when you already have one — the bomb-bay hull. It doesn't take that large a piece of sandpaper, so find a smooth section of hull, hold the paper against it (back side down), take the latch in your other hand and sand until the contours match. Do it seven more times and install them.

Two parts mount on the front of the bomb bay hatch. While their purpose isn't identified, torpedoes and concussion missiles are launched through the front port, so it's not unreasonable to assume that they're part of the targeting system. In any event, you'll have to contour their base for proper fit against the hatch. There's also one question I can't find an answer to. Namely, are the two parts positioned for equal separation or should the separation diminish the further you get from the hatch? It's pretty much your call, since no one is likely to tell you if you're wrong.

These two components that are probably part of the missile/torpedo tracking system are installed on the front of the bomb bay. IC-GEL is ideal for this.

At this point, I shot the inside of the hull with gray primer, as well as the inside surface of the tailpipe/exhaust cone. Then I scraped the dried primer away from the outer 1/4-inch or so of the tailpipe's inside face, did the same for the back edge of the hull, and then installed the tailpipe. Again, pay attention to alignment. In this case, the three blunt spikes should line up left-to-right. The same orientation will be used on the crew hull when we get to it. Finally, you'll find an indentation on the lower right rear quadrant of the bomb-bay hull. Drill a 1/4-inch diameter hole there. You'll eventually mount the targeting sensor pylon in this location.

Better now than later. I drilled the 1/4-inch mounting hole for the bomb-targeting sensor much earlier than the instructions would advise you to.

Central Hub

My kit came with the central hub partially assembled on the tube. Yours may or may not, which can affect some of your construction sequences. Regardless, a more or less H-shaped frame will have to be mounted on the bottom of the hub, centered both fore-and-aft and side-to-side.

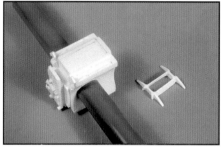

Look closely and you'll see guide lines drawn on the central hub as an aid to installing the H-shaped frame.

Since there's no dimple, recess, or other way of knowing where the frame should go, you'll have to lay it out yourself. It's actually quite easy. Measure the width (or length) of the frame, then the width (or length) of the hub bottom. Deduct the width (or length) of the frame from the width (or length) of the hub bottom and divide the result by two. This tells you how far in from the side (or end) of the hub bottom you need to be for the frame to be centered. Draw a pencil line down one side and across one end at those locations. Apply CA to the back of the frame, position so that a side and one end butt against the pencil lines you drew and the part is centered.

One Hull Deserves Another

With the bomb bay hull built, it's time to tackle the crew hull. There's a little more to this, but not much. A frame lattice has to be mounted on top of the Ion engine covers, but their location was a complete mystery initially. However, after spending some time on the Internet, I found enough information to show me exactly where they went, as well as the fact they're 1/2 inch too long. That was easily remedied by simply cutting off the surplus portion. Proper location was easy as well since the frames are full span. Just locate the butt end of the open frame even with the back edge of the Ion cov-

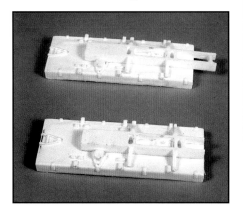

Both Ion covers are seen here. At the top is the unaltered lattice frame after installation, compared to the corrected frame at the bottom.

ers and everything falls right into place.

The completed Ion covers can now be added to the top and bottom of the crew hull. Alignment is crucial here as well. Look closely and you'll find some very light scored lines running left-to-right on the forward end of the crew hull. They're only on the top and bottom, their width being equal to the width of the Ion covers. This is where the front edges of the Ion covers need to be positioned. Locate the top cover, check it again, and yet again, then while holding it in position, run a bead of Super Gold CA down the seam and hit it with a shot of InstaSet. Repeat for the bottom cover.

There are four long fittings (part T) that mount on the outside of the crew hull and butt against the forward half of the cover/hull joint. The forward end is exactly even with the front edge of the Ion cover. Look closely at the center of the fitting (between the two arcs) and you'll find a couple of very lightly scribed lines. If you have everything positioned correctly, those lines, if cut out as a slot, should fall precisely over the groove between the sixth and seventh ribs when counting from the front.

Both inboard fittings do *not* have slots cut where the scribed lines are, but the outboard fittings do. Keep in mind that the outboard sides of *both* hulls have the triple rib that projects out from the hull side about 1/4 inch. Beyond that, the hulls won't fit against the hub if you reverse things.

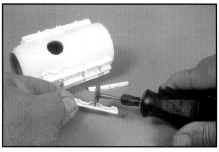

Because of the relative brittleness of thin resin parts when compared to styrene, my Dremel with a diamond cutting wheel is the ideal way to open up the slot on these fittings.

The instructions tell you to cut a slot between the two lines, but they don't tell you how. The obvious method would be with a knife, but the fragility and relative brittleness of that small a casting makes me nervous with that method. Instead, I resorted to my Dremel-powered diamond cutting blade. It cuts literally like a hot knife through butter. After verifying that the slots would line up where they should, they were installed and it was time to deal with the interior.

Cockpit

There really isn't a lot of detail in the cockpit assembly, nor does there need to be. Interior colors range from dark gray to black. Besides, the pilot is dressed in black, and there's no way to know what the interior really looks like, so you simply don't need to worry about it. What is there makes it plenty busy.

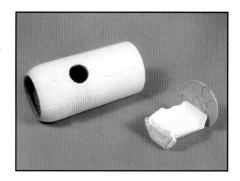

This is the crew hull and interior module ready for installation. Note that I robbed the rear bulkhead from the Darth Vader kit instead of using the resin version.

Three parts form the basic cockpit. I did replace the aft bulkhead with the one from my MPC kit. Once I had the assembly together, it was slipped into the hull (from the rear) to make sure I would have clearance for the cross tube. Satisfied that I would, I added the seat and painted the whole thing flat black. Before the pilot was cemented in position, he was painted Floquil Engine Black so that he would have a little sheen for contrast with the flat black. In the meantime, I'd sprayed the hull interior a dark gray. Now the completed cockpit assembly was inserted for the last time. A bead of CA around the perimeter of the aft bulkhead would hold it firmly in place. Finally, the remaining tailpipe/exhaust cone was CA'd in place.

Mating the Hulls

I slipped the bomb-bay hull (the right one when viewed from the front) onto the tube, checked for proper fit against the hub box, and made whatev-

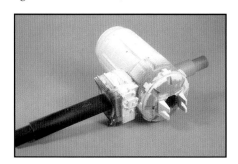

I've installed the bomb bay hull on the central hub. Don't forget that there are specific parts for the right and left, and also an up and down. Get it right or you'll have bought yourself a lot of grief.

er adjustments were needed for a gap-free fit. Then I pulled it off, added a coat of IC-GEL to the hub, and reinstalled the hull.

Note that the IC-GEL was used only on the hub side. Thinner Super Gold was run around the tube where it protrudes through the outboard side of the hull. I repeated the process to install the crew hull, making sure to sight the front, back, *and* sides to make sure the two hulls are in line with each other.

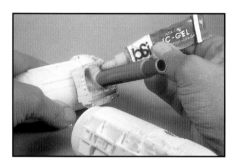

Add a little more IC-GEL to the opposite side of the central hub and install the crew hull.

Fins

There's a group of fins that mount on the tube between the outboard sides of the hull and the wing mounts. My instructions were relatively clear on the first set. They mount on the top and bottom centerlines of the tubes. The fins butt against the outboard curve of the hull (as do the opposite ones), but they also fit into the slots that were cut earlier in those fittings. Just keep test fitting and trimming until they seat properly. Also, be aware that they extend further toward the wing than is necessary. This allows you to trim them to the correct length and angle to fit against the wing mount.

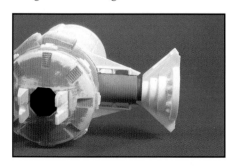

The wing mounts can be temporarily slipped in place in order to trim the top and bottom fin castings for a proper fit.

The other fins fit on the front and back of the tubes, 90 degrees from the vertical fins. They butt against the hull sides. You'll find some trimming needed there, but not on the outer ends. Where things get tricky is in getting the back edges to fit against the tubes. Each set of fins is comprised of two long ribs joined by two small vertical bars, and those small bars are delicate.

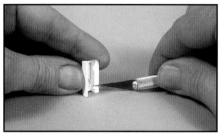

Use a brand new #11 blade to bevel the insides of the paired fins for a proper fit against the cross tube. Gently, gently — the vertical connecting bars are very delicate.

If you clean up the flash around those bars first, you stand a very good chance of snapping them when you start beveling the back edges of the ribs. So, bevel the ribs first and *then* clean up the bars. In either case, start with a brand new #11 blade in order to minimize stress and pressure.

When properly trimmed and installed, this is what all the fins should look like.

Targeting Sensor

The sensor's mounting pylon has a large resin peg on one end that fits into the hole you drilled previously. Again, watch the pylon's orientation. It projects at about a 45-degree angle towards the *center* of the ship, not towards the wings. Once it's in place, all that's left is to mount the sensor itself. Since I

would have to center the sensor on the bottom of the pylon, and the sensor base was larger than the pylon, I decided to pin the two together. This meant I'd have to find the center point of both surfaces. That's easily done by drawing lines connecting each pair of diametrically opposed corners on each surface, essentially forming an "X" on each. Where the lines intersect is your center point. I drilled a couple of holes, inserted a pin, mounted and aligned the sensor, and that was that.

After installing the targeting sensor's mount, I drew an "X" on the mating surfaces of both the mount and the targeting sensor itself in order to find the center points. By doing this, I could drill the appropriate-size holes and pin the parts together.

The Wings

Now it's about time to tackle the things you bought that MPC Tie Fighter kit for — the wings (parts 3 and 4). You'll need to install the SMT-provided resin inner panels in place of those from the MPC kit. As usual, test fitting first will keep you out of trouble. I found that I had to sand the back down a ways to get a proper fit. Depending on your personal preference, you can do the job by either holding the back down on a sheet of 100-grit sandpaper, or by wrapping a piece of sandpaper around a block and sanding the back while holding the part still. Either way, be sure to constantly alter your sanding pattern in order to maintain an even thickness. And because of the amount of ultra-fine resin powder you'll be creating, be sure to use some sort of breathing protection.

When you're satisfied with the fit, they're installed with IC-GEL. A couple of clothespin clamps made sure I got a good bond. Next came the wing

I had to sand the back side of the resin inner panels so they'd fit properly on the styrene wings from the MPC kit. Don't forget your particle mask.

root attachments (parts Q). Again, test fit. Clamping will definitely be needed here to get everything tight — and there's a problem. Because of the location, along with the size of the jaw opening needed, most clamps modelers have on hand won't be large enough. The solution? Use a 3-inch Pony spring clamp. These are large, heavy-duty clamps familiar to anyone who's ever done woodworking. Some of them are so large and powerful that it takes two hands to overcome the spring strength. You find them in most lumber yards and big-box home improvement centers.

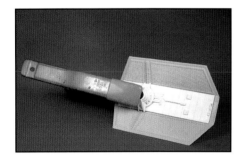

Once the inner panels are installed, the wing mounts come next. I ended up using (very carefully) a large woodworking clamp to attain a good, tight joint.

Wing Struts

Each of the wings features a pair of hydraulic adjustment struts, one forward and one behind each wing root attachment. They're also the only parts in the kit that are rough enough to be considered useless. Therefore, I chose to replace them with scratch-built copies from brass tubing. The process is exactly the same as that used for the B-Wing and Starfury guns, so I won't repeat that description here. Only the

dimensions and exact configuration change. Keep in mind that you will want to remove the angled ends and mount them on your replacement struts. And don't forget to add the resin replacement fitting (part V) to the outside of the wings.

Look closely and you can see the rebuilt hydraulic struts in place on the wing mounts. Just below, on the gray wing panel, you can see the other pair that is ready for installation on the other wing mount. The construction technique for the replacements is identical to the Starfury and B-Wing guns. Only the dimensions change.

PRIMER/PAINT

The finishing process began with the usual priming session: prime, examine, putty, sand or otherwise correct any flaws, prime again, and repeat until satisfied. In the case of the TIE Bomber, I'd suggest two other things. First, wrap some tape around the stepped ends of the crosstube to protect it from the primer and paint. Fail to do this and you'll be spending time scraping the built-up paint off so you can mount the wings. It also helps to stuff a little bit of paper towel or tape into the wing root attachment socket for the same reason. Be sure to protect the cockpit as well, so no primer gets inside.

First Paint the Solar Panels

After spraying the entire model, including the wings, Model Master Aluminum Non-Buffing Metalizer, the solar panels were given a shot of Model Master FS 37038 Flat Black. When that dries, grab your knife and a roll of low-tack tape and mask all 20 solar panels on the wings. This is also the time to install the canopy (or windscreen) from the MPC kit — but not the canopy frame. Be sure to mask the canopy off as well.

The Final Color

While we're now at the point of painting the overall color, one question begs an answer. What's the correct color? And the answer, as with the B-Wing, is — who knows? Between the 15 seconds of film time and various web sites, the answer is anything from light primer gray to a deep blue-black. SMT recommends Hyundai Jamaica Blue, though the truth is that it's pretty much your choice. Since the TIE Bomber is operated by the Empire, which in turn, serves the dark side of the Force, a color that would project a rather ominous image seemed appropriate.

Except for the solar wings, the TIE Bomber uses a monotone color scheme. Do note that I'm spraying the surface color over aluminum to enhance the appearance of a hard metal surface.

The result of all this philosophical/religious analysis was a more or less dark blue-gray. It is a 50/50 mix of Model Master FS 35164 Intermediate Blue and Floquil Gunmetal. To make identification easy, let's call it TB (TIE Bomber) Blue-Gray.

With the color to hand, all parts were sprayed with TB Blue-Gray. And don't forget to spray the canopy frame taken from the MPC kit. When the paint dries, install the canopy frame, strip the masking from the solar panels, and clear coat everything with Butyl Acetate.

If you're not familiar with this stuff, it's actually marketed by Testors as Metalizer Sealer. It dries almost instantly and is a true neutral clear. In other words, it has no effect on the appearance of whatever you spray it over and also does not cloud clear plastic. Put another way, it does the same thing Future floor wax does without the gloss.

One wing has been completed and the solar panels unmasked. In the foreground, I'm beginning to unmask the other wing.

Why use it? In this case, I used it to protect the underlying paint from weathering washes. Incidentally, keep in mind that most of the time you *don't* want to protect the base paint from your weathering techniques *because the whole purpose of weathering is to affect the finishing paint*. One more thing. I weathered the TIE Bomber *before* installing the wings. Normally the model should be totally built and finished prior to weathering, but installation of the wings would have prevented access to certain areas. It just goes to show that no approach, method, or technique is set in stone.

WEATHERING

No two models will ever be weathered exactly the same, partly because you'll never find any two machines (aircraft, spacecraft, tanks, etc.) exposed to absolutely identical conditions. The TIE Bomber, for example, will generally display relatively mild weathering.

Keep in mind that the Empire is a totalitarian society that's ruled with an iron fist. As a result, their military forces would be the epitome of spit-and-polish, much the way Hitler's military appeared in the early days of the Third Reich. Equipment would be maintained in near-immaculate condition. Obviously, craft on combat missions would acquire noticeable wear and tear. If nothing else, the extreme temperature swings of space and planetary atmospheres would have an effect,

never mind the near misses of plasma cannon. All of these factors have to be considered before you start weathering.

About all the weathering I did to the TIE Bomber was to touch the tip of a wet brush (that was fresh from my dirty thinner bottle) around the seams and anchor points of the hydraulic struts on each wing. It happened that my bottle of dirty thinner had taken on somewhat of a reddish cast as the result of cleaning a brush loaded with red. By the time it mixed with the rest of the crud in the bottle, the result was a very dull brick red tint.

As for the logic involved, consider this: If there is anything on a machine,

be it a car, aircraft, or spaceship that is likely to leak — it is the hydraulic lines and/or connections. And since the hydraulic/power steering/transmission fluid that we're all familiar with tends to be reddish in color, I simply projected that color into the world of the Empire.

With the weathering finished, I added the wings, made sure they were aligned properly, added a little CA to the joints, and the TIE Bomber was built.

SAME SONG, SECOND VERSE

As with the B-Wing, you're going to have to come up with a display base for the TIE Bomber. *Unlike* the B-Wing, you actually have three choices. Since the TIE Bomber *did* have landing gear/pads, you could cobble up a set by analyzing the configuration on the MPC kit of Darth Vader's Tie Fighter. Secondly, because of its compact configuration and straight edges on the bottom of the wings, simply set the thing down on a shelf and forget it. Or do what I did and create a base that will support it in flight position. That approach is very similar to what I did for the B-Wing, but easier. Either cut a base plate in whatever design you wish or buy a plaque from a craft store such as Michaels, drill a hole in the center and a matching one in the bottom of the Tie's hub box, cut a short piece of 1/8-inch diameter music wire, put everything together, and you're done.

Weathering, in the case of the TIE Bomber, is very light. A powerful totalitarian society such as the Empire would not look favorably on any maintenance crew that would allow a ship to look even slightly dirty, never mind shabby. Here I'm adding a few hydraulic leaks (very few) around the struts.

Finished at last, all this TIE Bomber needs is a stand.

Despite the fact that it got a mere 15 seconds of screen time, this "down the throat" view gives a good idea of just how imposing the TIE Bomber really is.

How to Build Sci-Fi Model Spacecraft

DIORAMAS AND VIGNETTES

Most modelers are content to display their finished projects on a wood or glass shelf, sometimes protected by a display case, sometimes not. Tracked and wheeled vehicles simply sit on their tracks or wheels. Aircraft are usually built with their gear down, which means they're displayed sitting on their landing gear.

Spacecraft are a whole different animal. I'd guess that some form of display stand supports a good 98% of them. Why? The main reason would have to be that *most spacecraft don't have landing gear*. If they do, there usually isn't enough information to figure out what the gear really looks like, which leaves the modeler creating landing gear out of whole cloth.

Be that as it may, there's an alternative to simply displaying your finished models on a shelf or in a display case — a vignette or diorama. Vignettes and dioramas both contain realistic groundwork and/or other scenic details. The difference between the

two is size and, to some extent, content. Dioramas are generally larger, sometimes *very* large, and can contain numerous models as well as extensive detail. Vignettes, on the other hand, are usually small, normally focusing on a single model and a limited amount of detail. There's also a blurred line between the two where it can be difficult to tell whether you're looking at a vignette or diorama. Both tell a story and both depict a specific moment frozen in time. It can be a very effective way of telling a story and displaying your finished models at the same time.

The downside — you knew there had to be one — is twofold. First, they take up more space than the model alone would. Secondly, a dust cover or some other form of enclosure absolutely must protect them. Besides keeping dust away, such covers also protect all your hard work from 40-year-old children who can't resist trying to touch it or pick it up.

ROSWELL

Early in 1947, Ken Arnold spotted several flying discs, which he referred to as "flying saucers." Thus was born the modern era of UFOs or unidentified flying objects. Then in July 1947, a spacecraft carrying seven aliens crashed on a remote ranch near Roswell, New Mexico. First reported factually — and confirmed by the military — as being real, it was later covered up with claims that trained observers had mistakenly identified a destroyed weather balloon and that the unidentifiable metal scraps — complete with indecipherable hieroglyphics — were nothing more than tin foil.

Since that event, there have been world-wide reports of UFO sightings by the thousands, claims of alien abductions, medical experiments, hybrid births, infiltration of civilization by a variety of alien species, crop circles, and more. Are *any* of these reports true? Was there more truth

than fiction to *The X-Files*? What about the Stephen Spielberg miniseries *Taken*, which focused on alien abductions? Is truth really stranger than fiction?

In any event, episodes such as the Roswell crash are ideal subjects for art posters, such as this one by Tony Weddel. It depicts the Roswell UFO during a night-time electrical storm just before the ship made the first of two impacts in July 1947. The 20- x 26-inch poster is currently available from ProWeb Fort Worth (see appendix for address and website).

Artists aren't the only ones who gravitate towards UFO events. Modelers find that they also make for fascinating vignettes or dioramas. Sometimes you don't even have to scratch-build such a scene because a garage kit manufacturer will produce a complete resin diorama kit. And if you get *really* lucky, a major plastic kit manufacturer will market such a kit under their own label.

Fortunately, that's exactly what's happened where the Roswell event is concerned. Testors has created a dandy all-resin kit of the crash scene that includes five alien and three human figures, a limestone/sandstone arroyo, and the damaged spacecraft. Since it's still listed in their 2002/2003 catalog, it shouldn't be too hard to track one down even if it goes out of production.

GETTING STARTED

Because all parts are resin, you need to open that sturdy box some place where you won't lose any small pieces if they fall out. Even though this is a 1/48th scale kit, the gray aliens are only some 3/8 inch tall.

Construction begins by joining the two large base sections to form an L-shaped base. However, first you have a bunch of casting sprue to remove. Resin is brittle when compared to styrene plastic, so you can't just cut through the gates as close to the parts as you can get.

For anyone wishing to replicate the final Roswell crash scene, fortune has smiled. Testors offers a complete resin kit of that exact scene. As to whether the ship is accurate, that's for you to figure out. Many UFO researchers tend to agree that it is. It's your choice.

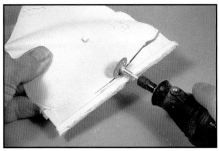

Many resin parts have quite a lot of casting sprue to get rid of. In many cases, the familiar sprue cutters will be all that you need.

In other cases, such as this heavy sprue on the edge of the wing, a Dremel with Diamond cutting wheel is a better choice. Its speed minimizes the risk of chipping.

Here the two-part resin base has been assembled and sprayed with a base coat of Dupli-Color Red Oxide Primer.

ROSWELL, NEW MEXICO
JULY 1947

This photo-realistic painting of the purported Roswell UFO just moments before its first impact during an electrical storm in early July 1947 is the work of renowned aviation artist Tony Weddel. It's available as a 20- x 26-inch lithographic art poster at a most reasonable price from ProWeb Fort Worth. Full ordering information can be found under the ProWeb listing in the appendix.

Sometimes yes, sometimes no. There's enough room on the base parts so that sprue cutters take care of the problem. An Excel knife and sandpaper handles any remaining stubs.

The sprue attached to the edge of the ship's wing is another question entirely. In order to avoid any chipping of the part, I switched to my Dremel MultiPro with a diamond cutting wheel. Then the usual knife/sandpaper method finished the job.

THE BASE COMES FIRST

Satisfied with the cleanup, the base was built. How they go together is pretty obvious, but I did spend some time test fitting and making slight adjustments so I could get a nice, tight seam. Then the two parts were joined using IC-GEL CA, which was also used, along with Super Gold +, throughout this kit's construction. Despite the rapid cure time of the CA, I gave it a shot of accelerator while holding the parts tightly together to prevent any possible rebound. After cleaning up the two outside seams, the entire base received an overall coat of Dupli-Color Red Oxide Sandable Filler Primer Surfacer and was set aside while my attention turned to the ship. Incidentally, the red oxide color gives just the right tone to the final sand color. If you can't find red oxide, use rust.

THE SHIP

Because the ship was a biomimetic creation grown in a zero-gravity vat, the damage inflicted when hit by a lightning upstroke resembled a large gash in human skin when slashed with

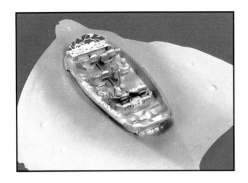

The cockpit tub has been completed and installed in the bottom half of the ship. Note the two dead aliens still in their seats.

a butcher knife or sword. In the ship's case, a large portion of the left upper fuselage and part of the left upper wing skin disintegrated, leaving an opening about two-thirds of the length of the ship. As a result, you could see into the ship from outside. What's the bottom line to all of the above? Simply: The kit has an interior that you have to build.

The interior is really pretty simple. Seven parts, six of them being seats, install in the interior pan or tub, and it's built. What takes your time is the fact that you can't just slap 'em in place and be done with it. There are recesses in the floor for each part, but they aren't large enough for the seat pedestals. Solution? Rather than spend a lot of time trying to carefully enlarge each recess to match the pedestals, I simply whittled down the edges of the pedestals to fit the recesses. This works just as well.

After the tub was installed in the lower fuselage/wing half, I fired up my

Add the top half, and the ship itself is about 90% complete. Only the vertical fins are left, but leaving them off for the moment makes it easier to clamp the halves together. In this case, a combination of wooden clothespins and a pair of 90-degree hemostats gave me the best clamping pressure.

Aztek A470 airbrush and sprayed the entire tub with Model Master Aluminum Non-Buffing Metalizer. I also sprayed most of the upper half's exterior. You'll see why later on. Metalizer is a lacquer and designed strictly for airbrushing (though it can be hand brushed if you have sufficient experience), but it is also available in a spray can for the airbrush challenged. Once dry (and it won't take long), it's time for the decals.

DECALS

I've already discussed decal techniques in earlier chapters, but the ones in this kit are different enough that they deserve a little extra attention. The instructions warn you that the decals are thin and tear easily. That's an understatement! Beyond that, the "dip in water for five seconds, wait one minute and slide off" application description can be ignored. Whether my sheet was old or otherwise some kind of anomaly — or a fair example of every kit — I can't say. Regardless, I soaked mine for up to twenty seconds, let 'em sit literally for many minutes, and still had trouble getting them off the backing paper. When I did get them on the model, some had to be reassembled like a jigsaw puzzle. Finally, it took Solvaset (the hottest solution around) to snug 'em down.

In fairness to Testors, I've had exactly the same problem from time to time with many different manufacturers. Remember, most kit manufacturers outsource (order from decal manufacturers) their sheets. Learning to overcome these little problems is what makes you a model builder. And as far

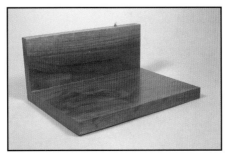

While waiting for other things to dry, I built up this walnut base to eventually mount the completed diorama on. See Chapter 8 for construction details.

Before starting the final detailing of the resin base, I drilled a couple of holes in both the bottom and back of the resin base. Try to pick some spots that can be easily camouflaged later.

as the Roswell ship is concerned, you won't be able to see the decals when the model is finished anyway, so you may not want to even bother with them.

BACK TO THE SHIP

All that's left to do to the interior is to put a couple of aliens in the seats. Pick any two seats at random. You'll only be able to see a hint of them through the gash, so spray them light primer gray and install them.

With that, you're ready for what is probably the trickiest part of the kit: joining the upper and lower halves. What makes it tricky is the fact that the two halves don't line up exactly, a problem that's fairly commonplace where resin kits are concerned. Since the upper half is slightly larger than the lower in some spots, it turned out not to be too bad a job. By the way, notice that I waited on installing the vertical fins in order to have fewer problems clamping the halves together.

There are no mating pins, sockets

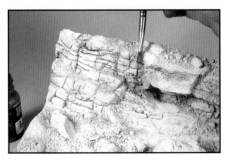

After initial painting and toning, I slopped on some dirty thinner and other assorted grit, allowing the stuff to follow cracks and crevices where it wished.

A light sprinkling of pumice stone helps blend everything in. Most of it will wind up being blown off, but you don't want a uniform coat anyway.

While tedious and time consuming, picking out all the bits and pieces of debris molded into the base will help separate your diorama from the run-of-the-mill versions.

or other alignment points, so your Mk. I eyeball computer comes into play again. I wound up aligning the edges of the crew compartment (fuselage?) and the wing leading edges to the extent possible. Knowing how the final position would be, the halves were separated and IC-GEL applied along the fuselage seam, then the halves were quickly rejoined. Precision is crucial here because you'll only have five or ten seconds to get things right before the CA grabs. If you miss, it'll be necessary to use a knife to slice the seam apart, scrape the CA off, and try again.

The edges of the wings were still loose all the way around. I ran a bead of Super Gold + CA along the loose seam, clamping as I went with wood clothespins or anything else that'd work. Because the upper edge overlaps the lower, a small bead of Super Gold + could be flowed in to fill the discrepancy. Finally, accelerator was sprayed on all seams and things were left to cure for awhile.

After removing the clamps, the CA on the mismatched seams (mostly on the underside) was sanded down and the vertical fins added. Then a small strip of masking tape was slapped across the fuselage gash to protect the interior before the entire ship was sprayed with Model Master Non-Buffing Aluminum Metalizer. Remove the tape and move on to the base. By the way, this is the reason I sprayed the upper half before cementing them together.

The Base, Part 2

As provided in the kit, the resin base would not sit perfectly flat. Besides, I planned to eventually put a

dust cover over the finished diorama. As a result of this, I built up an L-shaped wood base from walnut that would be large enough for the resin base to mount on and be enclosed by a Plexiglas cover. See Chapter 8 for particulars on how to create this and other bases.

Turning my attention to the resin base, I drilled three or four holes in the base that would be used later to mount it to the walnut base. Hole size will depend on the screws you decide to use, but somewhere around 1/16-inch diameter should do. Two holes went through the bottom and another two through the back. Exact placement is up to you, but try to find locations that will make them easy to hide.

Once the holes are drilled, the fun begins, because you can turn your creativity loose. If you've ever done any scenery work on model railroad layouts, I don't have to tell you how to get realistic terrain. For those who haven't a clue, the following works quite well and is easy to boot:

Airbrush or hand brush the entire base (which has already been painted red oxide) with Model Master Sand. Follow that with areas of Model Master FS 30219 Dark Tan. Keep in mind that the idea is to blend the Dark Tan into the Sand so that you get tonal changes without having obvious demarcation lines. This type of work is very subjective, so just keep at it until it looks right to you. Don't be afraid to try other brownish/tanish shades if you think it'll get the result you want. In other words, consider yourself an artist.

Even when you're pretty well done with the color blending, you're not done. Come back with a fair-size brush and a bottle of dirty thinner. Choose a brush like a 1/4-inch chisel point that's seen better days. Scrub the brush around in the bottle so that you pick up some of the grit that accumulates in the bottom, then simply drip or slop the mess on selected areas of the base detail. Being thin, it'll run down the vertical walls, into the cracks, and around some of the molded rocks and debris. Since it's also a solvent, it's possible that some of the sand blend you've already applied will thin to the point of allowing the red oxide to show through. You can either leave it or lightly spray some more sand over it to blend things back together.

After you've pretty well gotten the results you're after, you can sprinkle some pumice stone (try your local lumber yard) along the vertical walls and elsewhere, then blow off the surplus. What remains will blend right in with all your other efforts, increasing the realism you've been striving for.

Before you mount the resin base to your wood base, one more thing remains to be done. Take a fine-tip brush, such as a 10/0 or 20/0, a bottle of Floquil Bright Silver, and a steady hand, and carefully paint all those little pieces of metal debris that were torn off the ship when it hit the arroyo wall. Take your time, because the longer you study and stare at the base, the more debris you'll see.

When all the debris has been painted, go ahead and permanently mount the resin base to the wood base with screws through those holes that have already been drilled. However, don't

Though the aliens only need a shot of gray primer and a dash of black for their eyes, a little more effort will be required for the three humans.

just center the base on the base. If you temporarily add the ship to its final position, you'll find out that it extends beyond the right edge of the resin base. In order to have the entire diorama centered, the base itself will be off-center. This is particularly important if you intend to add a dust cover.

Now camouflage the screw heads by smearing a little putty over them and blending the soft putty into the surrounding terrain. Use an artist's spatula or the back of a knife blade to gently sculpt the proper configuration, and then let things dry. Touch up the colors with your airbrush, then finish off with a little dirty thinner and you're done. It won't be long before you won't be able to find the screw locations, and you're the one who put 'em there!

FIGURES

There are six figures left to paint and detail, three aliens and three humans. I had already painted the aliens gray, so all I had to do was carefully paint in the black, almond-shaped eyes. In case you're wondering, the eyes remained very prominent even after the aliens died. The three humans run the gamut, from a civilian to an Air Force officer and a G.I.

I chose to put kind of a brownish suit, brown shoes, white shirt, and maroon tie on the civilian. His fedora (snap-brim hat) was made just a little darker than the suit. Skin color in all

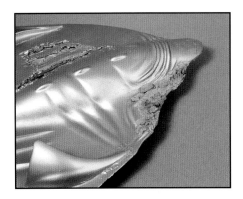

On the leading edge of the right wing, you'll find an area of dirt and small rocks. After the ship hit the arroyo, it rebounded slightly, resulting in rock and dirt falling onto the ship and staying there. Detail that small area to match the surrounding terrain.

Final detailing is done with Tamiya Clear Orange, Clear Red, and Model Master Clear Transparent Black Window Tint.

cases was blended primarily from Model Master Skin Tone Light and Model Master Skin Tone Warm Tint. Don't forget a tiny ring of white at the end of the left sleeve. The civilian is extending his arm towards a dead alien, so the shirt sleeve is beyond the jacket sleeve.

The air force officer wears a khaki uniform, black tie, black shoes, leather jacket, and an officer's hat. Note that the hat should be khaki with a black visor with a leather strap just above the visor and gold braid on the front peak.

As for the G.I., he's the simplest of all. I painted him Model Master ANA 613 Olive Drab with black shoes. The web belt, pouches, and leggings are Model Master Faded Olive Drab. Model Master FS 30117 Military Brown and Floquil Steel took care of the rifle. Don't forget to do a little dry-brushing on each figure in order to bring out the folds and creases in the clothing. Just don't overdo it. And a very, very light dusting of Floquil Dust is in order as well. Remember, Roswell in 1947 was a very dusty place (still is), especially in the middle of a sprawling ranch. It's also hot in July and air conditioning in vehicles was still a rarity. All this means that they drove over dirt roads with car and truck windows open. The last thing you want are figures that look so perfect and clean that they could've stepped out of the pages of a men's fashion magazine!

SHIP DAMAGE

Since the ship was a biomimetic organism, there's the question of what kind of damage it would have displayed. Frankly, there's no way to know. However, due to the fact that part of the

fuselage/wing "skin" disintegrated and what initiated the damage was, in essence, a massive electrical overload, certain assumptions aren't unreasonable. At the very least, there would likely have been discoloration around the edges of the "wound," probably similar to an electrical burn. And as the ship lost power and began to die, its molecular structure would have been less resistant to the heat of air friction. The molecular weakening would have also affected its structural integrity. As a result, when it impacted the arroyo wall, the right leading edge would have crumpled to some degree, though there would have still been enough residual strength to cause a slight rebound from the point of impact. As the ship came to rest, a small quantity of dirt and sandstone would have rained down on top of the right wing.

Testors replicates this on the model, so you'll also need to paint the debris that's molded onto the top of the right wing. Use the same methods and colors on this area that you did on the rest of the groundwork.

Turning to the "burn" surrounding the wound, I switched my Aztek A470 to a fine line nozzle and broke out a couple of Tamiya acrylic paint colors. Starting with X-26 Clear Orange, I sprayed a narrow line around the edges of the wound. Then I did the same along the leading edge of the wing and fins.

I followed the same process with X-27 Clear Red. Instead of trying to

Two dead aliens are lying on the ground. Be sure to pick positions that provide support so that they look naturally dead. The civilian (probably a newspaper reporter) is trying to work up the nerve to touch one.

The third alien collapsed and died on top of the wing. Notice how the three transparent colors (orange, red, and black) blend to create an electrical burn on the edges of the gash.

keep each color separate and distinct, the idea is for them to blend into each other. Finally, I took some Model Master Transparent Black Window Tint and blended that into the previous colors. Since the Black is a very thin color, I also misted it very lightly over selected areas of the ship, such as the wrinkles in the trailing edge of the right wing. When I say "mist," I mean it. You want enough to leave the impression that something's there, but not enough that you can actually see it.

As previously mentioned in Chapter 3, the Window Tint is only available in a spray can. You'll have to spray some into a 35-mm film can or small paper cup in order to pour it in your airbrush.

FINAL ASSEMBLY

There are two dead aliens lying on the ground. I added them to the base first. And don't just plop 'em down. Take your time and make sure that they're lying naturally. You want the bodies to be in contact with the ground, perhaps with their heads draped over a rock.

However you do it, make sure that they *look* dead. Remember, dead bodies are limp, not stiff. The last thing you want is to see daylight *under* their bodies!

If you examine the base closely, you'll find shoe prints impressed in the surface. You'll find these useful for the positioning of both the civilian and the officer. Also, I'd suggest adding only the two aliens and the

civilian to begin with. When that's done, it's time to install the completed ship. There's a little square tab on the bottom of the ship that keys into a socket on the top of the tall rock pile. Since the ship's nose fits into a recess in the arroyo's side, there are plenty of hidden areas for a couple of dollops of IC-GEL. Put one dab on the bottom of the nose, another on that belly tab, install, and hold 'til cured.

Add the last dead alien to the top of the ship and position the kneeling G.I. next to him. The instructions show the G.I. with his hand on the alien. I chose to reposition him so that his hand would be resting on the ship. After all, how anxious would *you* be to touch something that'd just changed every belief you'd ever had?

The finished crash scene looks realistic enough – you can almost imagine the conversation between the scale figures — "This is a weather balloon?"

Finally, position the officer on the ground near the left wingtip, his hand braced against the wing, and you're done.

"If it is, then what are these almond-eyed aliens? Some kind of specialized meterological instruments?"

"You know we're not going to be allowed to talk about this. It'll probably wind up at Area 51 and no one will ever know what happened here."

BIRD OF PREY

The climax of *The Search for Spock* has Admiral Kirk recovering Spock's regenerated body from the Genesis planet and returning it to Vulcan. Since Dr. McCoy is a temporary host for Spock's essence, karma, soul, life-force (and talk about your split personality), the purpose of the journey is to reunite body and essence, basically returning Spock from the dead. Along the way, the original *Enterprise* is destroyed, most of the Klingons are killed, and their Bird of Prey (BOP) is captured by Kirk and company. When they reach Vulcan, the Bird of Prey lands on a high plateau surrounded by barren rock crags. With its wings raised for landing, it looks to all the world like, well, like a prehistoric, predatory bird. And it's a perfect scene for the subject of a vignette.

FIRST, FIND THE KIT

As with most out of production kits, this is your initial problem. Since availability changes on a daily basis, I can't point you toward a specific source. It's basically a snipe hunt, but one where you'll actually find the snipe. Start by going through the ads in model magazines. If you're an IPMS (International Plastic Modelers Society) member (highly recommended), browse through their wants and disposals listings or add a wants listing of your own. If you have access to the Internet, there are all kinds of sites offering old kits, discussion forums where you can pursue the subject, and more. Of course, as I've mentioned elsewhere, there's also E-bay.

CONCEPT

The concept for this vignette was quite simple. I was essentially going to replicate the scene on Vulcan of the Bird of Prey roosting among the crags. Most of my work would be concentrated on creating the plateau and surrounding crags from scratch. As for the Bird of Prey, it could be built straight out of the box (or the bag, since I had a bagged kit with no box), with two exceptions. The wings would have to be modified to an angle 30 degrees above horizontal, and I would have to create some landing gear.

RESEARCH

There are times when research doesn't get you very far, or raises questions that you wish hadn't been raised. In other words, forget it or ad lib. This is one of those times. Research was pretty well limited to two movies, the Internet, and some of the *Star Trek* publications. You'd think that would have been enough. Not so.

As it turned out, the two films, *The Search For Spock* and *The Voyage Home* wound up being my primary sources. When it came to creating the scenery for my Vulcan vignette, they gave me everything I needed. You'll find the most useful scenes to be located near the end of *Spock* and the beginning of *The Voyage Home*. What the movies *don't* give you are any clear views of the Bird of Prey landing gear configuration, and if you're gonna have it on the ground, you've gotta have landing gear.

After a couple of hours on the internet, I had plenty of photos of BOP models, images, 3-views, drawings, etc., none of which showed the gear — except for a single frame capture from *The Search For Spock*. I finally found a front view color illustration of the BOP in the June 1999 issue of *Star Trek: The Magazine* that depicted the gear — and that's when things got worse.

It turns out that the BOP appears to be a different size in different areas, depending on the scene. For example, if you try to project a given dimension based on a human standing next to it, the next scene will scale out differently even with the same human in it. When Kirk and Bones are seen against the BOP (which Bones — Dr. McCoy — rather uncharitably referred to as a Klingon flea trap) on Vulcan, the ship appears to be a certain size. However, the image you're seeing is neither a full-size prop nor a 3-dimensional model — it's an artist's rendering. Beyond that, the whale tank that goes in the cargo bay is 60-feet long, but the ship isn't big enough to hold it, unless it's bigger than it appears. Depending on what overall length you assign the BOP, the location

and configuration of the gear will change with some of the changes being physically/mechanically impossible.

Confused? Me too! The bottom line is this: Unless you simply want to give up and move on to a different project, all you can do is design your own landing gear to fit the model you have in your hand. Aside from the fact that no one is going to be able to prove you wrong, you just *might* get lucky and hit the nail on the head. Besides, what really matters are the techniques used to create this vignette.

Of course, with my luck, detailed drawings of the gear configuration will probably be available from someone by the time you read this!

CONSTRUCTION

Construction is entirely conventional and according to the instructions *except* for the radiator assemblies, so there's no need for me to repeat myself on that aspect of this project. Chapter 2 covers styrene construction in considerable detail. The only things I didn't install during the regular assembly phase were the torpedo conduit, cloaking generator, and the warp-drive housing. At this point, you should have both wings and the main hull built, but the wings are not yet attached. You need the radiators to do that, and they have to be modified to landing configuration first.

Radiators

The kit provides you with two different sets of cores and end plates. One set creates the cruise mode where the wings are basically level and the other drops them to 30-degrees down. You can modify either set, but it's a little less work to start from the cruise mode.

There are several ways to determine the correct angle, including the use of a protractor. But why do it the hard way when there's a relatively easy way to do it? Each end plate is a stepped design, with the inboard part having recesses molded into them. The other part is smooth. Its length and angle also determine the wing's final angle. As luck would have it, the straight edge where the step occurs just happens to be a 30-degree up angle.

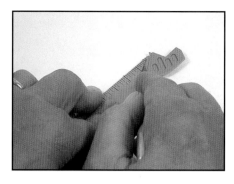

To modify the end plates, first scribe a line as described in the text, then snap the surplus part off.

So, all you have to do is measure out onto the smooth part a distance of .15 inch, mark the location, position a straight edge, scribe the line with your knife, and snap the surplus part off. Now repeat the process for the other three end plates.

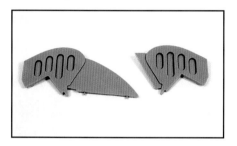

On the left is the original end plate with the modified version on the right. All four end plates receive the same treatment.

Mount the end plates on the radiator cores and allow them to dry. Don't worry about the surplus core; we'll take care of that in a minute. When everything is dry, just score a line from one end plate to the other, snap off the excess, bevel the edge, and install your new radiators on the wings.

Once the radiators are installed, one more modification needs to be made. The radiator ribs don't extend far enough out onto the top of the wing. It's easy enough to create that extension by simply cutting about a 1/2-inch wide strip of that surplus radiator, bevel the underside edges, and cement it in place. Not only have you extended the radiator ribs the correct distance, you've also restored the correct arc to it. Do keep in mind that you'll also have to install a gusset at each end of the radiator to blank off a gap created by the extension of the radiator ribs.

After the cement has dried good and hard, mount the wings to the hull and you now have a Bird of Prey with its wings up 30 degrees, ready for landing — as soon as you extend the gear.

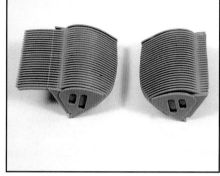

After building up the radiator assemblies, score a line connecting the ends of the modified end plates and snap off the surplus radiator. You can see the score on the left assembly. The one on the right is completely modified.

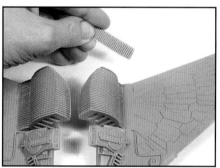

One more modification is needed before mounting the wings: the addition of a radiator-rib filler strip. On the right you can see the configuration of the filler strip before installation. On the left is the completed modification.

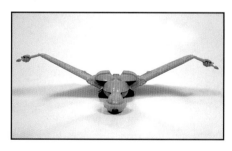

There you have it. A Klingon Bird of Prey with its wings raised to 30 degrees for landing. Considering its appearance, it makes you wonder if the prehistoric pterodactyl wasn't the inspiration for this ship's design! There is no landing gear yet, but we'll get to that before long.

THE BASE

The base starts out as an 18- x 20-inch piece of 3/4-inch thick plywood. Because you're creating what is essentially an eyrie for a predatory bird, you'll also need several feet of aluminum screen, Elmer's Carpenter's Wood Glue, at least a quart (which eventually turned into a gallon) of Bondo Body Filler from your neighborhood auto parts store, scrap wood blocks, and a staple gun.

Once you've watched the two movies enough times to get an image of what you want to do in your head, it's time to make a mess. Remember, you're not going to be able to create an exact duplicate of the scene all the way down to the last rock. For one thing, you wouldn't have enough room. And the way those scenes were filmed precludes it anyway. What you're after is the effect.

Basically, the Bird of Prey was going to be more or less in the center, its nose (or head) pointed at the left front corner. The largest group of rock spires would be behind the ship, generally in the upper right corner, with the height gradually dropping as the rocks stretched out along the top and right-hand edges of the base. Along the left and front edges would be a lower batch of rocks, everything blending into a slightly rolling but more or less level central section where the ship would land.

The first thing I did was position the model about where I wanted it on the raw base, then used a felt tip pen to roughly draw the contours for the high terrain. Roughly is the operative term

Base work starts by simply sitting the BOP model on the plywood and drawing the contours for the mountains and rough terrain with a Sharpie.

here, because you're going to be using a lot of artistic license. Anyway, after the contours were determined, the model was set to one side and I got ready to turn myself into a carpenter/landscape architect (or motion picture set designer/builder if you prefer to think of it that way).

Although the actual mountains/rocks would be created with window screen and Bondo, you have to have some way to support the screen in the first place. That's done easily enough by simply whacking off a few pieces of 1- x 2-inch lumber to various lengths. No need for any two to be the same length, nor does the length of any given piece matter for the most part. There is the occasional exception and the one in this case is to make sure that at least one of them is as tall as you want the tallest spire to be. I stopped at about 10 inches.

Scraps of wood created a rough frame (or armature) for the window screen.

Now cement the various pieces you've created onto the base in whatever pattern suits your fancy. As you can see from the photo, where you place anything depends strictly on what you want the final result to be. Incidentally, when gluing wood to wood, you can't find anything better than Elmer's Carpenter's Wood Glue.

Glue dry? Good. Things are about to get a little sticky in more ways than one. I picked up about a 4-foot long piece of 28-inch wide aluminum window screen that would be used to form the final contours. While ordinary scissors will cut it readily, you'll wind up with rough edges that can make your skin itch like crazy. If you lean towards sensitive skin, I'd suggest either some light cotton or leather gloves. *Do not* use latex disposable gloves, because those rough edges will simply tear 'em up.

The aluminum window screen is crumpled, twisted, pinched, and otherwise mangled into the desired shapes and then stapled in place. Use gloves unless you want your skin to itch for the next couple of hours.

Cut some of the screen into a manageable size that more or less fits the area you're planning on it doing. Then sorta scrunch it around until it starts to take on the shape you've envisioned. Now staple it to the base, making whatever changes in configuration you want as you go. Wherever some of the screen comes in contact with the support strips, either drive a staple through the screen into the side, or even into the top. By the way, I used an Arrow T-55 staple gun and 1/4-inch staples. Both are commonly available at your local hardware store or big-box home improvement stores such as Lowes or Home Depot.

Once you've worked up the nerve to actually start stapling the screen, you'll find that the whole process is really quite easy. Between stapling the screen in strategic places and simply using your fingers to form desired contours in other areas, it won't be long before you've built up a basic form, or armature, as a foundation for the final surface. After I was satisfied with the vertical contours, I stapled a final piece of screen over the flat central section. This was as much to give the Bondo something to grab, as it was to impart a realistic, slightly uneven surface to the center of the base.

I'll grant you that the preceding description detailing creation of the basic base probably sounds like you just opened a Greek dictionary, but it really isn't all that difficult. In actual fact, these methods, or others very similar to them, have been used for decades by model railroaders to create realistic scenery for their train layouts.

Some of the terrain can be created by simply wadding up the screen and then stapling. However you do it, this view shows the final contours ready for putty. Geez! I feel like a model railroader!

You just have to get the nerve to *start*. The worst thing you can do is make a mistake, which just might accidentally wind up producing the result you were looking for in the first place!

It's Bondo Time

For those of you who don't know what Bondo is, it's a two-part, gray body filler (or putty, if you prefer to think of it that way) that's used extensively in automotive and boat repair shops. When it comes to repairing holes and/or dents in just about any kind of metal or fiberglass surface, recontouring surfaces, and so on, this stuff is about as universal as duct tape.

Anyway, because it's a two-part system, it has to be catalyzed with a cream hardener (that comes with the filler). Working time depends on how much catalyst you use and what the ambient air temperature is. How much catalyst you use for your particular situation is something you'll have to figure out from personal experience. It doesn't

Glop some Bondo onto a piece of scrap plastic, cardboard, or whatever, add a dollop of hardener, and mix until the color is uniform.

take a lot of catalyst, as evidenced by the fact that a quart can comes with a 3/4-ounce tube of hardener. On average, you'll wind up with somewhere around four minutes working time, so don't get overly ambitious. You can always mix up another batch.

Then there's the question of what do you mix it on. Basically, use anything you can throw out later. Scrap pieces of cardboard or envelopes from some of those bills you haven't paid work quite well. If you want to get fancy, check around the auto parts house for some polyethylene mixing boards and spreaders. Since cured Bondo doesn't stick easily to them, you can flex them back and forth to remove the cured putty.

Whatever quantity you're going to work with can be mixed with just about anything you have handy. Sticks, flat strips of wood, one of those polyethylene spreaders, and so on. The plastic spreader (polyethylene) is ideal for applying the mix to your base. Putty knives and large artist's spatulas also work well, though they're a pain to scrape the hardened putty off of.

Now Let's Putty

After mixing up a quantity of Bondo I was comfortable with, things got started by spreading the stuff across that flat (more or less) central plain. No attempt was made to get complete coverage or worry about the final contours. Right now all you're trying to do is form a hard skin over the screen armature. You'll need some patience, because you're gonna be mixing batch after batch of Bondo for a while. Once I was out of the central plain, I started working my way up the main mountain sec-

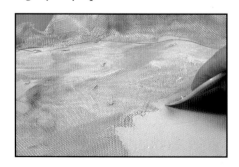

With your weapon of choice, which is a vinyl spreader in this case, start spreading the mix over the screen.

tion. Again, I was only worried about an initial hard skin at this point.

From here on, things settled down into a rhythm of mix and spread, mix and spread, until you wonder if you're ever going to finish. It also takes a lot more Bondo than you think it will. I wound up using almost an entire gallon, even after building up the basic shape with wood strips and window screen.

Here I've more or less gotten the plain covered and am working my way up the mountain. All I do now is continue repeating the process until everything has been puttied.

In any event, the one thing you *don't* have to worry about is having to smooth the rock forms down into soft-edged contours. Remember, this is Vulcan and you're dealing with rough, raw, hard-edged volcanic-style terrain. If you want an area of Earth to use for comparison, a combination of Monument Valley on the Arizona/Utah border and the Valley of Fire in Nevada would be a good place to start.

Now Paint It

Based on the two films I used for reference, most of Vulcan is reddish in color. Essentially, the planet is one giant chunk of iron that has been weathered and oxidized over thousands of millennia. That'd certainly account for the sculpted spires, wind-swept plateaus, and rugged terrain.

As a result of the preceding paragraph, it turns out that the perfect base color just happens to be Bondo Easy Finish Primer 722 Red Oxide. Once you have a solid coat of Red Oxide on, or something approximating that color, it's time to break out the old airbrush and a variety of similar but different shades of the basic color: rust, British crimson, red-brown, and so on.

With all the groundwork configured, a can of Bondo Easy Finish Red Oxide is sprayed on next, and it'll take the best part of an entire can.

Remember, you can also take the different shades and lighten them by adding various quantities of white to the mix, and so on. And when you start spraying, don't try to get uniform coverage. Allow the rough areas to self-mask, thus creating natural areas of lighter and darker shades.

Dirty thinner, which usually winds up being some kind of a dark, dirty gray, can also be slopped on here and there and allowed to run where it will. Then you come back over that with one or more of the rust, oxide, or crimson colors. In this case, the idea is to change the dirty thinner back to a reddish color, simultaneously obtaining a darkish, shadowy tone imparted by the underlying dirty thinner. It sounds strange, I know, but you'll see what I mean if you try it.

And if you're interested in adding a slightly pebbled or gritty texture to certain areas of the base, here's another stunt you can try. After you've slopped on some dirty thinner or other color, while it's still wet, sift on some pumice stone. Just grab some in your hand and kind of toss it around, then sit back and wait for it to dry. Now airbrush the desired color on top of the pumice stone. Most of it will simply blow off, but what sticks to the dried paint or dirty thinner will then be colored by this last airbrushing. The result is both realistic and subjective, which also means a lot of what I'm talking about isn't visible in the photos.

At least there's one thing you won't have to deal with where this diorama is concerned. There is no foliage, not so much as a weed shows up in either of the films when the Bird of Prey is sitting on Vulcan.

Frame It

When the base was finally finished to my satisfaction, I dropped it into a picture frame that I had acquired to hide the raw edges (see the "Frame It" heading in Chapter 8). It would also give me a way to mount a dust cover later on.

After a trip to the lumberyard, hardware store, craft store, auto supply store, and a few hours time, I had my landing site built. Now where's the Bird of Prey?

Even though I did use a modular picture frame kit as discussed in Chapter 8, an interesting little problem reared its head. In order to get a wood frame with a smooth, flat side (which would allow me to fasten a dust cover with screws later), I had to buy what was described as a "gallery frame." What does that actually mean? The recess on the back of the frame was a full 1-inch deep, and my BOP base used 3/4-inch thick plywood. In order to shim the recess so that the top of the groundwork would be even with the surface of the frame back, I simply cut an 18- x 20-inch piece of 1/4-inch thick plywood and glued it into the bottom of the frame recess. Then when I added the BOP base, everything would line up the way I intended it to.

All that remained was to finish the Bird of Prey and mount it on the base.

Landing Gear

This is the only truly nasty part of this project, and for exactly the reasons I mentioned earlier. But accurate or not, the BOP has to have landing gear in order to replicate this scene, so let's get to it.

One thing you can say about the Klingons is that they tend to overbuild.

Thick and heavy seems to be their philosophy. If nothing else, their designs won't fall apart due to being too light! Between that philosophy and what little I could see of the gear in the movies, I took the same approach to designing the gear for my model.

What you won't get in this section is an exact description that will allow you to duplicate my gear concept. Not only might yours be more accurate than mine, I'm not about to deny you the fun (or agony) of doing your own design work. However, that won't stop me from telling you how I came up with my particular concept.

Basically, I transmuted the legs and feet of a pterodactyl into a mechanical configuration. I also noted that the Bird of Prey sits relatively close to the ground. This is obvious from ramps that allow the crew entry from the ground. If they were *too* steep, they'd be unusable. That observation alone told me the landing strut would have to have a sharp bend in it so that it could retract into the lower hull. Remember, the wings incorporate variable geometry, so the gear can't be attached to them.

The result of all this is that I began by creating a flat, rectangular footpad from .020-inch sheet styrene. Then a triangle was mounted on each long side of the pad, angling in much like the sides of a pyramid. In the center of the pad, I installed a 1/2-inch long vertical piece of an H-beam (Plastruct makes them) and cemented the tip of the triangles to the sides of the beam.

A longer piece of H-beam was cut to form the strut that would run from

It's amazing what you can do with a few pieces of scrap styrene and structural shapes, isn't it? I may have cut this gear design out of whole cloth, but you'll soon see that it wound up being a perfect fit for the ship.

the knee (the top of the vertical H-beam) to the hull. Length doesn't really matter here as long as you have enough extra to extend through the hull wall. Then I cut an appropriate angle (somewhere around 45 or 50 degrees) on one end of this beam and cemented it to the top of the vertical beam. At this point, I had my basic landing gear. But there was still more to do.

A couple of pieces of channel were cut to size and cemented on the outside edges of the angled strut (H-beam). Check out the photo and you'll see what I mean. It's a lot easier to depict than describe. When I had repeated the entire process another time, I had a pair of landing gear ready to install.

When a spacecraft winds up sitting on only two footpads, you're forced to conclude that the struts have to be located at the center of gravity. That point, fortuitously, just happens to be smack in the middle of the long, raised plate immediately under the leading edge of the wing. Find the center by drawing lines between diagonal corners, and X marks the spot. Now all that's necessary is to rough out an opening just slightly smaller than that H-beam extension and then finish it to the correct size with a knife.

Test fit (you've heard this before) the gear strut, adjust slightly, and continue repeating until you're satisfied with the fit and alignment. Then go ahead and install the struts. Do make sure that both of them match, both laterally and vertically, and that the footpads are parallel to the ground. Let everything dry good and solid, then set your Bird down on a flat surface. If

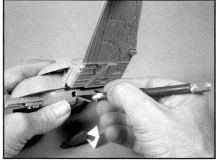

Between a Dremel and a knife, it doesn't take long to hog out an opening for the gear strut. That ever-popular test fitting will be needed in order to get things oriented correctly.

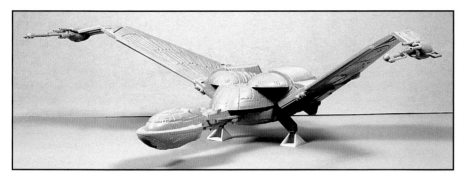

Nearing the end, all that remains is to add the warp-drive housing.

With the gear securely installed, proof of the pudding is whether or not the BOP will sit on its landing pads without tipping either forwards or backwards – and it does. Yippee! I must've done something right for once!

you've done everything right, you now have a Bird of Prey sitting proudly on sturdy legs. All that remains is to paint it and install it on the vignette base.

COLOR THE BIRD

We've already discussed painting techniques in preceding chapters, so there is little point in repeating the process here. Particularly since I did a completely stock paint scheme, literally following the instruction paint guide to the letter. The only thing I didn't do was use Testors Acrylic paint. Instead, I used Testors Model Master Enamels.

I found FS 34227 Pale Green to be a perfect match for the BOP's base color. As for the detail colors, only two will give you any problem: the dark green that is used on the underside of the hull, and yellow-green. Dark green is pretty much up to you, though I'd suggest something along the lines of FS 34092 Euro I Dark Green. As for the yellow-green, it's a lot more green than yellow. As a matter of fact, it's basically a lighter version of FS 34227, and can be found in the Model Master line as FS 34258 Green.

Incidentally, I painted all the detail panels by hand with a conventional brush. If you care to try your hand at masking and airbrushing multicolored panels, jump over to Chapter 5 and check out the detailed information on replicating the *Defiant*'s pattern.

The landing gear, based on scenes from *The Voyage Home*, is the same pale green as the rest of the ship. The radiator baffles are steel, and you'll probably want to finish them off with a light wash of dirty thinner instead of the black wash suggested by the instructions.

Decals

There are only four total in this kit. Since they were missing from my bagged kit, I had none. An insignia is engraved on the stand upright. This is what needs to be reproduced on the outside of the wing gun pylons. Then you have a series of Klingon letters on the trailing edges of both wings. As usual, there were two choices: forget about it, or try to reproduce them another way.

I didn't bother, mainly because this BOP had been in heavy combat with the Enterprise and it wasn't unreasonable to assume that the markings might have faded or been otherwise damaged. Beyond that, she sat on Vulcan for three months before Kirk and company made the decision to return to Earth. It would be bad enough to return in an enemy vessel, but no Star Fleet crew would want it to be wearing their markings as well. Three months is plenty of time to remove them.

However, if you want to take a shot at creating the missing decals from scratch, Klingon letters bear a close resemblance to hieroglyphics, which means you stand a fair chance of writing them by hand and coming pretty close. *Star Trek* devotees who have spent the last several years studying the Klingons will take you to task if the result isn't perfect, but as far as anyone else is concerned, it'll be good enough for government work.

Trot down to your friendly art supply store and pick up a Staedtler pigment liner. They come in a variety of tip sizes and colors, but a dark gray or black one with a .005-inch tip is what you want. Now practice copying

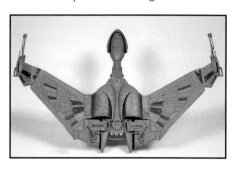

This is the Bird of Prey from the top, completely finished.

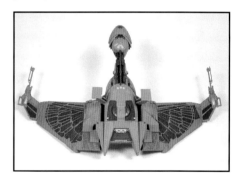

And here is a view from the bottom. Note that all of the detail painting, other than the pale green base color, was done by hand.

the Klingon letters that you see in the wing assembly stage (step 4A) until you feel confident. Now switch to the model and do it for real. An alternative approach is to write the letters on a piece of clear decal, then apply the decal in a normal manner. See? Nothing to it. Staedtler ink is permanent and won't fade.

The pylon insignia is a different story. This one's going to take a steady hand and your Opti-Visor. You'll also definitely want to create them on clear decal and then transfer them later. You do have one thing going for you, and that's the fact that the insignia is engraved on the stand upright.

Final Details

There are four items that have to be added before your BOP is finished. The torpedo conduit and cloaking generator need to be painted Model Master Rust and installed. At this point, shoot a light coat of Model Master Semi-Gloss Clear Lacquer and let it dry. All that remains are two clear parts: the warp drive housing, and the photon torpedo emitter. Detail them per the instructions, install 'em, do whatever weathering you wish, and you will find yourself with a Bird of Prey looking for a roost.

Landing on Vulcan

Adding the BOP to its eyrie is simplicity itself. All you do is drill into the center of the landing pads (so that the hole goes into the bottom of the vertical beam), then insert a pin cut from a jumbo paper clip. Leave about a quarter of an inch or so sticking out. For an in-depth description of how to pin components together, see Chapter 6.

Then position the ship on the base, noting where the pins contact the surface. Drill matching holes, add some CA to the bottom of the pads and the projecting pins, then insert the pins in the base holes. Just make sure the pads are in full contact with the surface or it won't look natural.

With that, your Klingon Bird of Prey is in its Vulcan eyrie and Spock's spirit is about to be reunited with his newly regenerated body. Three months later, this same BOP will carry Kirk and company as they time warp 300 years into the past to bring two Humpback whales the same 300 years into the future to save Earth from the devastation of an alien probe.

Think it didn't happen, or won't happen, or, oh, never mind. Time paradoxes cause severe headaches. Just watch *The Voyage Home* and decide for yourself.

Here you get a good view of how well the landing gear design worked out. It's also very obvious that the prehistoric Pterodactyl had to have been the inspiration for the Bird Of Prey design.

Viewed from the top, the modified radiators are easily seen. And ain't it amazing what a gallon of Bondo and some window screen can do to create realistic volcanic scenery?

How to Build Sci-Fi Model Spacecraft

BARE METAL OR PAINTED PLASTIC?
ONLY YOUR MODEL BUILDER KNOWS FOR SURE

Bare-metal finishes are the bane of most model builders. The majority of natural metal finishes you see are anything but natural, despite the fact that their creators *think* that they are. Aircraft have a patchwork of toned panels that replicate a pattern of contrasts rivaling agricultural fields from 20,000 feet. While aircraft *do* depict that patchwork of toned panels, the differences between panels are usually subtle rather than obvious. Bare-metal spacecraft shine like a new dollar, with *some* of them being polished to the point that you can use the surface for a mirror. They may be beautiful and perfect, especially in a custom-built display case, but they darn sure ain't realistic. This is not to say that some spacecraft (and aircraft) shouldn't be that shiny and perfect, but they're the exception, and not the rule.

Painted surfaces are a slightly different critter. We generally wind up painting colors over a primered surface. The result is usually quite realis-

tic, especially when you take the time to add weathering. However, you can improve the realism by first applying a basic natural metal finish *before* the final color goes on. Also, the various panels on a painted spacecraft can benefit from the same toning methods used for a natural metal aircraft finish. Only the colors used will change.

S4 UFO

Interested in a model of the classic disc-shaped flying saucer? Then take a look at this Area S4 UFO kit produced by Testors. It's big, simple to build, and has the easiest monotone metal finish you'll ever hope to find. Beyond that, if you're a believer in UFOs/extraterrestrials, it's a must for your collection.

Is this model based on a real interstellar spacecraft from the Zeta Reticuli star system? Does the ship utilize antimatter reaction to create a gravity "warp" drive, not dissimilar to what is used in the *Star Trek* universe? Has

some of the ship's technology been reverse engineered to create some of the exotic consumer products that we now take for granted? Are we dealing with fact or fiction? Testors includes a 16-page booklet with details of the ship provided by Bob Lazar, who claimed

The Area 51 UFO is a classic disc-shaped flying saucer, and an ideal subject for an easy, polished-metal finish.

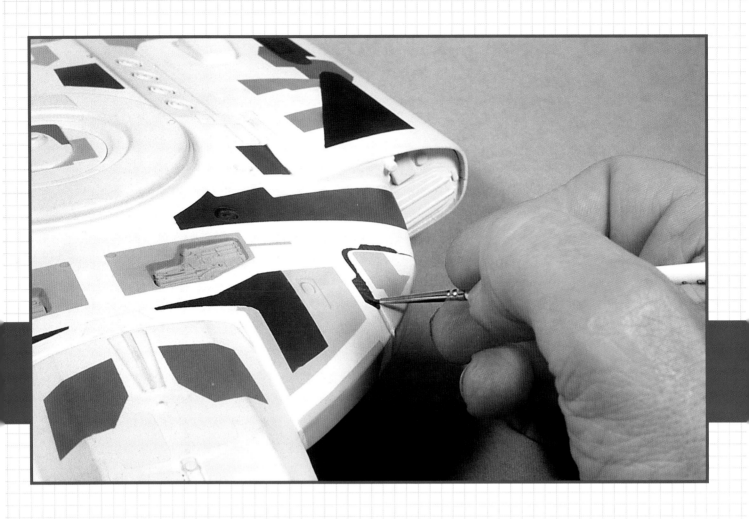

to have worked on the ship for some two years trying to ferret out some of its secrets and says all of the above is true. The choice is yours.

CONSTRUCTION

Even though its 13 inches in diameter, this kit is about as simple as you can get with only 23 parts. It gets even simpler the way I approached it, reducing the total parts to 5. The reason for that was my plan to demonstrate a monotone bright silver finish. To do so, no interior details or figures would be needed.

With that in mind, construction is simplicity itself. All you do in install the floor into the lower half (the two halves are clear styrene), then add the upper half to complete the basic shell. No need to worry about fogging the clear either because everything will be painted. Add the upper deck housing and that delicate little wave-guide terminator, and the model is built. It can't get much simpler than that.

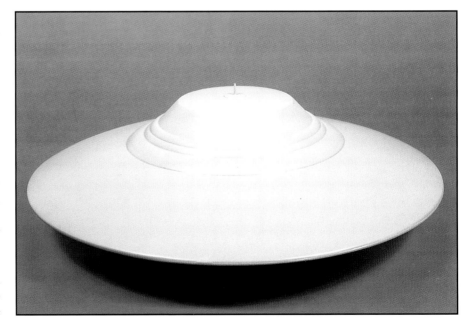

You need to do exactly three things to get this little puppy ready to paint. Build it, eliminate the equatorial seam, and prime the heck out of it until you have a smooth, flawless surface that you're happy with.

Seamwork

If you've been reasonably careful in your construction, you have a single seam where the upper and lower shell halves join. Simply scrape the seam down with the edge of your knife blade, then grab you a chunk of 150- or 180-grit sandpaper and sand 'til the seam disappears. Minor gaps can be filled with CA or Model Master Red Putty.

PRIMER

Construction of this kit was a breeze. Painting will take a little longer, but not much. As always, primer comes first. In this case, the first couple of coats brought out some parts of the seam that needed more work, which is what primer is for. Those problems were quickly cleaned up and more primer applied.

Now I went over the latest primer coat with fine grit sandpaper (about 320 or 400), sprayed more primer, and then went over *that* coat with crocus cloth to obtain a smooth, polished surface. About the only thing you have to worry about during this entire process is to make sure you don't snap that wave-guide terminator.

PAINT

The S4 UFO, when sitting on its bottom (no landing gear or skids) unpowered, is a uniform bright silver that looks like it was cut from a solid block of metal. This means that duplicating its appearance couldn't be easier. Oh, in case you're wondering about windows, they're not visible unless the ship is powered up. Then part of the skin becomes transparent.

The final finish is done with a spray can of Floquil Bright Silver, described as a "plastic-compatible lacquer," a phrase that's an oxymoron if I've ever heard one. Lacquer, unless you know how to use it (auto modelers in particular fit this description), doesn't particularly like plastic. What makes Bright Silver "compatible" for those who don't normally use lacquer is the fact that some of the chemicals were replaced with alcohol. Result? A paint that dries to a very hard, self-shining surface that's perfect for this particular project.

Anyway, all you do is spray the top of the ship and let it dry. Then flip it over, spray the bottom, let it dry, and keep repeating the process until you have a solid bright silver ship. About the only mistake you can make is to start or stop spraying while the can's nozzle is pointed at the ship or spray too wet a coat. Pull those stunts and you could be sanding down some paint splatters and/or runs.

That's it. You're done. The instructions would have you add a small American flag decal to the ship, claiming that someone at Area S4 did that. I chose not to because I wanted to represent the ship in its original appearance.

Floquil Bright Silver from a spray can is the only thing you'll need to get the results you see here. Sometimes the unbelievably simple methods will do a better job than all the complicated, sophisticated methods you can imagine.

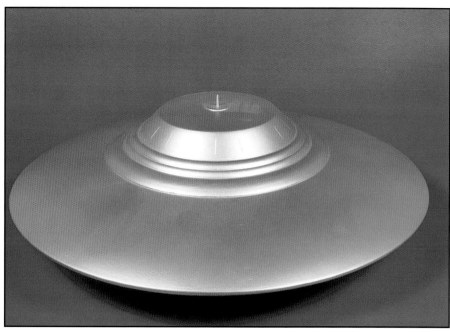

If you're looking for a simple, silver metal, this is about as simple and silver as you can get.

BUILD, PUTTY, SAND, AND PRIME

Construction of this kit requires nothing more than the normal styrene building techniques. However, you will need a fair amount of putty due to the fact that the fit in certain areas could be charitably described as rough.

There are only 16 parts plus the stand, and three of the parts can be left off until after it's painted. As a result, you'll spend more time puttying, sanding, and priming this thing than you will building it. Put another way, Model Master Red Putty, 100- to 220-grit sandpaper, and surfacer/primer will become your close friends before you're done.

PAINTING/MASKING

Once a base coat of bare metal has been applied and allowed to dry, final finishing can begin. Despite the kit's lousy fit, AMT provides an excellent two-page layout comprised of a five-

Designed for the Star Trek: Deep Space Nine *series, the* Defiant's *design was dramatically different from most* Star Trek *ships. AMT produced a very nice kit of it.*

U.S.S. *DEFIANT*

Ships that are painted a color are frequently fairly easy. As has already been described in previous chapters, you can obtain a nice, realistic painted surface that looks like the model was built from metal by simply painting over an undercoat of silver/natural metal. That's fine for a monotone scheme or maybe a couple of small, contrasting color sections. Masking and airbrushing, or even hand brushing those small areas isn't all that difficult for anyone. *But* many spacecraft, especially those in the *Star Trek* universe, tend to wear complex, multi-colored — and very specific — patterns. The various *Enterprise* ships are a prime example of this, but there are stencils available from the aftermarket to help you solve that problem, or at least part of it. Beyond that, you're pretty much on your own.

For instance, the U.S.S. *Defiant* from *Deep Space 9* is a very compact design, totally different from most of the other *Star Trek* ships. So is the pattern, which means that building the AMT kit of the *Defiant* will introduce you to a masking nightmare. Let's see if we can get you through it.

Basic assembly has been completed and putty applied. As you can see, you're going to spend some time with putty and sandpaper.

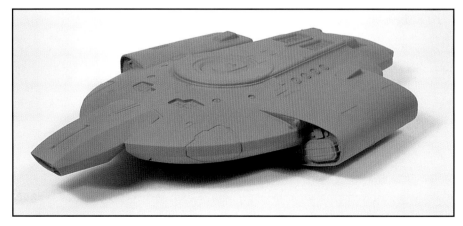

A final coat of primer finishes up the easy part of this model: building it. Now for the tedious part.

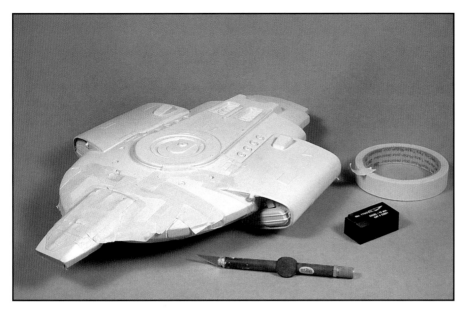

After the base color and subsequent clear coat has dried, masking of the pattern begins. Most of the masking was done with Scotch 230 Drafting Tape and a knife (along with a generous supply of replacement blades). Oh — and patience. Lots of it.

view drawing of the ship, a nine-language color chart, and clearly flagged arrows showing exactly what section is painted what color. I wish every manufacturer would take this approach. It would make things a lot easier. If you're looking for any more info on the *Defiant* beyond what you can find from tapes of *Deep Space 9* episodes and the Internet, track down a copy of *Star Trek: The Magazine* for October 1999. Page 29 has a very nice 3/4 right front shot of the *Defiant* that you may find useful.

The *Defiant*'s color scheme starts with an overall coat of light gray that's a 50/50 mix of Model Master FS 36495 Light Gray and FS 37875 Flat White. Then a coat of Floquil Crystal Cote creates a smooth glossy surface that you can start masking on.

By the way, if you've been in the habit of cleaning empty paint bottles and reusing them for custom mixing, or even spending money to buy *new* empty bottles for the same purpose, let me suggest an alternative. Get friendly with the people behind the counter of your local film processor, and then ask them for a bag of those leftover plastic film canisters that 35-mm film is packaged in. No, not the metal canister that actually holds the film, the plastic canister with a snap top that the metal canister is placed in. Film processors either throw them out or send them off for recycling, so why not offer to do some of the recycling for

them? They accumulate by the hundreds, even thousands, so one request can easily get you a couple or three hundred in a box or bag.

If you're still wondering where I'm going, it's simply this. Those plastic canisters make the greatest little custom paint containers you've ever seen. They hold close to an ounce of paint, the snap lid makes it easy to shake up your mix, and you couldn't ask for a better way to pour the mix into your gravity or side-feed airbrush cup. And when you're done, throw 'em out. Free and disposable, what more could you ask for?

What Kind of Masking Agent?

That depends on you. You've got everything from ordinary masking tape to all kinds of liquid maskers. Other than your personal preferences, it's a matter of matching the masking medium to the specific requirements.

For example, liquid maskers range all the way from specially designed films to plain ol' white glue. All of them are brushed on and do an excellent job of protecting the masked area. For all practical purposes, you don't have to worry about paint bleeding under. When it comes to removing the dried liquid maskers, unmasking is usually as easy as removing masking tape. Stick the point of a knife blade under one edge and lift. Over the years, I have run into a couple

(can't recall their brands) that ranged from difficult to flat-out stubborn. That problem can be caused by either an outdated bottle or leaving it on too long.

Many manufacturers recommend Scotch Magic Tape. If you can adapt to it, it does an excellent job. I can't. I personally find it way too difficult to remove.

Frisket Low Tack Masking Film from Badger (of airbrush fame) comes in 8 1/2 x 11-inch sheets. It's available in either gloss or matte finish, and there's no residue to worry about. It works great on flat or nearly flat surfaces, but it's a little stiff for contoured surfaces.

One of the more exotic masking agents originated in chemical laboratories (when model builders say they'll use anything that works, they mean it) is a little item called Parafilm M that's marketed by Testors. Though it's actually a non-adhesive adhesive film designed to seal retorts, beakers, and the like, it has a property that can be invaluable to the modeler in specialized circumstances. It sticks to surfaces by contact *without the use of any adhesive*. You do have to stretch it in order to activate that trait, so be prepared to play with it a little before beginning any masking.

Me? While I've used 'em all (as well as some very strange methods that I haven't bothered to discuss), and probably ninety percent of all my masking has been done with a variation of plain, ordinary 3/4-inch wide tan masking tape — Scotch 230 Drafting Tape. It looks, feels, and behaves exactly like everyday Scotch Masking Tape, except for having a substantially lower tack. It's not the best thing if you're taping a box together, but highly desirable when you're trying to avoid stripping paint off a model. If you can't find it at hobby shops or office supply stores, try looking at places that carry artist supplies. Can't get anywhere but the local hobby shop? Then check out Tamiya masking tape. While I've never used it, it's supposed to possess a low tack similar to Scotch 230 Drafting Tape. Just be prepared to get a smaller quantity at a higher price.

BACK TO THE *DEFIANT*

Other than the base color, probably the dominant detail color is the one flagged with the letter D. You make it

With masking of the first color complete (or as much as I could reasonably handle), the exposed areas were airbrushed.

By the time I'd finished masking all the "D" panels, no matter how I'd tried to protect all the exposed surfaces that *didn't* need to be painted from overspray, something that shouldn't have been sprayed was. So I ended up spraying as many of the "D" panels as was practical while protecting the rest of the ship. After those panels had dried, I shifted my attention to another section, adjusting the overspray protection as appropriate, and repeated the process 'til all "D" panels had been sprayed.

Once all the "D" panels were finished, the ship was carefully unmasked and the next batch of panels were masked and sprayed. And so on and so on until my back was numb, my eyes were crossed, and I was wondering if I'd ever get all those miserable little panels painted!

with a 50/50 mix of Model Master FS 35164 Gray Blue and FS 35044 Dark Blue. Mixing the color is the easy part. Now you have to mask off the appropriate panels.

As I said earlier, the paint schematics are excellent. They're also very busy, due to the variety of panels that have to be painted. Fortunately, most of the colors are standard shades and the three that do have to be mixed are keyed to FS numbers. Despite the fact that there's nothing technically difficult about masking and painting all those panels, the tedium can easily bore you to tears if you try to do it at one sitting.

Everyone has, or has to develop, their own approach to this amount of masking. Some try to mask every panel on the entire ship at one time. Others will mask one or two panels, paint them, strip the masking, then repeat the process endlessly until they're done. Me? I've found that it usually works well for me to mask all panels *of a particular color* at one time, spray them, remove the masking and let things dry. Normally I use my favorite Scotch Drafting Tape for most of the work, repeating the process for each successive color until I'm done.

However, sometimes things work out in ways that prevent you from taking your preferred approach. The *Defiant's* panels fall in that category.

The first pattern on the Defiant has been completed — or at least most of it has.

Each time you strip tape from a masked area, it's another moment of truth.

With the second pattern complete, the Defiant is beginning to look like its old self. Just keep repeating the process 'til every color pattern is complete.

At long last, all of the multi-colored panels have been successfully masked and painted. A final coat of Crystal Cote has it ready for decals.

This is the Defiant displaying her full complement of markings. All that's needed is a stand.

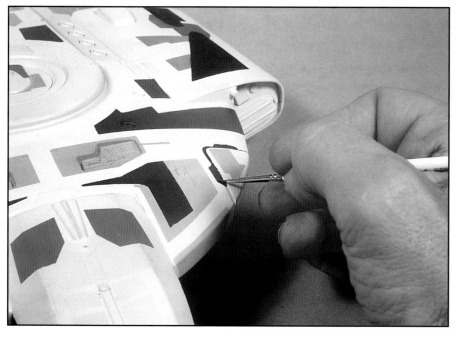

Small details don't lend themselves to masking. For them, you'll need a small brush and a steady hand.

Because of the configuration of the panels, you're inevitably going to wind up doing a little trimming after the tape (or whatever masking agent you use) is in position. Keep a knife with a *brand new* #11 blade close by, as well as a pack of replacement blades. The idea is to keep the sharpest possible tip on your knife blade. This way, minimal pressure will cut through the tape that you need to trim *without cutting into the underlying paint*. When you're

doing this kind of trimming with a knife, the rule for replacement blades is change early, change often. Spare blades are cheap compared to the pain of damaging a nearly finished model.

Once you've finished masking and painting all the panels (how long it takes you will depend on your level of patience and how well both your eyes and back hold up), there are a few small detail areas that will need attention. These will be primarily recessed areas

that simply don't lend themselves to masking and airbrushing. Here you'll have to revert to old-fashioned, high-quality, sable-hair or synthetic-bristle, fine-point brushes.

With all the detailing done, the entire model gets another shot of Floquil Crystal Cote.

After that's dry, you're ready for a decal session. When *they're* dry, a final coat of Testors Semi-Gloss Lacquer Clear Coat will finish out your *Defiant*.

THE STAND

The stand is a nice, sturdy two-piece design that's actually big enough to hold the finished model. Base colors are silver and gold, with the letters using that 'D' custom mix that you used on some of the *Defiant*'s panels. If you've been wondering what you were going to do with the left over mix, now you know. Use it to paint the raised letters on the display stand. Slip the *Defiant* in place and you're done. Now turn the page and we'll tackle some advanced detailing.

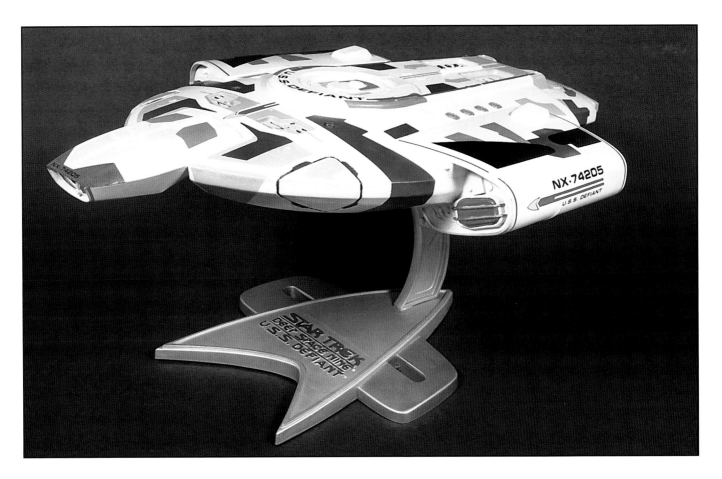

Mounted on the kit-provided stand, the Defiant is ready to lead another mission against the Dominion.

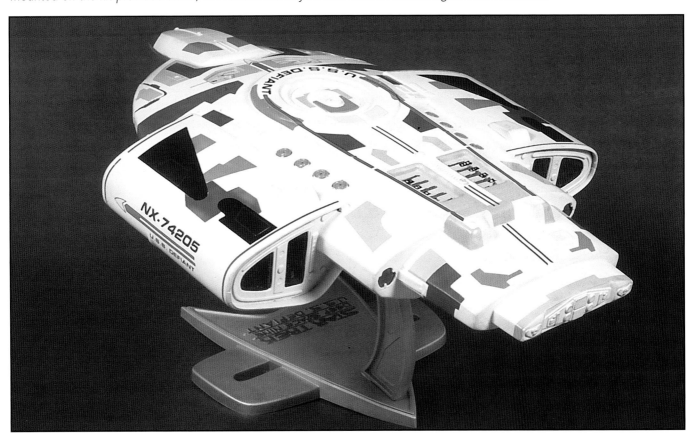

Even from the rear, the Defiant was a distinctly different and beautiful design. Unfortunately, she was lost in action during the Dominion War.

How to Build Sci-Fi Model Spacecraft

ADVANCED DETAILING

Many modelers go along for years creating a collection of finished models built straight out of the box. If that's you and it makes you happy, fine. However, when the creative juices start flowing, you frequently want to do something to your latest project to make it just a little — different. Maybe you want alternate markings, or weathering so that it has that realistic "used" look. Lighting would be good, if you can do it in such a way that the wires and light source are hidden. Then there's battle damage. Finally, some kits come with quite a lot of interior detail — or you could scratch-build a fancy interior — that can only be seen if part of the outer skin is removable. How do you hide a removable section when it's been replaced on the model? There are answers to all these questions if you simply take your time and start thinking outside the box.

MARTIAN WAR MACHINE

Anyone who's ever seen the 1953 film *War of the Worlds* (the one starring Gene Barry before he became famous for portraying Bat Masterson) has been mesmerized by that manta ray shape that floated over the landscape destroying everything in its path with a death ray. Over the years, several garage companies have produced models of the beastie in various sizes. But now Monsters In Motion has produced an outstanding resin kit of the War Machine, complete with sections of a street and a badly damaged building.

There's also a separate lighting/sound kit available if you want to go that far. I wanted to light mine, but I didn't want to spend all that extra money, which meant I had to find another way. Since the kit is in 1/35th scale, which gives the War Machine a span of some 12 inches, designing my own lighting was feasible. It also didn't hurt that I knew an excellent electronics

Monsters In Motion has produced a gorgeous 1/35th scale Martian War Machine diorama. If you have anything approaching fond memories for the 1950s vintage movie, War of the Worlds, you need to give serious consideration to this model.

technician by the name of Don Pyeatt. He agreed to keep me out of trouble and I couldn't have done it without him.

FIRST, BUILD IT

For all practical purposes, you're dealing with two separate kits (the base/building and the War Machine itself) that are then combined to form the whole.

The base/building uses some 8 resin pressure-cast parts, while two resin parts and several vacuformed clear parts form the War Machine. Since the instructions are geared to their lighting kit that I wasn't using, I glanced at 'em, and then did it my way.

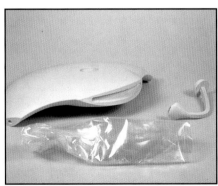

Two resin parts form the War Machine itself. The basic ship is a one-piece spin casting, while the cobra head is a separate casting. You also get vacuformed parts for the transparent areas.

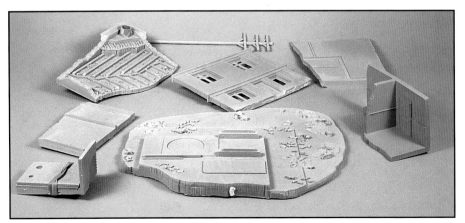

Here you see all the parts for the base and building, including a telephone pole that we won't be using. All parts are cast in a baby blue resin.

Chapter 6 – Advanced Detailing   77

Anticipating the Wiring

The obvious approach is to hard wire everything together and run it off a battery. While that method works, there are two problems. First, you'll eventually find yourself needing at least five hands to hold various finished and painted components while everything is pinned and glued together during final assembly. This ain't the easiest thing in the world to begin with, besides being fraught with all kinds of potential for damage. Secondly, if you keep the lights running for extended periods, you'll have to keep changing batteries. Besides, I wanted to get the War Machine off the built-in support mount that had the Machine sitting on the edge of the building, and position it a couple of inches above in midair. It's tricky, but not *all* that difficult, as you will see.

Most of the wiring would be hidden inside the building and the ship, but how to run it under the building to a plug-in transformer? Simple enough. Mount the entire model on a wood base and enclose it in a dust cover. That way I could drill through the bottom of the resin *and* wood bases, cut a groove on the underside of the wood base to hold the wires, and mount a jack at the rear edge.

I started by drilling a hole near the inside of one wall, about where the instructions would have you mount the speaker from their lighting/sound kit. Size doesn't matter as long as it's large enough to let the wires pass through. You can always enlarge it if need be.

The wall sections will need to be cleaned up, especially the bottom edge

Since I was taking a different approach to lighting, I began by drilling a hole thru the base just inside the building wall. Since I changed horses in mid-stream, I never used this hole. So whether you need to drill it or not depends on you.

so you can get a tight joint where the wall meets the sidewalk. There's a recessed lip on the back lower edge of the wall sections designed to fit over the raised inside core. The recess isn't high enough to clear the foundation, so you'll need to do some trimming.

PINNING

This is the kind of model where pinning really comes into its own. My wall sections weren't perfectly straight by a few hairs. It really wasn't even enough to notice in most instances, but it showed up when you tried to get a flush fit against that raised core. Forget that heat gun! There isn't enough deflection for that. Instead, all you do is install pins in the base of the wall sections and force the wall straight during construction.

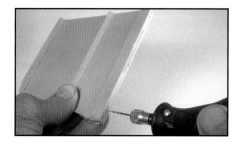

Before installing the building's walls, I drilled holes in the bottom edges with my Dremel to accept metal pins.

Using a drill bit equal in diameter to the pins you'll be using (.050 inch in my case since I was cutting pins from jumbo paper clips), drill three or four holes in the bottom of each of the wall sections. Now shove a piece of wire into the hole 'til it bottoms, cut the wire about 1/4 inch away from the bottom (I used a Xuron Hard Wire Cutter) and you have your pin. Repeat the process for all your other holes.

The pins were cut from jumbo paper clips using a Xuron Hard Wire Cutter.

The trick (if there is one) to getting a tight, straight installation is figuring out where to drill the matching holes. All you do is hold a sidewall (with the pins installed) in position, using a square to make sure the front edge is even with the raised core.

Here, the pins are in place, the wall is in its correct position, and pressure is applied to mark the pin locations. Then the matching holes are drilled.

Apply a little pressure along the bottom edge sufficient to press that edge back against the core while at the same time pressing down on the top of the wall section. This will result in the pins making slight indentations in the base, and you'll know where to drill the matching holes. It's sort of like rubbing your stomach and patting your head at the same time.

I drilled all the holes, added some IC-GEL, and installed the walls. Be sure to use a square on the inside of the side walls to make sure they're vertical. One thing you may discover when test fitting the front wall is the need for a pin near the top of each corner to help

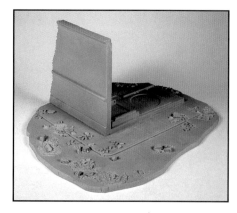

Finally, the wall section was installed with CA. The result? A nice, sturdy joint that won't ever separate. You can literally pick the model up by the building wall without worrying that something will come apart.

After you get the rest of the walls in place, you may find it necessary to add a reinforcing pin up near the top of the wall. Just drill straight thru the face of one wall into the intersecting wall, install the pin, and patch the hole with a little putty.

hold the side/front corners together. If so, just drill straight through the front face into the edge of the side wall and install a pin.

A dab of putty will eliminate the hole. Once the outer walls are secure, add the second floor section and the partial rear walls. However, do not add the roof section at this time. There's a lot of other work that has to be done first.

The front portion of the building doesn't have a second floor; it is open its complete height. To correct this, I installed a couple of pieces of square plastic tubing along the walls at a point where the second floor would be. I later used a piece of sheet styrene for the floor.

I had already built up a walnut base (see Chapter 9), so it was time to figure out the location for the building/street base. As with the Roswell diorama, there would eventually be a dust cover built for the finished model, so the trick was to figure out exactly where to position the base in relation to the War Machine while keeping everything within the base borders. This is entirely dependent on where you place the War Machine relative to the building. Use the cast-in mount, and you can pretty well center it.

GET THE WAR MACHINE OFF THE ROOF

Using a cast-in mount as part of the roof structure in order to support the War Machine is certainly not an unreasonable approach. Trouble is that

by doing that, all of the heavy roof/wall damage is at the other end. The end result is that the War Machine winds up looking like it's actually *sitting* on the roof. Considering that the War Machine was a *flying* machine that floated on a repulsion field and never physically touched a building until the Martians died and the machines crashed, this approach is more than a little unrealistic. This presents a rather interesting problem. Exactly how do you support a model War Machine in midair? Electromagnetic repulsion? Hidden wires? Invisible thread? What?

I got on the phone with Tony Weddel and we brainstormed more than a few ideas, discarding most of them for one reason or another. Then it hit us. The answer was right in front of us. It so happened that Monsters In Motion had included a resin telephone pole, snapped off at the base, which was intended to be placed on the ground as part of the street damage. Its location was at the right side of the building (looking from the front) at the street corner. All I would have to do is to replace the kit's resin telephone pole with a brass-and-plastic (or brass-and-wood) version. Rather than the pole being on the ground, it would be in the act of being pushed over by the War Machine. At least it would appear that way. In actual fact, a section of the brass tubing would extend *into* the War Machine. Not only would the War Machine be supported in midair, the tube would allow wiring from the ship's lighting to be fed through the tube and under the base.

What Diameter?

Before you locate it, it helps to figure out what diameter you need. The kit-provided pole is just less than .190 inch in diameter. This scales out to a 6.65-inch diameter in real life. That's just a tad skinny, particularly when you consider the one in my back yard is 8.1 inches in diameter, and I've also seen larger ones. Scale that one down to 1/35th and you're looking at a pole that would be .231 inch in diameter. In case you're wondering why I'm agonizing over a .40-inch difference, it's because I'm engaged in a balancing act. To get the War Machine off the roof, I needed

the largest diameter tubing possible in order to support the ship. At the same time, it has to be small enough to fit the scale of the model.

So, 3/16-inch tubing (.187 inch) scales out to 6.54 inches, 7/32-inch tubing (.218 inch) equals 7.63 inches, and 1/4-inch tubing (.250 inch) calculates to 8.75 inches. What's the bottom line? After arguing with myself for a considerable period, I settled on 7/32 inch. Despite the fact that 1/4-inch diameter would only scale out to just over 1/2 inch larger than 7/32 inch would, it seemed a little fat to me when placed next to the corner of the building.

Locate the Pole

Since I wasn't going to use the roof mount, the base was shifted to the left (when viewed from the front) on its wood base. Exactly where it was shifted to was determined by my holding the War Machine in the air in the approximate position that I wanted it to wind up in, and then sliding the base around 'til everything was in the correct position. Once the base was in position, I drilled a couple or three holes through the resin base in order to temporarily screw it down to the wood. There wouldn't be any problem hiding the screws, because the craters in the street would be perfect for the purpose. Drill through the bottom of the craters and drive the screws home.

Because of my mid-stream change of horses (which allows me to suspend the ship above the building), I drilled a 7/32-inch diameter hole thru the resin base where the telephone pole would have been located. Note that I have temporarily mounted the model on its wood base so that I can extend the hole all the way thru the wood. You'll also need a regular power drill for this stunt, because a Dremel won't handle a large enough bit.

Then I took a 7/32-inch diameter drill bit, found the location on the sidewalk where the telephone pole was located, and drilled all the way through the resin *and* the wood base. The exact angle will depend on precisely how you want the War Machine to be positioned. You also don't want the pole *too* far off vertical because the greater the angle the more weight and stress you impart.

I wound up leaning the pole about four or five degrees off vertical and positioned it so that as it continued to fall, it would collapse into the street away from the front of the base. This would allow the War Machine to be positioned as if it were traveling from the back to the front of the building, just low enough to hit and begin to push over the telephone pole. That also provides an explanation for the partially demolished building (due to it's being too close to the repulsor field). And because the hole you've drilled goes all the way through the wood base *and* the resin base, you have more than enough support to keep the tube from deflecting under the weight of the War Machine when you add it.

Back the screws out, separate the building/street base from the wood, and then we can turn our attention to painting and detailing the resin base.

BRICKWORK

Before you can paint the brick, you need to know what color. There are companies that market premixed 'brick' paint for the modeler. The problem is that there's more than one shade of brick. Buildings that were erected in the 1930s and 1940s (such as those depicted in the movie) or earlier were, more often than not, some shade of "brick red." But depending on the kiln they were produced in, the exact shade varied all the way from a fairly bright red with a touch of brown, to a dark, near-brown with a touch of red, and everything in between. I wound up taking a half bottle of Model Master FS 31136 Insignia Red, to which I added a little bit of Model Master FS 37038 Flat Black and an even smaller amount (just a touch) of Model Master FS 33538 Insignia Yellow. The exact amounts will depend on what shade of brick looks right to you. Take it slow, adding a few drops at a time.

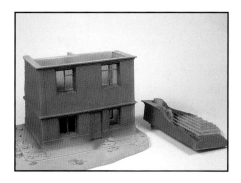

I sprayed the outside of the building a basic brick color to start with. Note that the roof section is still separate. It will stay that way for some time to facilitate any interior detailing desired.

Once I had the color mixed, the entire outside of the building was sprayed brick red. This includes the broken edges of the building walls and both sides of the roof parapet.

Remove the Mount

Since I had no need for the cast-in mount on the roof, I whacked the majority of it off with my Dremel and diamond cutting wheel.

Having determined that I had a way to get the War Machine off its rooftop perch, I reverted to my Dremel and diamond blade to remove the mounting post from the corner of the roof.

What remained was cleaned up with a knife. That left me with a good-sized hole in the corner of the roof to eliminate. Rather than try to fill the hole with a circular plug, all I did was slap a piece of .020-inch styrene over it and trim the long edge to match the irregular contour of the destroyed surface.

After removing the mount, a piece of .020-inch styrene was installed to cover the opening. I trimmed the outer edge to match the contour of the damaged roof.

The Street and Sidewalk

After the basic brick color had dried, I wrapped some paper towel around the building and taped it in place. Then the street was airbrushed with a wet-on-wet-on-wet mix of Floquil Grimy Black, Floquil Concrete, and Floquil Weathered Black. The idea is to create an asphalt pavement that's seen quite a bit of traffic on it. To do this, you have to break up the monotone appearance of Grimy Black.

At this point, the building was masked off and both the streets and sidewalks were airbrushed. In case you're wondering, most of the masking seen here is nothing more than paper towels wrapped around the building and then taped at the bottom.

Start with a solid coat of Grimy Black, and then come back over it (while it's still wet) with random streaking and misting of Concrete. Repeat the process with Weathered Black. I even went so far as to spray a little bit of thinner here and there. Also, there's no need to be overly neat. Remember, this scene depicts past and current destruction (in other words, combat) and it's going to be grunged up a lot more before we're through. What you're doing now is creating the base colors.

Before removing the masking from the building, the sidewalk was airbrushed freehand with Concrete. Try to be as accurate as possible, but if you wind up with a little overspray on the edges of the street, it won't matter.

Concrete Trim

The cornices, corner trim, and cement ledges are basically cast concrete. In order to get a little separation when compared to the cement sidewalk, I added some Model Master FS 17875 Insignia White to the Floquil Concrete. This lightens the concrete slightly and, because FS 17875 is a gloss paint, it adds a little bit of sheen to the color.

After masking off all the concrete trim and cornices, I gave them a coat of Floquil Concrete with a little Gloss Insignia White mixed in to create a slight sheen.

After masking off all the trim, spraying my modified concrete color and then stripping the tape, it was time for the next step: brick mortar.

Mortar Lines

Brickwork is installed with mortar, which is basically nothing more than a thick cement, or concrete mix that's slathered onto each course of bricks before the next is added. Color can be anything from plain old natural concrete color to white. For model purposes, I like to use flat white to provide a little definition for the individual bricks.

There's more than one way to do mortar. Some like to use watercolor and a wet brush so they can apply it exactly where they want it, removing any vestige of surplus. The result winds

White acrylic paint is being wiped on with a paper towel to create the mortar lines. Remember, it isn't necessary to highlight every mortar line. In fact, it would look phony if you did.

up being perfectly neat. That's fine for a new building, but it doesn't suit one with some age on it — especially an older building that's been on the receiving end of a heat ray.

So, after the enamel brick color was good and dry, I took a wad of paper towel and started wiping on some white acrylic paint. Either Liquitex Titanium White acrylic artist color or Badger Air-Opaque White acrylic will do. The reason for the acrylic paint is the fact that it doesn't affect enamel paint, meaning I could wipe it off unwanted areas leaving the enamel color untouched. At least that's the way it's supposed to work.

Anyway, I applied a little acrylic white onto my paper towel and spread it over a section of brick, then started wiping off the excess. Surprise! Surprise! Brick red started showing up on the paper towel and the model's walls began to look like they were being bleached! What happened?

To this day, I haven't got a clue as to what caused the problem. Acrylic and enamel have no relation to each other chemically because one is petroleum based and the other isn't. No way should there be that kind of reaction. But no matter, I was suddenly stuck with a pitcher full of sour lemons that left me with a very interesting problem. Do I go back to square one, re-prime the building and take a totally different approach, or try to figure out how to make lemonade out of the lemons? In case you're wondering, this is exactly the kind of unexpected surprise that separates the model builders from the kit assemblers. And if you've figured that I opted for lemonade, you'd be right.

Recipe for Lemonade

After looking at the disaster for a while, I noticed that it really didn't look all that bad. Matter of fact, it added some realism to the structure. Some areas remained a fairly clean brick red, while other parts I had wiped over were a rather light red, and still others were somewhere in between. It was actually a mix of random shades. In places, the white had flowed into the mortar lines and remained there. Other times it stayed on the surface, almost like faded whitewash, while the mortar lines remained a dark red. Hmmm-m-m.

I wound up taking some more paper towels and acrylic white, repeating the disastrous (I thought) process over the entire brick area. Obviously some of the white (and even the brick red that came off on the towel) managed to stain the concrete trim. All I did was let that dry, then hand brush some more of my cement mix over it to touch up. Wherever too much white was showing on the face of the brick, I used my Rich AB-100 airbrush to mist some brick color mix over it in order to diminish but not hide the white cast.

Are the mortar lines too prominent? Is there too much white on the surface of the bricks? Never be afraid to mist some of the base color over the area to tone things down.

The end result was a rather wellworn brick wall that was beginning to look like it had seen better days. Now, would I have used this method on a nice, clean building that was ready to receive its usual customers? Absolutely not. But when you consider that this building's latest customer was a War Machine and its heat ray, the method was entirely appropriate.

WINDOW FRAMES AND DOOR

Whenever models of buildings dating to the late 1800s/early 1900s are built, it's almost a knee-jerk reflex to paint the window frames and doors either white or dark brown. Aside from the fact that this wasn't a universal practice, I wanted something a little different.

Switching over to a conventional brush, the window frames and doors were painted Model Master Euro I Dark Green.

Quite a number of commercial buildings, both then and now, opted for some shade of green. Knowing this, I settled on Model Master FS 34092 Euro I Dark Green. Then FS 34095 was used on the inset door panels to provide a little contrast.

DON'T FORGET THE ROOF

Assuming you included the roof-side walls (the inside of the parapets) when you applied the mortar, all that remains is to detail the damaged roof. Aside from that little triangular section that covers the old mount hole (that piece should be painted Floquil Grimy Black) the rest of the roof is various shades of gray, grime, and assorted crud. If you want to see what I'm talking about in real life, crawl up in the attic of a 70- or 80-year-old house. Aside from the ever-present dust, the lumber has aged to various shades of grays. There's absolutely nothing bright or clean about the entire area and you won't look any better after you get out of there.

That's the look you're after, because all the roof detail, including ceiling beams, etc., had been hidden for decades before the Martians came. Basically, all I did was hand brush all of that detail with various shades of grays,

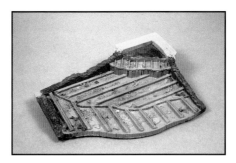

Aside from a little more detailing of the cast-in debris, the roof is pretty well finished.

Floquil Grime, Floquil Dust, dirty thinner, and anything else that came to mind.

You'll also find all kinds of molded-in debris, bricks, shattered pieces of cement cornice, and so on. These all need to be picked out with the appropriate colors. Take your time and remember that the more details you pick out, the more realistic the end result will be.

WINDOW GLASS

The kit-provided window glass is way too thick for my taste, especially when some of it is going to be shattered and broken. Instead, I dug out a piece of .010-inch clear styrene and cut several pieces to fit the various windows. They can all be installed with Super-Gold + with no concern about an occasional smear or fogged area. I also replicated shattered panes by simply breaking some of the styrene in my hands before installation. In other cases, you can do the damage before the fact. And don't overlook the fact that you can create a bunch of real fine clear shards by crushing and breaking small pieces of clear styrene, then scattering them on the sidewalk and street.

Assuming you have shattered at least one of the lower floor windows, think about what shattered it. I took a small piece of scale lumber from an old model railroad project and positioned it through the broken glass from the inside. A few more pieces of lumber and assorted debris was scattered around, then I inserted a piece of styrene inside the building to form the second floor (remember those braces I installed way back at the beginning?).

I repeated the process regarding

With shattered glass, part of a curtain blowin' in the wind, along with loose bricks and broken lumber laying around, its beginning to look like the real McCoy.

damage and debris on the inside and then added something else. Part of the framework of one upper window sash was broken out, meaning there'd be precious little glass, if any, in that window. If you take a small piece of lightweight cloth that's cut just larger than the window height and half its width, then cement the top edge on the inside just above the window, you have a curtain that hasn't torn loose. Now drag the bottom of the curtain through the glassless bottom sash and turn loose. Adds a lot of realism, don't you think?

THE BACK ROOMS

There are several partially destroyed rooms on the back side of the building. The two most complete

Same song, second verse. It isn't hard to visualize these second-floor rooms being occupied as the War Machine bore down on them. Incidentally, all those loose bricks are fixed in place by a somewhat unexpected method. Scatter them randomly, and then shoot them with some 3M Super 77 Spray Adhesive. I've had this one can for the last 30 years or so. I don't even know if it's still made, but it's perfect for the purpose. It's high tack, disappears completely, and doesn't blow the pieces around while you're spraying.

are on the second floor and are typical of what you'd see in a walkup hotel in the 1920s or 1930s. Both have wainscoting (wall paneling) on the lower half of the walls, while the upper walls can either be wallpapered or painted. Floors can be bare wood or cheap carpet. Each room also has a door leading to what we assume is a hallway.

On the lower floor, you're basically looking at structural walls with some of the plaster or wallboard torn away. You need to detail all of these areas to whatever level you wish. When you're done, install the roof casting, touch up any seams that might exist, and your building is pretty well done.

The Nitty Gritty

Go ahead and install the base permanently with the screws driven into the craters. Add a little putty on top to camouflage the screws and sculpt the putty to match the surrounding crater detail.

From this point on, it's simply a matter of sweating the small stuff until you get the results you want. Detail the rest of the molded-in debris, paint the craters, maybe add a fireplug, and so on. You might want to add water streaks to the building, assorted junk and lumber laying in the street and so on. Some of the lumber could even show signs of being burned. How about a poster plastered on the brick wall of the building that's in the process of peeling off?

One thing I ordered from Squadron Shop was a 1/35th scale set of bricks manufactured by Sol Model Corporation. What you get is a pack-

At long last, the War Machine base is completely finished. Now it's just a matter of getting the War Machine itself to the same stage.

age of, what else, brick. Made from plaster, you get individual bricks with colors ranging all the way from light gray through reds, pinks, and dark gray. There's also a bunch of dust and grit that results from the package bouncing around in shipment. None of the bricks are truly perfect in size and shape either, which makes them ideal for debris resulting from a Martian attack. Scatter the bricks and dust around here and there and it'll really add to the final appearance of the base. Finally, don't forget to spend some more time with dirty thinner and the Floquil weathering colors to tie everything together.

In case you're wondering how to keep all that loose brick and debris that you just scattered around the base in its place, the answer is surprisingly simple. The obvious approach, which I intended to use, would be to tediously glue each individual brick into place. Aside from the fact that it would take more than a few hours, it would also destroy the truly random appearance of scattered or fallen brick. Was there another way?

It turns out there was, though it took considerable nerve to try it. 3M manufactures a product called Super 77 Spray Adhesive. I wound up spraying it in short, narrow (they give you two different spay heads) bursts directly at the loose debris. The stuff simply bubbles up on the surface (like some kind of chemical boiling), then soaks in and disappears. And that's it. None of the loose debris is loose anymore, color is not affected, and in a few short minutes, it's completely dry and nothing else will stick to it.

While you couldn't ask for a better way to fasten loose junk, make sure you use this stuff where there's plenty of ventilation — and don't breathe it. Keep in mind that you're basically using contact cement in a spray can. That's not something you want in your lungs.

Now let's concentrate on the War Machine.

Lighting Parts

The nose and wingtips are reproduced in the kit as clear vacuform parts, though they glow a translucent green in the film. On the other hand, the lens for

the cobra head (also clear vacuform) is clear, though the ray itself is red. Since this is the location of the death ray, intensity varies as the ray powers up for firing. So how do you reproduce this effect on the model? Fairly easily it turns out, especially when you have the generous assistance of a skilled electronics tech such as Don Pyeatt. I literally cannot say enough about the help he provided. Could I have done it without him? Probably not, considering the fact that I haven't played with LEDs that much and I wouldn't recognize Ohm's law if I saw it painted on the side of a very large barn.

So, Don determined that the best approach would be five LEDs equally spaced across the nose recess, one in each wingtip and another in the cobra head. All would be green except for a red one to represent the death ray.

Then there was the question of the transformer. You know the kind I'm talking about. They're the little plug-in power supplies (also known as wall warts) that come with cassette tape recorders, cordless telephones, and the like. If you're like most people, when the equipment wears out, you toss the equipment but usually forget about the transformers. Granted, you could go buy a nice, new wall wart at Radio Shack, and pay anywhere from $15 – $30, but why bother if you've got a few spares laying around?

It turned out that the best one I had on hand was from an old BellSouth cordless phone. It converts 120VAC 60Hz 8W into 9VDC 300mA and has a female plug. All I would need would be a male jack of the appropriate size, the

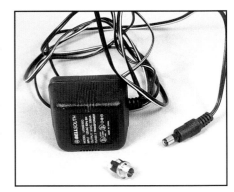

If you've ever worn out a cordless phone, you should have at least one of these transformers lying around. No? Then go buy one from Allied or Radio Shack.

LEDs, and Don's expertise, and we could get the show on the road.

Don gave me a shopping list and I hustled on down to Allied Electronics. If you don't have one near you, they have a web site so you can order by mail. I wound up with seven #10-41C 505 2103 green LEDs and one #932-9405 jack. As for the red LED, Don had a bunch on hand, so we used one of those. If you have to buy one, the best fit will be one of the smaller ones, such as 5 mm.

Before we get any deeper into the lighting segment, a word of caution — or warning, if you prefer. Despite your curiosity to make sure the LEDs work (either singly or after they've been wired into an array and before you've added resistors so you can connect the power supply), absolutely *do not* touch their leads to a flashlight battery just to see the little boogers light up. While it might not happen, you run the risk of burning them out, forcing you to order another set of LEDs.

It does little good to have all these parts if you can't connect them, which means you gotta have wire. Don dug out a couple of pieces of modular inside phone wire (techs and model builders are both packrats) that would do nicely. You can buy the same stuff at Radio Shack. It also wouldn't hurt to buy a pair of wire strippers because this wire is a four-conductor design and you're only going to use two: the red and black. Incidentally, the wires are extremely delicate, which means be very careful when stripping the outer sheath so that you don't nick the insulation on the wires.

PREPARE THE WAR MACHINE

Before you bother with doing any wiring, a little prep work on the ship itself is needed.

The hole in each wingtip needs to be drilled out, with the diameter being just slightly less than the countersunk area. Then you will have to cut a slot running the width of the nose recess.

You can pretty much eyeball it as long as it has sufficient room to clear the LED leads when they're oriented vertically. A Dremel with a carbide cutting wheel is ideal for this. And don't forget to clean out the flashed-over

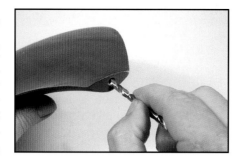

Each wingtip has a recessed hole. Drill each one out so the wires can gain access to the hollow interior of the ship. Be aware that one tip will have more material to drill thru than the other. This is simply the nature of spin casting.

Cut a lateral slot in the nose recess that will allow the completed wiring array to be inserted. Carbide cutting wheels or Dremel's diamond wheels are invaluable for this kind of work.

hole in the top of the ship where the cobra neck will mount.

So far, the prep work has been pretty tame but the cobra head/neck is a different story. Because I didn't opt for the lighting kit designed for this model, my cobra head has the recessed hole drilled for the LED, but the neck is solid. This leads to the obvious question of just how do you run the wires from the head, down the neck, and into the ship? Basically, you sneak in the back door, or the back of the neck.

First you take a #43 drill bit (which is about .100-inch diameter) and drill straight into the front of the cobra head until the bit comes out the back. If you've held it straight and level, it'll exit at the very back of the head just above where the neck begins.

Now switch back to the carbide cutting wheel on your Dremel and cut a wide groove all the way from the drill bit's exit point to just above the stepped fitting that plugs into the top of the ship.

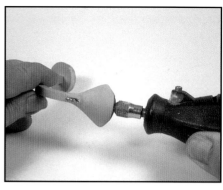

If you drill straight into the front of the head, the drill bit will come out perfectly centered directly above the neck.

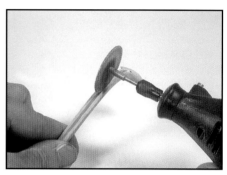

Switching back to our carbide cutting wheel, cut a square groove as far down the neck as you can without cutting into the base. Size it so that the wires will fit side by side.

Using the two wires as a gauge, make the groove wide enough for the wires to fit side-by-side and deep enough that they will be below the surface of the neck. There's plenty of room, so about the only things you have to worry about are getting the side walls of the grooves vertical, and not going so deep that you weaken the neck to the point that it might snap.

Now stand the cobra neck on its base and drill a hole straight down thru the base.

Once the groove is completed, stand the neck upright on the stepped fitting, place the drill vertically in the bottom of the groove, and drill straight down until you've gone completely through the fitting.

After the neck is wired, we'll spread putty over the groove, sand it, rescribe the recessed lines, and wind up with a fully wired cobra head/neck that works just a well as the one in the lighting kit, but costs a heckuva lot less.

The Pole

Still just a piece of brass tubing, the pole was cut to approximately 9 1/2-inches in length. I temporarily installed it (again) in the base and held the ship up about where I wanted it for its final position. This is strictly your choice, because it all depends on what kind of a scene you're trying for. It turns out that the location I picked was about 2 1/4 inches to the right (as you view the ship from the front) of the original mounting hole in the belly. And in case you're wondering, we'll eventually be plugging that hole.

A 7/32-inch hole was drilled, angling in at somewhere around 30 or 40 degrees. Then the ship is slipped over the pole (rod) until it butts against the inside of the upper surface. I had cut a bevel on the end of my pole, so I simply rotated the pole in combination with position changes of the ship until I had the position I was looking for. The ship would eventually be CA'd in place and an extra pin inserted for good measure.

The location of the extra pin would mainly be an educated guess. While the ship was temporarily mounted on the pole, I stuck my index finger in through the cobra mounting hole and felt around 'til I found the pole where it hit the upper surface. Then I drilled a hole through the top of the ship at the spot I hoped was in line with the pole. Be sure to drill at an angle that matches the pole. Incidentally, that same #43 drill bit will suffice, even though the pin will be cut from .080-inch music wire.

Slot the Rod

In case you're sittin' there screaming that an .080-inch pin ain't gonna fit

a 7/32-inch tube, quit hollerin' and read a little farther. First, cut a slot (using the carbide cutting wheel again) about an inch long in one side of the top end of the tube. Width isn't critical, but around 1/8 inch should do nicely. Now shove in a piece of styrene from the top so that it plugs the entire tube and extends beyond the side of the slot. Be sure to stop about 1/4 inch from the bottom of the slot, add some CA and then whittle down the surplus styrene until it matches the contours of the tube. Don't forget to deburr the exposed edges of the brass tube so that it doesn't damage the wire that you'll have to pull through.

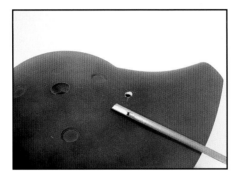

Look closely and you can see the styrene plug in the end of the brass tube, the opening on the side that the wire will pull thru, and the hole in the bottom of the ship that will slide over the tube when we get around to wiring everything.

Use the carbide wheel again to cut a slot in the styrene that fills the area above the opening you left for the wire. Make this slot only wide and deep enough to provide clearance for the wires as you insert the pole into the bottom of the ship. Finally, use the #43 bit to drill a hole on the opposite side of the slot, hard against the inside surface of the tube, literally forming a hole between the styrene plug and the inside of the tube. That reinforcing pin will eventually go into this hole, providing extra strength to the mount.

Now for the Wiring

Anyone who's ever done any lighted models knows that you have to solder wires together. If you have soldering experience, you're set. Don't know a soldering iron from a heat gun? Then it's about time you found someone to give you a crash course. The process is

really quite simple and can be learned in short order.

Assuming you've overcome the soldering hurdle, let's see what this thing is going to take. In order to keep the nose LEDs properly aligned and be able to install them after everything is soldered together, I cut a substrate (a piece of .020-inch sheet styrene) to fit the recessed portion of the nose. After marking the horizontal centerline, I determined the locations for five equally spaced LEDs. Using a knife blade as a reamer, I slowly created five holes, checking for fit frequently. You want the holes just large enough for the LEDs to slip through until they butt against the raised collar at the bottom of each LED.

Do not permanently install the LEDs into the substrate at this time. However, you can go ahead and either spray the front surface of the substrate with chrome silver or apply adhesive backed chrome foil. This will create a reflector for the LEDs, and since it's on the front of a piece of styrene, the risk of shorting the wiring is eliminated.

Soldering Time

The first thing Don did was insert (temporarily again) all five LEDs into the substrate, then arc the unit until it appeared to match the curve of the nose. This is strictly an eyeball operation.

Keep in mind that you have both a positive and negative lead on each LED. There are two ways to determine which is which, but the easiest is to look for the flat spot on the LED collar. That's the negative lead, also known as the cathode.

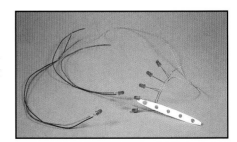

In this view you can see the nose array and wingtip lights after they've been wired. Also in the picture is the styrene substrate with self-adhesive chrome foil applied to the front. Note that the resistors haven't been added to the array yet.

After tinning the connecting wire he'd be using (this also burns off any varnish on the wire, making for a solid solder connection), the end of the wire was soldered to the first negative lead. As he moved to the next one, he began to pull the substrate back into an arc, soldered the second lead and so on until all of the negative leads were connected. A surplus length of wire with the insulation on it was left attached for the time being.

At this point, the substrate was removed and the array flipped over so that the positive leads (and also known as the anodes) would be on top. Then all of them were connected with another piece of wire. In this case, just a short tail of tinned wire was left beyond the array.

Each of the wingtip lights had long pieces of insulated wire soldered to their leads, as did the red LED for the death ray. It only takes about 1/8-inch of bare wire to make a good connection.

The Resistors

Resistors basically impede current to a level that individual components can handle. Since the LEDs operate at about .5 volt and .02 amp and the transistor can produce .3 amp (300 milliamps) and 9 volts, you have to find some way to keep the LEDs from getting the entire jolt. It turns out (according to Don) that each resistor needs to have a value of 390 Ohms. He didn't have any of that value on hand, so 320-Ohm resistors were used. The difference? LED current is a little higher (26 milliamp instead of 20) and the LEDs will burn a little brighter. Most modern LEDs can handle this extra current, especially for the limited time they will be operated in a typical model.

Individual resistors for each LED were used because their small size would allow everything to slip into place as designed. A single resistor could have been used, but no way could you have stuffed the thing through any of the openings.

One lead of each LED on the nose array was clipped out and replaced with the appropriate resistor. Note that you *really* want to do this one at a time. Otherwise, that array you spent time

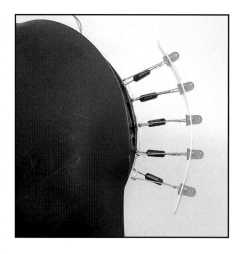

In the final stages of wiring, we're just preparing to slip the nose array into place. You have a clear view here of how each resistor is connected to the nose LEDs.

building up will inconsiderately fall apart. The fact that there are suddenly no wires to hold the thing together might have something to do with it.

A length of insulated wire was soldered to the short, tinned tail of the array and the unit was tested to make sure the lights actually worked. They do! In case you're wondering what about the other resistors, we'll get to those in good time. Right now it's time to start putting the thing together.

FINAL ASSEMBLY — AT LEAST FOR THE LIGHTING

The substrate is slipped back in position over the nose LEDs and a dab of CA added around the collar of the outboard lights. That's all it'll take to hold the substrate/reflector in place. Now install the array in the nose, carefully working the wiring and resistors through the slot. Don't be afraid to enlarge the slot a little instead of trying to force the wiring array. The two long pieces of wire will be fished up through the top hole and left alone for the moment.

Using the same process, more or less, install the wingtip LEDs and the red one in the cobra head. The long leads on the wingtip units will fish up through the top hole as well. As for the cobra-head light, feed the leads through the head, down the neck and through the base mount. Then set the cobra head/neck aside for the moment. Incidentally, you won't need CA for

either the wingtips or cobra head because the LED collars wind up being a tight fit. Or at least they did on mine.

We're not done threading wires yet. A final pair, somewhere around 20-22 inches long, has to be fed up the brass tube (from the bottom) and out the side slot. You'll want enough surplus above the top of the tube that you'll be able to feed the wires up into the ship, fish it out the top hole, and still have three or four inches to work with. What's left below the bottom of the tube, which should be a good 9 or 10 inches, will eventually wind up being fed through the hole the tube (rod, pole) mounts in, then running over to the back of the base where it will be soldered to a power jack that you'll plug the female end of the wall wart into.

A Hole for the Jack

Though we won't be using it for a while, now is as good as time as any to drill the needed hole for the power jack. Using a 5/8-inch diameter bit, I drilled straight into the back edge of

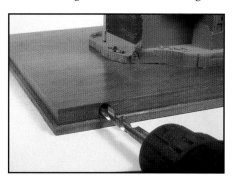

The hole for the jack is 5/8-inch diameter and goes straight into the back edge of the base. Note that there's just enough room above the rabbited lip so that it doesn't break thru the top surface.

the wood base.

You can drill the hole pretty much wherever makes you happy. Now stand the base up on edge and drill two overlapping holes of the same diameter into the bottom of the base. Don't go overboard and drill clean through the base. Stop when you break through into the horizontal hole, and then clean out the overlap with a knife so that you have a rectangular hole in the bottom of the base.

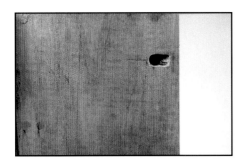

Two overlapping holes and a knife creates a slot that'll provide clearance for the wires.

The Rest of the Resistors and All the Connections — Except One.

Now the three remaining resistors are installed. The way Don did it was to lay the three resistors side-by-side, bend one lead across the two adjacent to it, and solder them all together into an array. This soldered end of the array becomes a tie point for the red (positive) lead from the power jack. There's nothing wrong with the method, but it's strongly suggested that, if yours winds up being done the same way, you insulate the assembly with some electrical tape. This layer of tape will not only insulate the bare wires and prevent any accidental short circuits, it will also serve to prevent the small telephone wire from bending at the solder joints. Remember, when you start shoving all this wiring down into the ship, if anything breaks loose, you won't be able to get to it for repairs. Better to make sure that nothing *can* break loose in the first place.

At long last, all wiring connections are complete. We did add a wire nut to the juncture of all the black (negative) wires for one very simple reason. It eliminates any chance of some of the other wires shorting out against it.

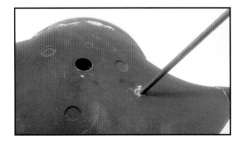

The brass tube (soon to be a telephone pole) has just been permanently installed in the underside of the ship.

STUFF IT AND BUILD IT

The moment of truth has arrived. Permanent installation of all the wiring starts by working the nose array back into place. A couple of gobs of IC-GEL in the corners of the nose recess just before you press the array home will be plenty to hold things in place.

The wingtip LEDs are pressed back into place, and then all the wiring sticking out through the top hole is carefully worked down into the body of the ship. That's followed by the cobra neck/head. In order to create a more dynamic appearance, I rotated the neck so that the head (and death ray) would be pointing between the fourth and fifth nose LEDs to the left (as you view the ship from the front). Once I knew what the position was going to be, I pulled the neck back out, added some IC-GEL, quickly reinstalled the neck, and then moved on to the underside.

That long .080-inch reinforcing pin was shoved in the top hole and out the bottom hole that's intended for the pole. Now fit the wires into the tube's recess and, at the same time, start the end of the pin into its hole. Believe it or not, the entire unit will slide very neatly into the underside hole until the top of the pole butts against the underside of the hull top.

Pull the pole back out about a half inch or so, add some IC-GEL, and quickly slide the pole back in place. Put a little more IC-GEL on the reinforcing pin projecting above the hull and (again) quickly shove the pin in until it's flush with the surface. And the result is a nice, solid installation that won't break loose or rotate.

You'll notice from the photos that I haven't yet cleaned up the puttied neck groove. Matter of fact, I didn't even *putty* it until after everything was wired and all the parts were hanging together. This turn of events is due to the fact that the wiring was done at Don's house (where his bench was), while construction and photography was done at mine — otherwise known as a slight problem in logistics. You can use the same approach if you wish, but it's definitely the hard way.

TROUBLE

When everything's running along smooth as silk, do you ever worry that something just *has* to go wrong? Occasionally there's good reason to feel that way because I just ran head-on into a problem. After testing all the lighting to make sure everything worked (it did), stuffing everything into the ship's hull, puttying seams, etc., I made one more test. The green LEDs worked like a champ, but not the red death ray. Hoo boy! What now?

Since I hadn't closed up the belly mount hole, the obvious answer was to fish the leads out and see if we could figure out where the problem was. That's what Don did, and the answer wasn't one I liked. All connections were solid, which told us exactly one thing. Somewhere between the last test lighting and stuffing all the wiring into the hull, that poor little red LED simply gave up the ghost. It happens, and there's really nothing you can do about it.

So, confronted with another lemon, and a very sour one this time, I had to figure out how to make some more lemonade. Fortunately, the answer turned out to be relatively simple. After watching the film another time or two, I noticed that the death ray crystal doesn't glow all the time, only when it's powering up to fire. While the nose and wingtips *have* to be lit at all times, the death ray doesn't.

CLEAR PARTS

The nose and wingtips are produced as vacuform parts. Rather than repeat the details on how to trim, fit, and glue vacuform components, refer back to the B-Wing section of Chapter 3. However, there is one other thing you need to do before permanently installing the War Machine's nose and wingtips. They need to be tinted.

You do need to be aware of a couple of tradeoffs that you'll have to deal with. In the film, the nose and wingtips glow a uniform, translucent green. If you light this model, whether do it yourself or with the manufacturer's lighting kit, the one thing you won't get is a uniform glow. To get the solid, uniform color you see in the film, your only choice would be to paint the outside of those parts a solid color. LEDs don't have a sufficient dispersal angle to create the glow you see in the film. Choose to install lights, as I have, and you'll have to live with LED hot spots. Impressive, certainly, just not identical to the film.

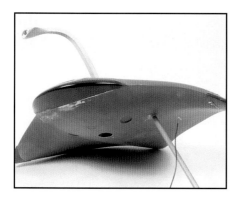

If you're not that used to working with vacuform parts, all I can say is that they will definitely teach you patience. Either that or make you want to throw the entire model against the wall! No matter, this photo proves that it really can be done.

In any event, the clear parts are easily tinted by spraying the interior with Tamiya X-25 Clear Green Acrylic. The more coats you spray, the darker the nose and tips will appear when unlit. However, the lighter your tint, the more obvious the LEDs will be when things are powered up. It's essentially your choice and about all I can suggest is that you tint some scrap clear plastic to see what the different effects are.

Speaking of scrap plastic, I wound up having to cut three 1/2-inch diameter discs from clear stock (.020 inch will do) that will be tinted the same transparent green and cemented into the magnetic repulsor recesses in the bottom of the ship. These discs are supposed to be provided in the kit but mine either didn't have them, or they got lost during construction.

After getting everything tinted (keep in mind that the death ray lens remains clear), all of the vacuformed parts were installed with Super-Gold + CA. Clean up the joints, mask the clear (and tinted) parts, including the discs on the belly, and it's almost time to paint the monster.

PLUG THAT BIG HOLE

Since we've eliminated the rooftop mount and found a way for the ship to appear suspended in midair, the last thing you need is that big hole in the belly. It's 5/8 inch in diameter, so all you have to do is cut a styrene disc that size, fit it carefully into the hole, sand the seam down, and you're ready to prime.

PAINT IT — AT LAST

Believe it or not, this is the easy part. Mask off the nose and wingtips, and then shoot the war machine with primer. Once you have a smooth prime coat on (and don't worry about masking or protecting that brass tube), the entire ship gets a coat of Model Master Steel that has had just a tad (like three or four drops) of Model Master Chrome Silver added to it. Your goal is metallic steel.

After masking off the lenses, a base coat of metallic steel is applied. If you prefer Model Master Metalizer, try Stainless Steel.

In case you're wondering why I don't spray the whole thing copper and forget it, it's because it wasn't copper. The electronic eye that pursued Gene Barry and his girlfriend in that demolished farmhouse was, but it also extended from inside the ship. If you watch the film closely, you'll see that the ship is actually the aforementioned metallic steel with copper highlights, which were essentially reflections from the numerous fires. Tony Weddel also had a chance to see the filming model when he was in California and gave the same description.

When the metallic steel was dry, I simply sprayed a mist coat of Testors Copper (in the small, square bottle)

over the ship. Just enough that you could see the color, but not enough to hide the underlying steel. Due to the metallic finish, there's no need to spray a clear coat on the ship. However, if you're simply married to the idea of clear coats, shoot the thing with Model Master Sealer for Metalizer. Being a true neutral, it won't affect the metallic tone.

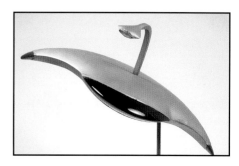

Testors Copper is then misted over the ship. Note that, since the intent is to replicate the effect of fires being reflected in its surface, you do not want an even, uniform coverage.

THE POLE (PART 2)

To turn a brass tube into a telephone pole ain't as hard as you might think. First, hand brush a heavy coat of primer and don't worry about the brush marks. In fact, you *want* brush marks. That'll help replicate the wood grain. With the primer dry, brush on a coat of Liquitex Acrylic Titanium White. Again, don't worry about the brush marks. In fact, you'll find that you can make adjustments to the surface as the paint dries. Basically, you're going to be using your artist's eye.

When you have the pole looking the way you want it, paint it a reddish brown (such as Model Master FS 30117 Military Brown) and then follow with a wash of grimy black or dirty thinner.

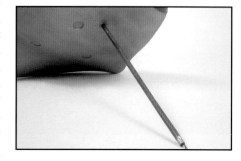

That pole is really a piece of brass tubing, but it sure doesn't look like it, does it?

Crossarms

Telephone poles (and power poles) have crossarms on them, sometimes two, sometimes three. The kit provided pole had three, so I used it as a guide. Using some more of my scale lumber (styrene strips will work as well), I cut three crossarms and six diagonal braces. Be sure to paint them to match the pole before installation. The two lower crossarms and their braces are installed in a position similar to that seen on the resin pole. A small dab of IC-GEL will be more than enough to hold them in place. It's the topmost crossarm that will make or break the impression of the War Machine truly being in midair.

I positioned the third crossarm right up against the bottom of the ship, slightly twisted to one side in relation to the other two. The part of the crossarm that would have continued into the ship had the ship not been there has been cracked at the midpoint, twisted back toward the street while still laying right up against the ship's hull. Check the photo to see exactly what I mean. Incidentally, this is what makes the ship look like it's pushing the pole over instead of simply being supported by the pole. And by using a piece of scale wood, you attain legitimate splinters and torn wood at the break point as well as fresh wood that hasn't been painted or stained.

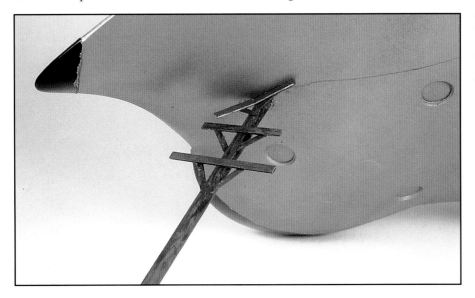

With the completed telephone pole impaled in the ship, I think you'll agree that it's going to add a lot of realism to the finished vignette. I still have to install the tinted repulsor discs in their recesses.

Install the Pole

Nearly done now, feed the power leads through the pole's hole, then slip the pole with ship attached into place. Rotate the pole until you have the ship is the position you want. Like the way it looks? Then pull the pole back out a little ways, squirt some IC-GEL into the mounting hole from the bottom, and shove the pole back into position. Remember, this stuff grabs quickly, so be sure to double check that you have the ship positioned the way you want it. As soon as the IC-GEL cures, turn loose of the pole and admire your War Machine suspended in midair.

WIRE THE JACK

Nothing will light without power. So thread the ends of the power leads through the slot in the underside of the wood base and out through the hole at the back. Solder the leads to the jack, then pull the jack back into position and keep tension on the leads until you staple them to the bottom of the base with an ordinary office stapler. Now carefully run a little bit of Super-Gold + around the edge of the jack to secure it to the wood. Finally, put a self-adhesive felt pad under each corner of the base. This will raise the base just enough to provide clearance for the wires that you have stapled to the bottom.

Plug the transformer into the wall,

Solder the power leads to the jack terminals, shove the jack into its recess, and staple the surplus wire to the underside of the base. Alternatively, you might just slap a piece of duct tape over the wires since the stuff sticks to everything.

plug the plug into the jack, and as they say — Let there be light!

THE REALLY FINAL DETAILS

At this point we're actually done, but there's one more thing you can do that'll really add a lot of realism to the scene — broken power and telephone lines dangling from the pole. And it isn't hard to do, either.

Get your hands on some 8- or 10-lb test fishing line. Cut several pieces (with three crossarms, you'll need at least 12) to varying lengths. Take a toothpick and apply a small dab of IC-GEL to the top edge of one of the crossarms. Be sure to equally space them, two on each side of the pole. Also, do it one dab at a time. Remember, you're dealing with a CA. As soon as the dab of CA is in place, add one of your lengths of line. Repeat the process 'til all of your lines have been installed. Then take a little bit of dark brown and paint each dab of CA so that they replicate the insulators they're supposed to be.

Be creative. Don't try to center the line so that each side has the same amount drooping. Longer on one side, shorter on the other. Maybe one will have snapped in such a way that it's lying on the roof, others are in the street, and so on. Don't be all that neat either. When a telephone/power pole is pushed over, lines snap under tension and get tangled with each other.

When the power lines have been installed, is your Martian War Machine vignette finally finished? Or will you spend additional days, or possibly weeks, adding all kinds of miniscule details to it, making it ever more realistic? Only you can say.

There you have it, a Martian War Machine, angling down over a destroyed building. Little did the Martians suspect, that shortly after this scene in the film, they would fall victim to Earth bacteria.

It's one thing to have a good-looking model, but little things such as these snapped power lines enhances realism.

You can see the telephone pole being pushed over by the dying War Machine. Actually, the pole is supporting the model.

How to Build Sci-Fi Model Spacecraft

THE *SPINDRIFT*

If you were watching science-fiction TV shows in the 1960s, you probably saw a rather interesting series called *Land Of the Giants* that was just beginning to show considerable promise when it was canceled. The premise had a commercial space shuttle called the *Spindrift* (whose design would have never survived re-entry), which, along with its occupants, winds up on a twin planet of Earth — with one slight exception. Humans on *this* planet were gigantic. Hence the title of the series.

Even though the name doesn't appear on the Polar Lights box, this is the old Aurora Spindrift kit, complete with ill-fitting removable upper hull.

Aurora released a model of the *Spindrift*, complete with a very nice interior. The forward upper half of the hull was removable, though the snap-fit section didn't fit all that well. Unfortunately, Aurora eventually went belly up and their various lines of kits became collector's items — and very pricey. Some thirty-odd years later, the *Spindrift* is back, repopped by Polar Lights and carrying a reasonable price. Also back is a removable hull section that still doesn't fit all that well.

Any time a manufacturer produces a kit with removable sections, panels, or whatever, the potential for fit problems isn't far behind. Most of those problems are the result of production limitations and/or the behavior traits of plastic. Sometimes it's a design flaw. Whatever the cause, if you're going to build a model with removable sections to expose hidden detail, you have two choices: either build the kit the way it is and live with it, or improve the fit through homegrown engineering and your own model-building skills. When it came to the *Spindrift*'s hull section, I chose the latter.

CONSTRUCTION

Taking first things first, the kit was built pretty much by the numbers. There are plenty of websites with photos of *Spindrift* models, each one seemingly using different interior colors. And there's no reason you can't. Being a commercial shuttle, décor would change from time to time. Add to that the fact that the series was shot in color but frequently viewed in black and white (because color TV ownership wasn't particularly widespread in the mid 1960s) and you have an awful lot of latitude where colors are concerned. Of course, this doesn't apply to the exterior, but we'll deal with that later.

I did find that construction went a little easier if I mounted the exhaust to the top rear hull, installed the combo onto the lower hull, and *then* added the intake. Before long, I had a completed *Spindrift*. All that remained was to fit the removable hull in place and that's where the fun began. Incidentally, I installed the sliding door but left off the antenna and clear dome for the time being. *Spindrift* will also be painted and detailed after the upper hull has been properly fitted.

If It Doesn't Fit, You Must Refit

The *Spindrift* is basically a clamshell, which means that the top edge of the lower hull has a very slight arc — or actually a reverse arc — to it. You'll find the low point in the center with the front and rear being slightly higher. Rather than the bottom edge of the removable upper hull matching the lower arc, it's straight across with the rear edge forming a 90-degree angle. When you try to put the upper hull in place, the front end pitches up slightly when you butt the rear edge against the intake wall. Result? A gap between the lower intake wall and the upper hull. Additionally, the molded studs that are supposed to snap into sockets to keep the hull in place actually fall ahead of the sockets.

I suspect that most modelers who build the *Spindrift* will simply display the finished model with the upper hull set to one side so that the interior is visible. This is perfectly logical, but the model would make an even better

impression if you could reach over and remove a tightly fitting hull section to reveal the interior.

First Make It Fit

Using a pair of sprue cutters, I removed the plastic studs from the upper hull that were supposed to make the section removable. You'll also want to remove the raised rib that runs along the bottom edge of the intake. Due to the changes that have to be made in the hull section, that rib will actually prevent you from obtaining a proper fit.

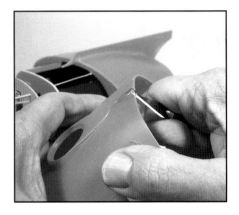

Refitting of the hull begins by carefully recutting the contours at the rear of the upper hull. Note that there's no way you can follow the advice of the safety police and push the blade away from you. Just be careful.

Now for the tedious part. Butt the back edge of the hull section against the intake and take note of where it begins to lose contact with the intake. Between a new #11 knife blade and sandpaper, *carefully and slowly* cut down the section that's *in contact* with the intake.

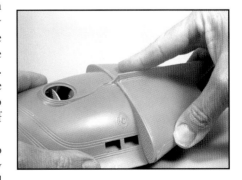

Slow and steady does it. By the time you've done your fifteenth test fit, things are looking pretty good.

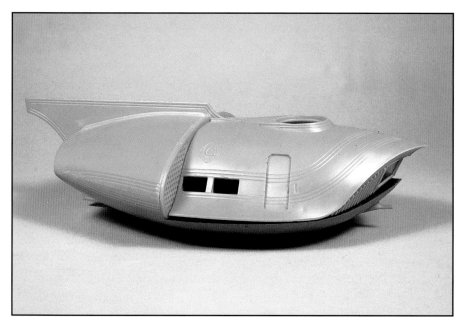

Did someone say it couldn't be done? The bottom edges haven't been pulled down yet (magnets still need to be installed), but you can see how well things are going to fit.

Constantly check the fit as you go, removing more material as needed until you finally have the entire rear edge of the hull section against the intake. And as the hull section moves back, it'll be necessary to slightly trim the front of the fin fillet that fits into a slot in the rear of the hull section. Don't get ambitious, just trim it back as needed.

Even as you work on the fit of the rear edge, you'll have to simultaneously be aware of a couple of other things. As you trim the edge to mate with the intake, the relationship of the inside of the hull to the interior wall sections will change. I found it necessary to trim the height of the main bulkheads before the hull section would drop down to contact the top edge of the lower hull. The same problem existed on the cockpit bulkheads as well.

What Kind Of Fasteners?

Once you have the hull section trimmed for a proper fit, you can't just sit the thing in place without still having gaps. There has to be a way to hold it. I had planned from the beginning to use rare earth magnets that were (I thought) readily available from Radio Shack. I'd seen them every time I'd been in one of their stores — until I needed them. Then I found out that none of the Radio Shacks in my area were stocking them anymore! That

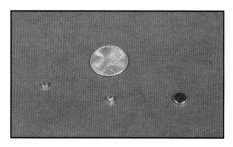

Three different size rare earth magnets compared to a common penny. I would be using the 1/8-inch diameter size (it's on the left). Even though it's the smallest, it has plenty of power for this purpose.

threw a huge monkey wrench in the works and more than a little panic — until I discovered an Internet site called Forcefield. They carry an incredible range of surplus rare earth magnets ranging in size from near-microscopic to some large enough to kill your TV or computer monitor if the things are in the same room. Even better, prices are dirt-cheap.

A quick phone call got six each of three different sizes (1/16-, 1/8-, and 3/16-inch diameters) on their way to me. Three days later, they arrived and I could get back to the *Spindrift*.

Where to Mount Them

That's the $64 question. Logic would suggest that the magnets be located in the same sockets on the lower hull that were intended to receive the snap-fit pins on the upper hull. All I had to do was enlarge the sockets to a 1/8-inch diameter and insert the 1/8-inch magnets to a depth that would leave their top surface flush with the sockets.

No need to worry about the polarity on the magnets that go in the sockets, but that will be a concern if I decide to use magnets on the upper hull. A dab of IC-GEL in each socket, followed by the magnet, would be enough to hold them in place.

Now for the tricky part — where and how do you mount the fasteners to

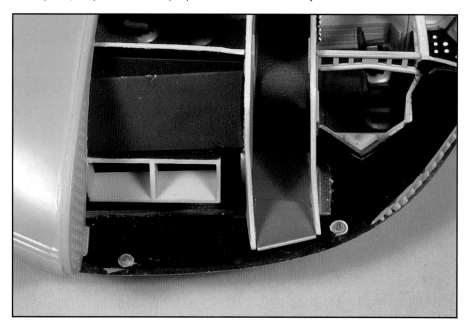

Here the magnets have been installed in the lower hull.

the upper hull? Considering the strength of rare earth magnets, there's also the question of whether to use a small piece of metal or another magnet. That question would be answered by experimentation, but the biggest problem was how to mount the fasteners in such a way that they would be parallel to the lower magnets. When the inside surface of the upper hull slants up at about a 45- or 50-degree angle, it's a definite challenge.

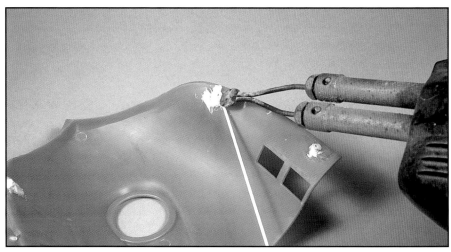

In order to get a secure bond, I welded the two plastics together with a soldering gun. Use caution so you don't wrinkle the outer surface of the hull.

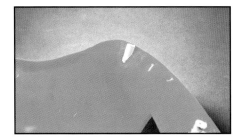

When you install the upper mounts, it's pretty much cut and try. The inside slope of the upper hull changes constantly as you move from back to front.

I finally settled on 1/8-inch diameter Plastruct plastic tubing. After cutting off the plastic snap-fit pins flush with the underside of the upper hull, four pieces of the tubing were installed in their place. This is strictly the cut and try method when it comes to figuring out the angle needed for the mating end of the tubing. And because of the way the hull contours change, the angle on the front tubes will be steeper than the rear pair. While tedious, it's really not all that difficult to do. Since one length of tubing will be far more than you'll need, if you make a mistake, or lose one of the short pieces, just cut another one.

Cut each piece longer than necessary, then install them over the original pin locations and let them dry. What really matters is that the tubes be reasonably close to vertical when the upper hull is installed. Right now the upper hull won't fit because of the tube's surplus length. We'll fix that shortly. Assuming this idea of mine actually works.

Once the tubes were in place, I started to cut them down with a diamond wheel on my Dremel. Bad idea. As soon as I started to cut, the tube popped loose. Aside from having to make another one, it identified a prob-

lem. Plastruct tubing is made from ABS, not styrene. The two plastics don't bond readily, which left me with the problem of getting a solid joint. I decided to try something that would be tricky and messy, but should work.

After I had four tubes glued in place again, I pulled out a Weller soldering iron with a flat cutting blade on it and a length of Evergreen .030-inch styrene rod. If you've ever done any electric welding, you know what comes next. All I did was heat the rod so that I could bend it around the base of the tube, and then blend the warm styrene into both the ABS tube and styrene hull. About the only really tricky part of the operation is to make sure you don't get the styrene hull so warm that it warps or wrinkles. Tool control is the key here. The result isn't pretty, but the tubes are secure, which is the whole purpose of this exercise anyway. Most people will never see the underside of the upper hull, but if it bothers you that much, it's not all that hard to smooth things down.

Adjusting the Height

Rather than try the cutting wheel again (once bitten, twice shy), I tried another approach that turned out quite well. I simply used the flat side of the cutting blade on my soldering gun to *melt* the tubing down to the desired length. Quick, easy, and if you make a mistake (of course *you* wouldn't, would you?), it's easily correctible by welding another piece of plastic onto the stub.

Final adjustment of the mount length is also done with my soldering gun's cutting blade.

I melted the tubes down to a point where they were level with the bottom edge of the upper hull, and then did a test fit. Though I had to make a couple of very slight adjustments, I wound up with all four tubes being barely in contact or just a couple of thousandths of an inch away from the top surface of the magnets in the lower hull. So far, so good. Now to add a metal contact.

Magnet or Tin?

Even the little 1/16-inch magnet, when placed on the 1/8-inch magnet, had so much grab that I decided not to use them on the upper hull. Instead, I dug out a piece of tin that was actually a leftover piece of flashing from having my house re-roofed.

Using a neat little tool called a nibbler (Radio Shack is one source, as well as some mail-order hobby suppliers), I cut four small pieces of tin. Size and shape is pretty much up to you, but

A metal nibbler makes it easy to cut pieces of tin for magnetic contacts.

make them as large as you think reasonable. That way the upper and lower mounts don't have to be a perfect match.

I used CA to install one piece of tin on a rear mount, shot it with accelerator, and then slipped the upper hull into position. Lo and behold, the tin clicked into position on the magnet! Once I had the other three in place, I'd have my removable hull section.

However, before I could do that, one final bit of adjustment would be needed. It would be necessary to pop the tin off the mount and shorten the mount an amount equal to the thickness of the tin. Otherwise the seam where the upper and lower hulls met would be forced open. This would be a little tedious, particularly since each mount would have to be adjusted individually, but nothing all that difficult.

With all the mounts adjusted, the tin contacts were reinstalled for the last time. Instead of my regular Super Gold+, I used IC-GEL for maximum strength. When I test fit the upper hull for the last time, it snapped into place just the way I wanted it to.

Keep in mind that installing these kinds of mounts is a highly individualized proposition. So much depends on your particular skill, ideas, access to parts, and more. One person will wind up with a perfectly fitting hull section, and the next will never be able to close the gap. The whole point of this discussion is to show you that it *can* be done. And, as always, if it doesn't work

out the way you want it to this time, learn from it so you can do a better job the next time.

NOW FINISH THE MODEL

I taped over the window and dome openings in the upper hull from the inside and also taped the sliding door shut. Cockpit windows were masked from the outside. Then I snapped (magnetically) the upper hull in place, installed that delicate little antenna just behind the dome, and gave the model a shot of primer.

The configuration of *Spindrift* leads to a rather interesting problem when it comes to spraying this thing. Just how the heck do you hold it and prime/paint it in a single step? Well, you don't. I wound up holding it by the tail fin and priming the rest of the model with the exception of the very bottom. That way I could set it down to let things dry. Then I changed my grip, sprayed the bottom (and the end of the tail fin), and mounted it on the kit provided display stand while the second paint layer dried.

After the primer was dry, I used the same process to spray the final color, which was Model Master FS 12197 International Orange. Incidentally, this color is a gloss finish. While appropriate due to the fact that most commercial airliners use a gloss or near-gloss finish, I did plan to overspray the finished model with semi-gloss clear for a more realistic appearance.

The completed upper hull with mounts and contacts installed.

After priming, the entire ship gets a coat of Model Master FS 12197 International Orange. Be sure to mask off the opening for the observation dome so overspray doesn't get inside.

Masking all the stripes is quite easy due to their pattern being engraved, but it will take some time.

Paint the Stripes

If you're looking at painting those contoured gray stripes with more than a little trepidation, relax. A practice common in the early 1960s that is normally disliked by modelers comes to your rescue here. That practice was the engraving of markings *into* the model's surface so that you'd know where the decal went or what the paint boundaries were.

Fortunately (this time), the *Spindrift's* stripe patterns were engraved, making masking simplicity itself.

If you study the box top, you'll see that there's a large center stripe of medium gray, then a narrow orange stripe on each side, followed by a narrow dark gray stripe on each side. All you do is lay down strips of masking tape so that the entire stripe area is covered, and run your fingernail over the

tape along all of the grooves. Run a new knife blade along the same grooves, remove the tape from both the wide center and narrow outer stripes, leaving the narrow orange inner stripe masked, and you're ready to paint. Nearly. Before you reach for the airbrush, be sure to do whatever other masking is necessary to protect the rest of the model from overspray. By the way, I found it easier to remove the upper hatch and paint its stripe separately from the section on the sides of the main hull.

The entire stripe area was sprayed with Model Master FS 35237 Medium Gray. Once that was dry, I masked over the center stripe and sprayed the narrow outer stripes with Model Master FS 36081 Euro I Gray. *Do not* make the mistake of spraying the single narrow stripe on the fin. It remains medium gray.

After removing the masking and discovering that the stripes actually turned out the way I wanted, I did a little more masking around the dome. There's a partial stripe of Euro I Gray that wraps around the front.

The Logo

Probably the trickiest part of the entire paint scheme is the company logo located on each side of the upper hull, just above the passenger windows. Molded as raised detail, your only choice is to very carefully hand paint it with about a 20/0 or 25/0 brush. The colors are the same as the stripes. The ribbed grille on either side of the cockpit windows will also need to be painted medium gray.

Painting that raised crest is another matter altogether. Your only choice is to use a very fine brush and a steady hand.

The engraved patterns make it a snap to produce sharp, crisp lines.

Shades of the 1960s! The finished Spindrift *mounted on that classic Aurora stand brings back more than a few memories.*

FINISHING TOUCHES

With the exterior completely done and all masking removed (except for the cockpit windows), the entire model gets a shot of Model Master Semi-Gloss Clear Lacquer. If you wish, you can then spray the inside of the removable hull section flat black. Just be sure to mask off the leading edge that's visible from the outside. Now unmask the cockpit windows, install the passenger windows, add the clear dome to the top of the hull section, and *Spindrift* is done.

There is, as always, the question of a display method. It's your choice, but all I did was add the kit's single decal to the familiar Aurora-style clear display stand and mount the *Spindrift* on it.

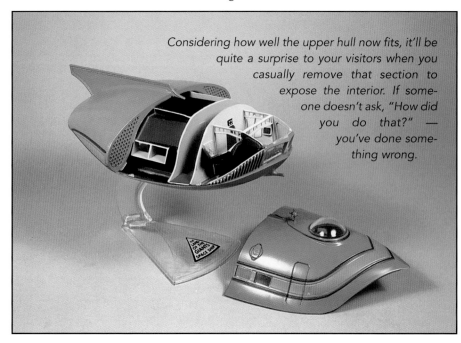

Considering how well the upper hull now fits, it'll be quite a surprise to your visitors when you casually remove that section to expose the interior. If someone doesn't ask, "How did you do that?" — you've done something wrong.

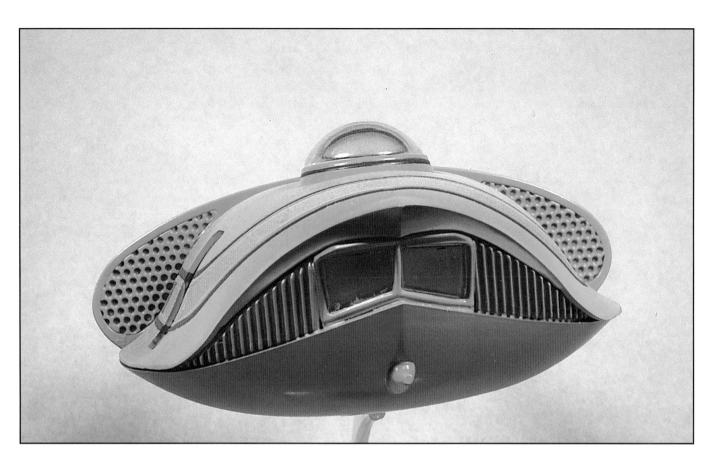

While not the most practical design for a sub-orbital transport that could survive re-entry, this head-on view is certainly impressive.

The front top half of the hull is easily removable, thanks to magnetic catches, along with a little whittlin' & sandin' to make things fit right.

ALIENS ARMORED PERSONNEL CARRIER

Of the four *Alien/Aliens* films produced by 20th Century-Fox, the second one — *Aliens* — can arguably be considered the best of the bunch. Boiled down to basics, the film was essentially the story of the cavalry riding to the rescue of embattled colonists. As it turned out, all colonists but one had been cocooned by the aliens. Ultimately, only three humans and an android escaped the carnage to return to Earth. Aliens very nearly turned out to be a high-tech version of *Custer's Last Stand*.

The Halcyon 1/35th scale Aliens Armored Personnel Carrier (APC) box.

Be that as it may, the cavalry of Colonial Marines rode to battle in a spacecraft (the *Sulaco*), a space shuttle, and, on the ground, a massive armored personnel carrier (APC). While the APC didn't survive halfway through the film, it made quite an impact, including absorbing quite a lot of battle damage.

Back in 1987, a company called Halcyon produced a very nice 1/35th scale kit of the Aliens APC. I got mine from Federation Models. Big and slab-sided with huge armored tires, it makes for an interesting addition to your collection just built straight from the box. It becomes even more interesting if you take the time to replicate its appearance after sustaining battle damage. All of which leads to the question of just how do you represent dented, bent, and torn steel on a plastic model. Believe it or not, it ain't that hard, so that's what we're going to do.

CONSTRUCTION

Construction is fairly straightforward, but you can definitely make your job easier with a few changes. Probably the biggest change I made was to alter the way the wheels mount. The kit provides little plastic stubs that go through the back of the sides and then into the wheel. This forces you to mount the wheels the very first thing *before* you even assemble the hull. Besides being a weak method and making vehicle construction cumbersome at best, it turns a simple paint job into a nightmare. There *has* to be a better way — and there is.

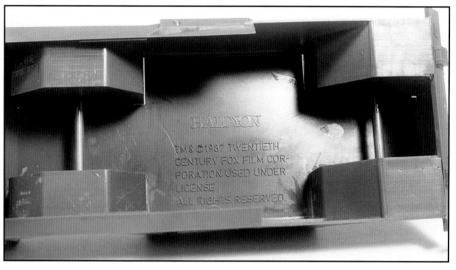

Viewed from the top with the sides and chassis assembled, you can see the .190-inch brass sleeves that were installed to allow later installation of the wheels and axles.

I built up the basic hull but left the top off. Then two pieces of .190-inch outside diameter (o.d.) brass tubing were cut to fit all the way across the hull with each end being flush with the outside of the axle holes This would allow

In this shot, basic construction has been completed. Neither of the gun turrets or the wheels have been installed and nothing has been primed.

me to cut axles from pieces of .155-inch tubing and permit installation of the wheels/tires at the very last, *after* everything had been painted and detailed.

Due to the kit's design, it's also necessary to install the running light and headlight lenses, along with the windshield, before the hull is buttoned up. Be sure you have a good, secure bond so that they won't pop loose when you mask them later. This is particularly important where the windshield is concerned, due to battle damage it will eventually suffer.

From here on, it's simply a matter of finishing up construction, *except for* a couple of more slight changes. Both the nose and top gun turrets use exactly the same method as the wheels in order for them to rotate. I took an approach very similar to my wheel modification in both cases, but with smaller diameter tubing. I'd suggest you do the same in order to mount the turrets at the very last. Matter of fact, my turrets can be easily removed and replaced any time I wish.

BATTLE DAMAGE

Before you actually start beating this thing up, you have to know where to beat. So, buy or rent a copy of Aliens and spend some time watching the APC action — particularly the part with Ripley at the controls, crashing their way out of the complex. That's where most of the damage in inflicted, since it's used essentially as a battering ram. Be sure to keep your thumb near the pause and frame-by-frame buttons as well, because some of the damage is visible in only one or two frames.

After an extended session with my VCR, about the only damage that shows clearly is the right front side, just forward of the right front wheel well. The sheet metal is rippled, dented, and crumpled to a fair thee well. Other damage doesn't show in the tape, but considering all the scrap metal, girders, and other trash the APC plowed through — not to mention the alien that was run over and crushed — you know the rest of the vehicle isn't going to be all that pristine.

Between all the physical contact, being sprayed with the alien's blood (hydrochloric acid) and having flammable liquid burning on top of the hull, you can pretty well give your imagination free rein. Now the question is exactly how do we inflict all that damage?

Dents, Dings, and Crumpled Areas

This kind of damage is best done before you do any painting. Exactly how you approach it depends on the precise kinds of damage and your own preferences. For example, if you're trying to create torn or bent metal with a thin edge, you'll need to thin down the back of the plastic to near paper thickness. Twist or bend what's left, and when properly weathered, you can't tell it from the real thing.

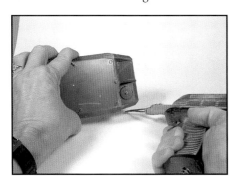

Battle damage begins by heating the plastic with a soldering gun. Note that you bring the gun close to the plastic, but not in contact with it. There is a place for direct contact, but we'll do that a little later.

As far as the side of the APC is concerned, I pulled out my Weller soldering gun with cutting blade again. With it turned on high heat (second step on the trigger), I held the blade under the right front side, checking frequently to see when the plastic would begin to soften. It doesn't take long, though it varies depending on how thick the plastic is and what kind of effect you're striving for. As it begins to soften, you can press in with your finger, piece of metal, end of a pencil, whatever will help you get the appearance you're after.

Crush in the softened section of fender using a section of girder, sharp piece of tubing, fingernail, or whatever.

Once I was satisfied with the appearance of the right front side, which took the brunt of the damage, I worked over the rest of the vehicle. Exactly what kind of damage you inflict is up to you, but can include twisted grab irons, bent corners, and so on. Since the vehicle took quite an impact to the rear at one point, I heated and twisted the bottom of the main turret guide rails and the ladder, which is mounted just to one side of the rails.

Here you can see how the main battery rail ends and the ladder have been heated, bent, and twisted. The thin edge of the fender has also been heated and allowed to distort.

The main turret needs to show substantial damage as well, since it was in its stowed position at the rear of the APC when Ripley rammed her way out of the complex. I went so far as to bend one of the gun barrels out of line, rendering the main battery inoperable.

In order to replicate the various scrapes and scratches, I simply drug the cutting blade along the surface in various areas, sometimes while the blade was beginning to heat up, other times after it was hot and starting to cool down. However much damage you do or do not inflict is entirely up to you.

NOW PAINT IT

When I was finished with the major damage, I airbrushed an overall coat of Model Master FS 34087 Olive Drab. This includes the two turrets and the outer wheel covers of all four wheels/tires. Since the wheel covers will be masked later and the tires painted, there's no need to be particular at this time.

Three of the wheels and tires are shown completed and painted. On the left, one wheel has been painted Olive Drab, then masked in preparation for painting the tire rubber.

Per the instructions, several small areas (actually grilles), of what's described as slate gray, were hand brushed. You'll find that Model Master FS 36118 Gunship Gray will do fine for that purpose. Then the gun muzzles were painted Model Master Steel. As long as I was in a painting mood, I masked off the wheel covers and sprayed the tires a rubber color, then pulled the masking.

Decals

Because there was more weathering to come, I didn't worry about getting a uniform gloss coat on the entire model. Besides, there were only two

With the nose turret is in place and the windshield in still masked, the APC has gotten an overall coat of FS 34087 Olive Drab. Also, the decals have been added to the nose plate.

decals and both were located on the front plate, so a shot of clear gloss in that area is all that was needed. Apply the decals, let them dry, and then follow with a shot of clear flat. You're done with the decals.

MOUNT THE WHEELS

The finished APC ready for weathering. Most of the battle damage can't be seen in this view, but it's there.

Since I had used .190-inch diameter brass tubing to create the axle sleeves, a slight problem was at hand. It turned out that if I enlarged the mounting holes on the back of the wheels (using a 1/8-inch drill bit), I could then use 1/8-inch brass tubing for the axles. The problem was that 1/8-inch tubing was too small for the axle sleeves. However, if I cut another pair of sleeves from .155-inch outer diameter tubing (which I had originally planned to use for the axles) the same length as the original tubing, then slid the second sleeves into the first ones I installed, the 1/8-inch outer diameter axles would fit perfectly. Problem solved.

FINAL DETAILS

The nose turret was simply slipped into position, remaining removable. But the main turret was a different story. Because all the damage was inflicted while the turret was in its stowed position at the rear of the APC, I mounted it into its sleeve with a dab of CA. If I ever needed to remove the turret, simply twisting it would be enough to overcome the CA's grip. There are times when no sheer strength is an advantage.

Finally, there are two red taillight lenses that have to be slipped under a pair of grab iron-like guards and a round lens that mounts on the front of the roof-mounted targeting sensor. The sensor has a bar guard in front of it. Instructions would have you add the lenses first, then the guards. I didn't do this in order to avoid masking them. If you take this approach, be aware that you will have to nip the mounting pin off the back of the taillight lenses in order to slide them under the guards. You also *may* find it necessary to do a little trimming on the underside of the guards to gain sufficient clearance. As for the sensor lens, you shouldn't have any problem slipping it into position. I also removed masking from the headlights and front running lights, but not the windshield. You'll see why before long.

Weathering

At this point, the APC is beaten, dented, dinged, scratched, and otherwise damaged. It also has a paint job that looks like it just came off the production line. Now it's time to get down and dirty.

Floquil Dust is being sprayed here. The Aliens Armored Personnel Carrier (APC) is really beginning to look like it's been through the wars.

I started out with my usual dirty thinner slopped here and there, particularly on the heavy damage on the right front. Then I ran some down the edges of the door, into the panel lines, and so on.

When the brush was nearly dry, I did a lot of vertical streaking that changes the tone of the base color but doesn't really add any. Don't forget to dirty up the wheel covers and tires either. The reason for the vertical streaking on the sides is the fact that weather conditions on the planet were abominable. Remember that they were in the process of terraforming a hostile planet to Earthlike conditions so it could be colonized. The result? Constant high winds, mud, and heavy rain. That much rain would wash most of the really prominent mud off the APC, but there would still be grime and grit.

After that, I came back and dry brushed steel into areas that were still wet, blending the two together until neither color dominated. I concentrated mostly on the damaged areas, sharp edges, and the rough scrapes and gouges.

Then there was the question of how to replicate damage from the alien's blood. Remember, their blood is highly corrosive hydrochloric acid. A Marine blew one apart as it was trying to get in the door, spraying blood inside the vehicle. Much more went on the outside. Also, more blood was sprayed from the one that Ripley ran over.

Less is more in many cases, so I tried simply splattering drops of Ambroid ProWeld onto the side of the vehicle where the door was, then left it alone with that side level to give the cement time to cook. It wound up with some fairly nice bleaching and blistering. I could have done more, including creating actual surface craters for the acid, but combined with everything else I was doing, I figured I'd leave well enough alone.

While all of that was still wet, more or less, I got another idea. While I didn't know how it would work, I decided to sprinkle a little pumice stone over parts of the APC (particularly the heavily damaged areas and the acid spray), and then blew off the surplus.

The result is a random gritty surface. That's just what you'd expect to see where damage was heaviest.

After that I came back with my Aztek airbrush and Floquil Grime. Once again, the previous treatments had not fully dried, so the Grime tended to blend into them. In areas I wound up with whitish/grayish streaks, which, as luck would have it, were very similar to the appearance of dried acid that had been streaked over paint. Then I switched to Floquil Dust and attacked the APC again. Don't forget to keep it very light, because it appears much heavier after it dries. You can use it for additional vertical water streaks, to blend other colors together, or anything else you might think of.

By this time I had a vehicle that actually looked like it'd been through heavy combat. But I wasn't through. Several scenes in the film show flammable liquid, maybe napalm, burning on the left front corner of the roof. This gave me a chance to do something I rarely do — burn some plastic. No, not the model. Scrap plastic sprue. Burning styrene emits a gritty black smoke containing particles that stick to anything they touch. If you ever burned a plastic model when you were a kid, you know what I'm talking about. What better way to put smoke stains on part of the vehicle?

If you're going to do this, do it outdoors. Not so much because it's dangerous. You'd have to make a conscious effort to start a house fire from a piece of burning sprue being held in your hand. However, your significant other ain't gonna take kindly to having

black plastic soot taking up residence on a nice, clean ceiling!

Light off the end of a piece of styrene sprue and when it's burning merrily, simply hold the APC above the smoke in a position that'll allow the residue to deposit itself on the proper area. It only takes a few seconds to do the job, but I'd strongly suggest you practice on an old model if you've never tried this method.

THE REALLY FINAL TOUCH

Only one thing stands between you and a finished APC — a shattered windshield. Huh? That's right. The alien that Ripley ran over was originally riding the roof of the vehicle. It leaned over the front and shattered the glass, trying to reach Ripley. Instead, she slammed the brakes, throwing the alien on the ground in front of her, and then ran over him (or it).

After removing the masking, I spun the tip of a knife on the windshield to create an initial opening. From that point, it was simply a matter of cutting straight lines and narrow "V" shapes in various directions until it looked like a shattered windshield.

The plastic is fairly thick (armor plate glass), so it'll take a little time to get a realistic appearance. This is also why you want to make sure the windshield's securely installed before you button up the hull.

And with that, the Aliens APC is done. All you need now is a *Sulaco* and a shuttle to have a complete set. Just be sure to watch out for alie..n..s…s….s…….

There you have it. Here is the front end of a mobile and heavily armed battering ram, otherwise known as an Armored Personnel Carrier (APC) of the Colonial Marines.

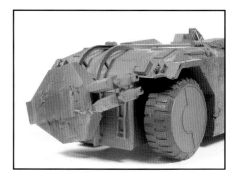

From the rear, you can see what kind of a beating the main gun battery took.

Here is a 3/4 left-front view of the completed APC.

That sooty smoke from burning styrene (the styrene in my hand isn't burning for safety reasons) creates a perfect representation of scorched steel.

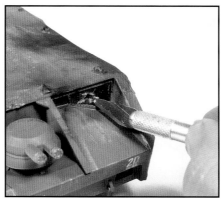

All it takes is a #11 blade and a few minutes patience to replicate a shattered piece of armored windshield glass.

This top shot gives you a good look at all the grime, grunge, streaking, and scorched areas.

7

How to Build
Sci-Fi Model
Spacecraft

ADVANCED KIT BUILDING
"OPEN THE POD-BAY DOORS, HAL."

K its can be found at every level of quality, complexity, and size. The same goes for instructions. Every now and again, all three coincide at the highest level. Such is the case with a truly superb 1/12th scale kit of the 2001 One Man Space Pod from Custom Replicas. Originally produced by Captain Cardboard, Custom Replicas has taken a very good kit and raised it to an even higher level. You get thirteen major urethane resin parts, a small bag of resin detail pieces, and another bag of white metal parts for the manipulator arms. A third bag contains instrument panels printed on translucent white Mylar, a couple of sheets of decals, and about a .030-inch thick piece of clear styrene. Also a couple of pieces of .060-inch white styrene and one .020-inch thick piece. Then there are the instructions and a couple of 4- x 6-inch color photos of a finished Space Pod model. The only thing you need to add is skill, experience, a videotape of *2001: A Space Odyssey* and any other reference photos

From the number of parts in this photo, it's fairly obvious that this is definitely not a kit for the beginner.

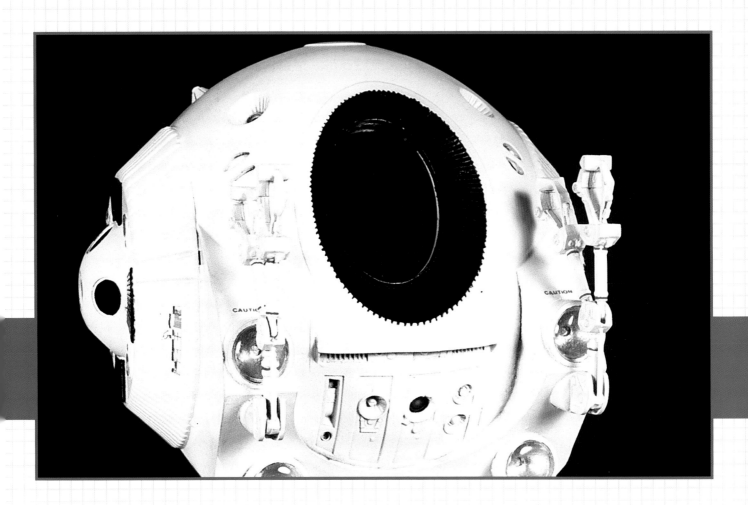

you can. No matter how good a kit is, you can *never* have enough references.

There's only one word for this kit — exquisite. That comment applies to everything from the resin casting to the instructions. The label states that advanced modeling skills are required. Believe it.

I'll grant you that this is not a kit for the beginner or even those with a few resin kits under their belt. However, don't let that keep you from acquiring a copy if it appeals to you. Set it on a shelf and use its presence for inspiration to improve your skills. Then, when you feel you're ready for it, open the box and build it. Now, follow along and see what you'll be getting into.

FIRST, READ THE INSTRUCTIONS

And this time, I mean *read* the instructions — all the way through. For starters, they're excellent instructions, complete with plenty of clear photos. However, because the kit is specifically geared to advanced modelers, the instructions also assume that you actually know what you're doing. If you're expecting to have your hand held every nitpicking step of the way, expect otherwise. Beyond that, certain components have to be installed at a certain time or in a specific way. In fact, the instructions actually state that the Space Pod is somewhat of a Chinese puzzle box, meaning that some of the components (such as the door) have to be completely finished prior to installation. The model is also designed to be lit (if you choose), so you'll need to take that into account as well. Does this mean you have to build the model exactly the way the instructions state? Not at all, because I didn't. But you darn sure better know what can be adlibbed and what can't.

INTERIOR PARTS

After doing the requisite cleanup of what little flash there was, I gave the door several light coats of primer and then set it to one side to dry while I tackled the interior. This pretty much followed the instructions, but you do want to make sure that the circular riser is correctly oriented under the floor. Botch its installation and you'll be in deep trouble.

I also wound up having to do some sanding on the back of wall A in order

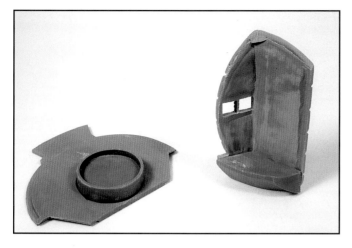

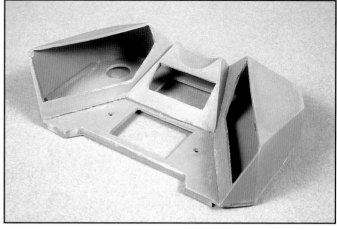

Construction begins by mounting the floor riser and wall block. Note that the floor is upside down so the riser can be seen. You can also tell where the back of wall had to be sanded flat to obtain a proper fit for the block.

Join the instrument panel and its base to create the instrument console. If you look close, you can see that the top line of the left and right housings are not perfectly level. We'll straighten that out before long.

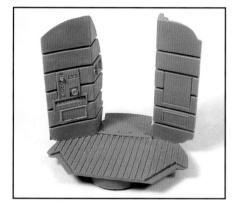

The floor/walls/riser assembly has been completed. It looks easy so far, doesn't it?

to get the spacer block to fit flush. With the block properly installed, both walls (A and B) were mounted in their appropriate locations on the floor.

Before building up the instrument console riser, first you need to cut the parts from the .060-inch sheet styrene that is provided with the kit. I've taped a copy of the patterns over the styrene to create an easy guide.

INSTRUMENT CONSOLE AND RISER

Building up the instrument console subassembly requires nothing more than joining two resin parts. Just make sure you add the instrument panel to the correct side of the panel base! Now flip over to page five of the instructions for a little scratch-building fun.

In order to properly position the console, a riser that mounts to the underside of the panel base has to be built up from the .060-inch sheet styrene that comes in the kit. Patterns for the riser parts are printed out for you on the last page of the instructions. I'd suggest you make use of the local copy machine or the copy function on

your computer's scanner to duplicate the patterns instead of cutting up the kit instructions. Then if you bungle something, you still have the original to make another copy.

Everyone has their own method of attaching paper patterns to styrene. Some use spray adhesive, others use glue sticks, still others go so far as to… you get the idea. You can use whatever gets the job done. My preference is to simply tape the patterns down to the styrene with ordinary masking tape. The edges of the pattern will be visible through the tape (and if you rub the

tape down, it'll also form a slight ridge). Then all you have to do is lay a straight edge down and cut through the pattern into the styrene. Don't try to cut all the way through the .060-inch thickness, either. After removing the pattern, the styrene can be easily snapped.

There are also the side patterns for a light box that fits under the center section of the panel base. In case you're wondering where the patterns are for the bottom and front of the box are, there aren't any. They're simple pieces, so you shouldn't have any problem cutting a couple to fit.

INTERIOR FORWARD WALL

Even though I wouldn't use the part until much later in this project, I went ahead and cut out the interior forward wall (or bulkhead) from provided .020-inch styrene. The pattern for it is found on page 3 of the instructions. What makes this one a little tricky is the fact that an oval opening has to be cut in the center of it that matches the window opening on the front of the Pod.

I laid masking tape over the oval section of the pattern, after taping the entire pattern to the styrene, drew a vertical centerline over the window pattern, and then duplicated the oval outline on top of the tape with the help of some ellipse drafting templates that I have.

When it comes to cutting ovals, or any continuous curve shape, a swivel tip knife is ideal for the job.

Finally, I cut the opening out by following the windows outline with a neat little knife I found in the Excel catalog — a swivel tip knife. Again, this is one of those tools that you use once in a blue moon, but is virtually essential for certain jobs.

BACK TO THE INSTRUMENT CONSOLE AND RISER

Once the riser was built and joined with the console, a nasty little problem reared its head. The instrument panel casting is thin-walled in order to allow for lighting. All you do is glue the Mylar instrument panel faces over the large openings. Then when you turn on the power, everything lights up like a Christmas tree.

I found that the top surfaces (walls) of the left and right panel openings were not maintaining a straight line. Since they were thin enough to be

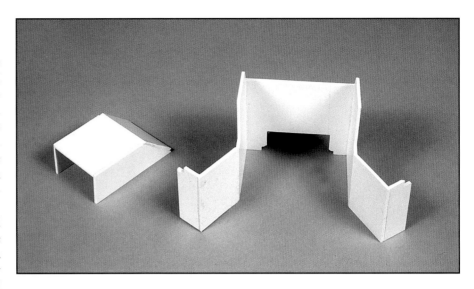

In short order, the instrument riser and light box are built up, ready for installation. That convoluted shape looks difficult but it really isn't.

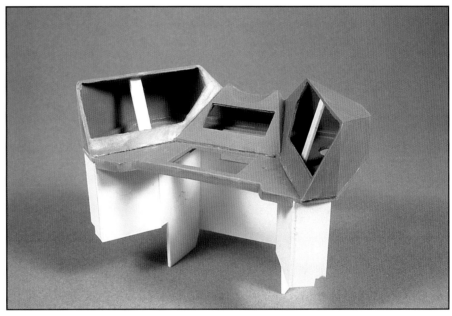

The console and riser have been joined, and they now lack only the light box. The two vertical braces you see make quick work of straightening out the top edges of the instrument housing.

flexible, I wasn't about to try heating and straightening them. For one thing, it wouldn't have worked. Besides, there was a better way.

All I did was cut a piece of scrap styrene to a length that would allow me to force the top edge up until it was level. In other words, I built a brace, or prop. This is strictly a cut and try proposition, but it doesn't take long to get it right. Then a dab of CA at the brace ends and you're done. If you're concerned about the white styrene forming a shadow when you turn the lights on, use a piece of clear.

MORE PAINTING

At this point, I shot the instrument console/riser and floor/wall assemblies with a coat of Model Master Flat Black from a rattlecan. That was followed, after it was dry, with a shot of Model Master Semi-Gloss Clear Lacquer in order to obtain a satin finish. Floquil Engine Black will get the same results without the need for a clear coat if you're using an airbrush.

I chose to forego lighting in my Space Pod. For those who opt for lighting, it really isn't all that difficult.

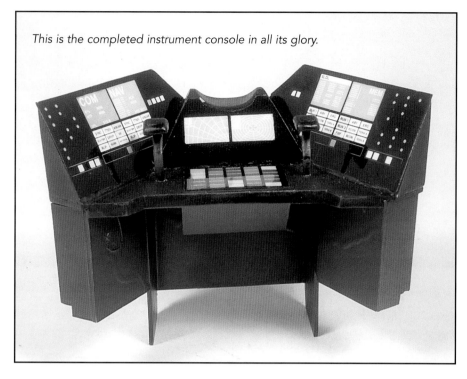

This is the completed instrument console in all its glory.

Though you'll have to make appropriate adjustments for the specific project, the wiring/lighting methods described in Chapter 6 should point you in the right direction.

Incidentally, lighting/wiring of the Pod is an area where you'll need some decent experience or know someone who does. Kit instructions do offer some excellent suggestions regarding the lighting of the Pod, but you won't find schematics or other wiring diagrams. Aside from the assumption that you have advanced skills, everyone has their favorite lighting method. Some use miniature incandescent bulbs, others miniature florescent tubes, and still others like to investigate high-intensity LEDs.

Not having to deal with lighting sped things up considerably. All I had to do was cut out the instrument faces, mount them over the appropriate openings, add the two control joysticks and the console/riser assembly was done.

THE DOOR

Since the door would have to be completely finished and installed before the interior is permanently installed, I wound up working on every part of the Pod at the *same* time. Well, not really at the same time. You work on one part until you either get

tired of it or have to let something dry, then switch to another part, then back to the first part, and so on. We've all had those kinds of projects, and this one definitely qualifies.

Anyway, after the door had been primed and an actuating rod installed on the inside surface, the outer surface and edges were sprayed with several coats of Model Master Bright White. Again, I used a spray can. In fact, the majority of my Pod model was painted with rattle-

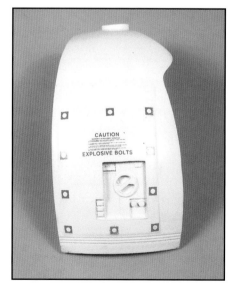

Other than the instrument console, the door is the first part of this model that will actually be completely finished. This is what the outside looks like with decals in place.

cans, though conventional detail brushes and an airbrush were used where needed as well. This had more to do with the Pod's sheer size and spherical configuration than anything else. It just goes to show you that the method that works is the one you use.

Model Master Bright White is a high-gloss paint and the Pod should actually have a satin finish. Just as I did with the interior, the white exterior would eventually be shot with a Semi-Gloss. But not until all the decals were applied. Also, I still had to paint the inside of the door and the inner surface of the hull, which led to another question: What color?

Whenever you see the Pod in the film, the interior is suffused with a red glow, very similar to the red safety lights in photographic darkrooms. The instructions include flat burgundy in their list of recommended paints, though there's no indication of what parts receive that color. A rare color photo of the Pod interior that I found on the Internet shows the inner surface of the Pod hull to be burgundy, with the rest of the interior semi-gloss black. However, in a conversation with Bill Lenches of Wilco! Models, I learned that he heard the interior walls of the Pod were actually a light beige when the red lights were off. So, I had to decide whether I wanted to represent the Pod in an occupied, powered-up mode, or unoccupied, powered-down mode. The difference? If powered-up, I'd paint the interior walls flat burgundy. The powered-down configuration would be light beige.

Due to the lack of a scale figure or seat (apparently no Pod seat was ever built for the movie set), I opted for the powered-down mode. Then came the question of what shade of beige. That's pretty much modeler's choice, so I wound up settling on Model Master FS 33613 Radome Tan for the inside of the Pod halves.

But what about the inside of the door? Perusing the Internet once again, I found a whole series of photos on the CultTVman website detailing an original Captain Cardboard kit of the Space Pod. A photo of the interior that was shot through the front window showed a door with a semi-gloss black inner surface. Considering that the

This is the inside of the door, complete with placards.

DOOR DECALS AND PLACARDS

What's the difference between placards and decals? They look the same, but placards don't come off their backing sheet when soaked in water and decals do. Just cut the placards to size and mount in their proper locations on the inside of the door. Apply a thin layer of Testors Clear Parts Cement, press the placards in place, and you're done. Decals go on the outer surface of the door.

Every now and again, you run across a bad sheet of decals. They look just fine, but after you've dipped them in water, they won't come off. Worse than that, the design starts breaking up, the cause being either insufficient clear coat or none at all. Mine appeared to have none at all. Rather than panic, there are two solutions to the problem. Either contact the manufacturer for a replacement sheet, or clear coat the sheet yourself. I chose to do the latter. You also may have no choice but to clear coat the decals yourself because it's not unusual for manufacturers of limited production kits to have no spares.

I sprayed a wet coat of Model Master Clear Gloss Lacquer over the entire sheet and let it dry. A test of one design proved that I now had decals I could use, but they were still just a tad

delicate. The solution? Another wet coat of clear gloss, and I could finally concentrate on applying decals. By the way, be aware that it will take substantially longer for each design to release from the backing paper. Patience. Patience.

In case you're wondering, decal setting solutions work normally over decals that have had to be clear coated this way.

FRONT/BASE ASSEMBLY

From the get go, the instructions have told you to temporarily assemble the three main parts of the Pod body by taping them together. Later on, which is about where we are now, you're to glue the front half and base together (but not the rear half) without removing the tape. I didn't. Matter of fact, I never bothered to tape anything together, though I did dry fit the parts to see what I'd be dealing with.

As it turned out, the part of the front hull that mated with the side of the base was warped in slightly. Not surprising, given the characteristics of resin, but taping the parts in place wouldn't have done a lick of good. Neither would CA, because there was too much shear tension. So it was back to the heat gun (Remember, it was first

door, when closed, would fill the space between the black padded walls, black seemed more reasonable than Radome Tan. After agonizing over the black/tan question for a while, and actually spraying the inside of the door Radome Tan, I finally took the bull by the horns and oversprayed the Radome Tan with Model Master FS 37038 Flat Black. Then a coat of Floquil Crystal Cote was sprayed over the Flat Black.

Incidentally, in case you're wondering why I use Model Master Gloss over some paint and Floquil Crystal Cote over others, it has to do, at least sometimes, with the brand of paint I'm trying to gloss. Model Master flat enamels tend to absorb Model Master Gloss Lacquer, resulting in a spotty appearance until you've come back with four or five additional coats. Floquil Crystal Cote, on the other hand, will produce an even gloss surface with only a couple of coats over the same paint. Does this mean Model Master flat enamel isn't a good paint? No way! In fact, I'm quite partial to it. It just has this little peculiarity that you learn to deal with.

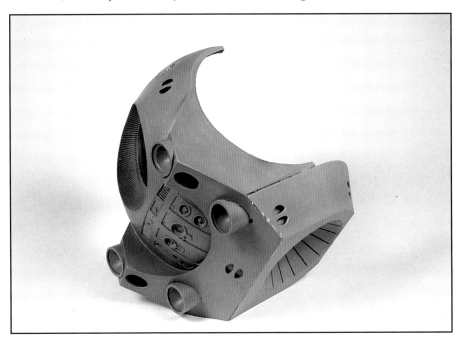

Actual construction of the Pod begins by joining the front half and the base. At the risk sounding like I'm repeating myself every five minutes, take your time and test fit, test fit, test fit.

used in Chapter 3). After a couple of minutes with a heat gun and my refrigerator's freezer, both parts lined up properly. By the way, I found that I had to do this on both sides. When I was satisfied that everything fit the way it should, the front and base were joined with IC-GEL. Besides having at least *some* shear strength (which most CAs don't), it can be applied to one surface like ordinary tube glue. Just be quick and accurate when you join the two parts. Some of the gel will squeeze out of the seams, minimizing the need for putty. If you feel the need for even more speed, a shot of Insta-Set accelerator can be spritzed on.

ALIGNING THE BACK

The instructions tell you that the Pod halves do not line up perfectly. Again, not surprising. However, you're told to correct the problem during final assembly when the finished interior and door have already been installed. There's an easier way.

After I had joined the front and base, I took the time to test fit the back section to see just how far off things were. They weren't off that far, as it turned out. I wound up dry fitting the back section into its correct position, forcing the top center into proper alignment with my hand and then using my heat gun to warm the areas that needed realignment. It became a sequence of heat and adjust, heat and adjust, and so on until things lined up correctly. Then, before turning loose of the model, it and my hand spent a little time in the refrigerator/freezer.

Used properly, a heat gun can work wonders when it comes to adjusting resin parts for a proper fit.

Don't get the idea that I did all this as a single step or that the parts were *way* out of alignment. You do it a section at a time, a little at a time, until you're satisfied. But it's better to correct the alignment problems now, when you can literally manhandle the parts, than to wait 'til final assembly and risk damaging fine details.

MANIPULATOR ARMS

The manipulator arms themselves are comprised of eighteen very nicely cast white metal parts. A pair of brass sleeves along with a pair of resin manipulator-arm collars complete the package.

White metal is malleable, meaning cast parts can be bent or twisted with nothing more than hand pressure. The thinner the part, the easier it is to bend. Realignments or slight adjustments can be easily done, but you can also damage fine detail parts if you don't watch what you're doing. The cleanup of fine parting lines is fairly easy as well. Most of the time, scraping with a knife blade or smoothing with fine sandpaper will do the job, but if you find too much of a step between the two halves of a casting, a small file can come in handy.

With the parts cleaned up, I built up both arms, minus the brass sleeves, in the stowed position per the kit instructions. While epoxy is recom-mended for assembly, I used IC-GEL. Either will work. By the way, the malleability of white metal can work to your advantage during assembly. You'll find that the fixed claws and forearms fit rather loosely into the wrists and elbows. Instead of adding epoxy or CA and then holding the parts together until they bond, use a pair of small pliers to gently squeeze the wrists and elbows before assembly. It doesn't take much, so be sure to test fit as you go. Done correctly, the parts will be held by friction as well as CA or epoxy, making for stronger joints.

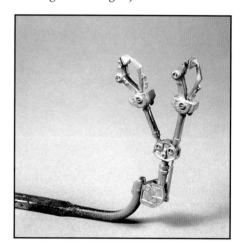

Here is one completed arm, configured in the stowed position. Be sure that the other one is an exact duplicate. And note the orientation of detail of the claws. It's very easy to reverse them.

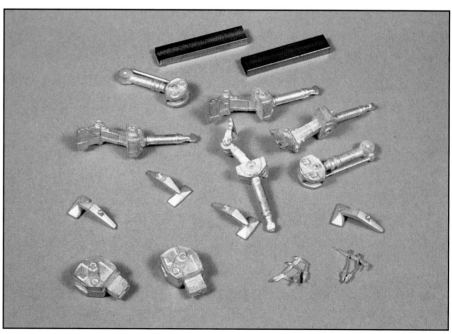

It takes all of these parts to build two manipulator arms?! It sure does.

Be sure to pay close attention to the three photos on page 7 of the instructions so that the pincers on all four of the fixed claws are properly oriented. You'll also need a pair of tweezers to install those delicate little actuator cylinders — and be sure to do the job someplace where you can find them if you drop one. There are no spares in the kit. Lose one, as I did, and you'll be forced to scratch-build a replacement. Finally, use one assembled arm as a guide to the second because the two arms have to be identical.

I clamped the studs that the sleeves would eventually slip over in the jaws of a couple of hemostats. That gave me something to handle while I sprayed the arms with primer and then Model Master Bright White. Be aware that it may take a couple of extra coats to obtain uniform coverage on all the nooks and crannies.

REAR DETAILS AND STEP

There are three resin details that mount on the outside of the rear Pod half: a TV camera, and two vents. Their installation is strictly by the book. The step, however, is a different matter. It has to be scratch-built from sheet styrene. Instructions specify use of the .060-inch styrene, but I used .020 inch

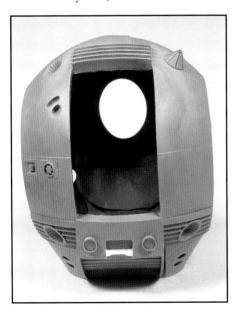

This view of the rear Pod shows the three resin details that have been added. Also, you can see how the gussets on the scratch-built step angle from the outside towards the center.

for a finer appearance. The reasoning behind that was the fact that .060 inch scales out to 3/4-inch thick, while .020 inch would be 1/4-inch thick. Assuming (a dangerous activity) that the step was made from a steel plate, 1/4 inch in real life would be more than enough to provide support.

Specific information regarding the exact configuration of the step is wanting, so follow the instructions and don't worry about it. I CA'd the step, after contouring the back edge to match the curve of the hull, so that the top surface was level with the bottom edge of the pocket. Gussets were cut 1/8-inch high at the back, tapering to a point at the front edge (think right triangle). They were attached to the underside of the styrene step with Ambroid ProWeld.

When I was satisfied with the detailing on the rear Pod half, it got the same treatment as the manipulator arms: primer and a couple or three coats of Model Master Bright White. As with everything else, all white surfaces would eventually get a final airbrushed coat of Boyd Gloss White. However, that would occur only after final assembly and cleanup of all seams.

COLLARS, BROW, AND SEAMS

I shifted my attention to the front Pod half/base assembly. The manipulator-arm collars have to be installed for starters. According to instructions, you want to carefully ream out the mounting holes (which are just under the upper floodlights) so that the collars fit snugly. Well, whether I got overenthusiastic during my initial cleanup of the parts or the holes were a little oversize to start with, I can't say. Whatever the cause, my collars fit anything but snugly.

At any rate, the loose fit never became a problem. After a little bit of dry fitting, I found that all I had to do was add CA to the collar sleeve, install, and then quickly align the collar so that the rectangular slot is precisely vertical. Repeat the process on the other collar, and you're done. All it takes is your Mk. I eyeball computer and a quick hand. A little experience doesn't hurt, either, but it's solving problems like this that creates the experience.

One last bit of scratch-building is up next. There's a brow (ledge, lip, etc.) that fits over a long, rectangular recess located just below the bottom of the window. The same page that contained patterns for the instrument console riser also has a pattern for the brow and its two support gussets. These three parts need to be cut from .020-inch white styrene.

After a couple of false starts, the eyebrow has been successfully installed. Note the orientation of the slots in the collars as well.

Installation of the brow is a little tricky, mainly due to the fact that the brow angles down and curves at the same time. At first glance, it seems that there's no way that it's going to fit. But if you get sufficient down angle, it will. There's no really easy way to do it, but the approach I took worked quite well. I installed the gussets first, one at each end of the recess. Then the brow was held in place and CA applied to the underside of the joint where the brow connected with each gusset, that being followed with a dab of Insta-Set accelerator before I released my grip. If everything was aligned to my satisfaction (and the first time it wasn't), a bead of CA was run along the underside of the brow from one gusset to the other and a similar bead on top to eliminate any gap. Once the CA had set, a little gentle sanding faired everything in. By the way, once the brow is installed, be careful where you put your hand. You'd be amazed how many times I cracked and repaired that brow seam before I finished my Pod! I'd never bothered cleaning up the seams that resulted from the front/base assembly. A little bit of Model Master Red Putty took care of any remaining gaps, then a sanding block and 120-grit sandpaper cleaned up everything after the putty had dried.

Finally, the backing flash on the hole for HAL's eye was removed and the now-familiar sequence of primer and bright white paint was applied. Amazingly, real progress is being made!

INTERIOR ASSEMBLY

If you're looking for something to do while paint dries, now's a good time to join the instrument console with the floor/walls assembly. You'll find that the instrument panel riser (the part you had to scratch-build from styrene) will fit the recess in the floor casting.

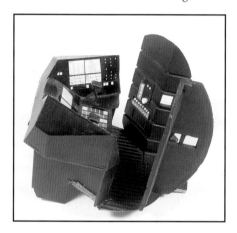

The completed interior is ready for installation.

All that you have to do is run a bead of IC-GEL along each recess, add the console, squirt a little accelerator on the area, and you suddenly have a completed Pod interior. You can't install it yet, but it's ready when you are.

Window and Forward Wall

After installing the window and just before adding the forward wall, the upper part of the front Pod interior, as well as one side of the forward wall, were sprayed Randome Tan. Just how much of the Pod interior needs to be sprayed can be easily determined by test fitting both the forward wall and interior assembly.

When it came to installation of the

window, I blazed my own path — again. The instructions want you to tape a square section of the clear plastic to the back of the forward wall, and then mount the complete unit against the window opening. The reasoning is perfectly valid, the idea being to avoid any blemish to the window. If you prefer to do it that way, go right ahead.

However, I opted to glue the clear stock directly to the interior window frame, using a combination of BSI Super Gold + and IC-GEL CA. At the risk of repeating myself, Super Gold + does not fog clear plastic. You *do* have to make sure it doesn't squeeze out onto the face of the window or you will have problems. Finally, I added some IC-GEL around the outer edges of the clear plastic to provide some added strength.

Rather than tape the window to the forward wall, I mounted it directly to the inside of the Pod's front half. In case you're wondering how I painted the interior color after installing the window, I covered the window temporarily with a piece of file card.

Once the clear plastic was in, I masked off the outside of the window. By doing this now, I could check from the back and make sure I hadn't missed a spot. With that done, it was time to add the forward wall. After test fitting again to determine the exact position needed for the oval cutout to align with the window opening, I put a small puddle of CA near each corner of the clear panel and then reinstalled the forward wall for the last time. Notice that the

clear stock is a rather large rectangle, so there's plenty of room to add the CA puddles without risk of flawing the actual window area.

Only one thing remains to be done

The forward wall and HAL's eye come next.

before adding the interior: installation of HAL's eye. This last piece of Mylar is simply positioned over the hole you opened up after the brow was installed. Holding it in place, I ran a bead of CA around it, gave it a shot of accelerator, and that was that. Since I wasn't lighting my Pod, I added a piece of duct tape over the Mylar to make sure it wouldn't ever come loose. If you plan on lighting yours, then you obviously have some more work to do.

Installation of the interior module comes next. If everything goes exactly according to plans, it'll drop neatly into place. Otherwise, you may have to make the kind of "adjustments" that I did.

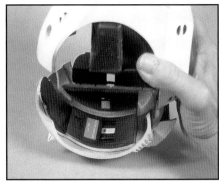

When you're satisfied that everything is going to fit, install the door and join the two halves.

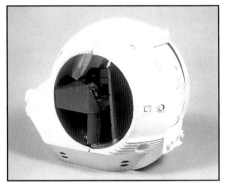

At this point, you have a basic Space Pod and a working door. Of course, there's still a lot more work to do before you can call it finished.

Considering the amount of putty I used on the top seam, you can tell that you're not exactly dealing with a perfect fit. But that's what putty is for.

ADD THE INTERIOR

Assuming I'd done everything right, all I had to do was add some CA to the locator studs, slip the interior into position so that the riser on the bottom of the floor would drop neatly into place, then step back and admire my handiwork. Good thing I decided to test fit first. Or to put it another way, "Houston, we have a problem."

While I did solve the problem, I still don't know what the actual cause was. I *think* dimension creep from making copies of the patterns was the culprit. It certainly makes sense, because a growth of .020 or .030 inch would be more than enough to throw a monkey wrench in the works. At any rate, I was left with a choice of either tearing down the interior and rebuilding everything a few thousandths smaller (assuming my assumption was correct) or figuring out how to make what I had work. Guess which approach I chose?

The solution turned out to be relatively simple. All I had to do was cut off the forward-most locator stud. This avoided the need for the riser rim to drop down in front of the stud, allow-ing the interior to slide forward into its proper position. At the same time, the two remaining studs prevented excessive lateral movement. Granted, this solution resulted in a little bit of slop that had to be addressed before adding CA to lock everything in place, but it certainly wasn't anything that couldn't be easily handled.

TWO HALVES MAKE A WHOLE

Joining the front and rear halves work pretty much the way the instructions describe. I would suggest that you spend some time test fitting the front and back halves *without the door in place* to become familiar with how everything is supposed to fit. When you're ready, lay the rear half on its back, add the door, and have at it.

Now the instructions imply that you're going to have tight seams that will require nothing more than thin superglue to secure. It may work out that way if everything goes exactly right.

But if you're not using Super Gold +, at least get your hands on a gap-fill-ing CA. You'll probably need it, especially on the upper seam. I did.

EARMUFFS

These are the side pieces that incorporate maneuvering thrusters. While I didn't install them at this point, I did check for proper fit. As you would expect, I wound up having to do a little bit of trimming here and there. My biggest problem was earmuff A (the right side as you sit in the Pod, left side as you face it from the front), the problem being directly related to the slightly oversized (I assume) instrument riser. Earmuff A has a half rim on the inner surface, the rim being used to locate the part. The earmuff wouldn't seat because the rim was hitting the side of the instrument riser. Solution? Trim out the offending section of rim to provide clearance around the riser.

DISPLAY MOUNT

When it comes to displaying the completed Space Pod, you have the same problem that you do with so many science-fiction models: How do you mount the thing on a stand? It really isn't that big a problem where the Pod is concerned. In fact, the method I used will work just as well if you light yours, because it will function as an invisible conduit for all of your wiring between the Pod and its base.

There's a 9/16-inch hole in the Pod base that is intended for a planned thruster opening, but it's also the perfect location for a support mount and power access. I dropped by a local hardware store and picked up four items: two 3/8 x 1/4-inch brass bushings, a 1/4- x 6-inch copper nipple, and a 3/8-inch flat galvanized nut. Now, things are about to get a little confusing because the sizes you're buying *are not* the sizes you're actually getting. Huh? Keep in mind that you're buying plumbing/gas fittings, and the way they're sized can easily give you a permanent migraine.

The bushings are actually step up/step down nipples that are threaded on the outside *and* inside, with a hexagonal nut cast onto one end. Although the *outside* thread is described as 3/8 inch, it's actually slightly larger than 5/8 inch, and the *inside* thread is really slightly larger than 1/2 inch, even though it's identified as 1/4 inch. Confused? It gets worse. That 1/4- x 6-inch nipple is a rigid piece of copper pipe that has threaded ends just a tad larger than 1/2 inch. However, it really is 6 inches long. And that galvanized nut? It's sold as a 3/8-inch nut, but has a threaded hole that's slightly larger than 5/8 inch — and fits the 3/8-inch outer thread of the brass bushing perfectly. Unless you're an expert at plumbing/gas fittings, take the

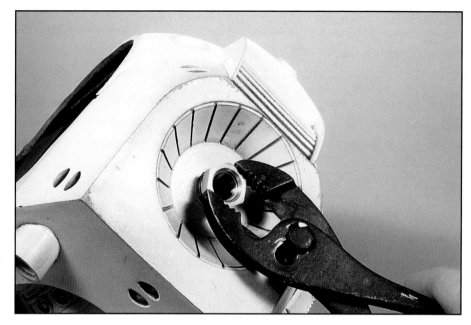

Installing the brass bushing at this time (before adding the earmuffs) allows you to see where to stop. Thread it in too far and you'd force the floor out of place.

cotton-pickin' model with you and sort through the fittings 'til you find what you need.

READY FOR FINAL FINISHING

With the Pod completely assembled (and the door installed), there's not a whole lot of construction left — but you still have a ways to go before it's completely finished. Remember that I said you'd probably need more

than thin CA? On my kit, not only was the top seam quite prominent, I didn't have a continuous curvature — especially front to back as the lateral curve approached the inner edges of the earmuffs. I was probably responsible for that as much as anything through over-enthusiastic sanding of the initial putty applied to the top seam. The manhandling of the front and rear halves, combined with a heat gun during the alignment phase, may well have been another factor.

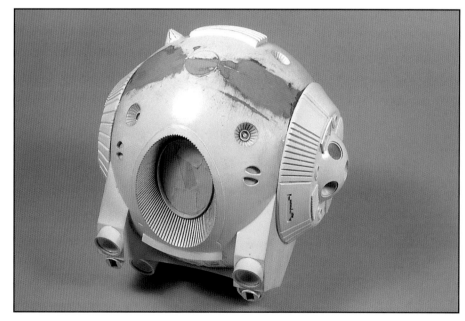

The earmuffs are in place, the putty has been sanded, and the window is masked off. Things are beginning to look good.

Whatever the reason, more putty and some very careful sanding finally brought out the correct curvature. There were also a couple of large seams on the back half just below the door where the front and rear halves would interface. Additional putty and sanding was necessary here as well. Once I was happy with the results, I masked the door with Parafilm M (no adhesive to mar the finish) and then airbrushed some Model Master Primer (out of a bottle) over the puttied areas.

More Paint

At this point, I screwed the 6-inch nipple into the bushing that had previously been installed in the base of the Pod. This gave me something to hold on to while spraying the Pod. It also didn't hurt that I'd be able to clamp one end in a vise when I needed to turn loose of the model.

First, all of the primed areas got a couple of coats of Model Master Bright White from its spray can. When that'd dried for a while, the entire Pod got a more or less overall light coat of the same paint — although I didn't bother with the door. Finally, I clamped the pipe in a vise and left things to dry for a few hours.

MANIPULATOR ARM SLEEVES

The manipulator arms mount into rectangular brass sleeves that then slide in and out of the collars. Again, the openings in the collars were too large for the sleeves. Whether you're interested in being able to slide the arms in and out or not, they still have to fit precisely, or the arms will sag.

Since the sleeves were too small for the collar openings, some way had to be found to shim either the openings or the sleeves. The obvious solution was to simply cut a length of the next larger size brass rectangle, install that in the collars and then be able to easily slide the original sleeves in and out. The trouble is, sometimes the obvious doesn't work. I picked up a length of next-size brass rectangle at the hobby shop and quickly made two discoveries — neither of which I liked. First, it was slightly too big for the collar opening. Second, the kit-provided sleeves would

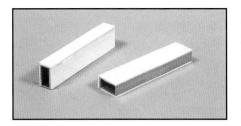

Bonding .020-inch styrene to three sides of each brass sleeve expands things just enough to make a perfect fit in the collars. Not the most orthodox way to solve a problem, but it worked — and very well, too.

bind when I tried to slide them into the new brass. Well, the obvious wasn't working, so now what?

After doing a bit of diddling, the answer arrived from an unexpected direction. All I had to do was CA a piece of .020-inch styrene onto both wide sides and one narrow side of each sleeve. The result? A perfect fit in the collar openings, along with the ability to readily slide in and out if that's your preference.

Incidentally, if you're planning on sliding the arms in and out, you'll want to spray the slides with a coat of your favorite bright bare metal paint.

THE FINAL WHITE COAT?

Although I didn't, you might want to spray the entire Pod a final thinned coat of Boyd Gloss White (marketed by Testors). The reason for this is that it

seems to be harder than other white paint, which reduces the risk of staining or otherwise dirtying the surface while working on final details and decals.

If you're running bottle paint through your airbrush and are in a hurry, or you just don't have the patience to wait for the white to dry, try adding a few drops of lacquer thinner to the paint. Just be sure you only add it to the paint you're spraying and not the main bottle.

DETAILS, DETAILS

I had downloaded all of those reference photos I'd found on CultTVman into a file on my computer. Now was the time to spend some time studying the various color details. Custom Replicas gives you a couple of 4- x 6-inch color photos of the finished model, but you really need more.

Adding some Model Master Chrome Silver completes the reflectors. If I had been intending to light my Pod, there would be light bulbs installed as well.

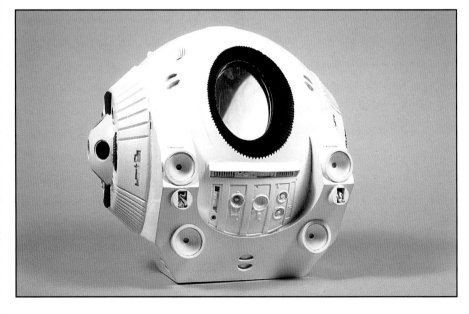

Now it's nearly finished. All that's left to deal with are the reflectors, lenses, and arms.

Most of the detail painting involves thruster recesses and other details on the earmuffs and the large ribbed recess surrounding the viewport. All of these are Model Master FS 37038 Flat Black. You'll also find a few other areas where small amounts of various colors are used.

By the way, *do not* try to paint all those little red bands that you find on the manipulator arms. There's a far easier way to do it — decals. This assumes that somewhere in your decal box you have a sheet of red decal stripes. If not, it's time for a trip to the hobby shop.

THE REST OF THE DECALS

Which ones you use will depend on the references you have on hand and how much time you want to put into it. The choice is yours. When you're satisfied with all of the decals, the entire Pod gets a coat of Model Master Semi-Gloss Clear Lacquer. Then, when that's dry, the Parafilm M masking is removed from the door, as is the tape mask from the viewport. And don't overlook the liquid mask you used on HAL's eye.

IT'S TIME TO GET GOOGLE-EYED

If you think I'm making something up, I'm not. First, paint the reflectors bright silver. While that's drying, head for your local arts-and-crafts store such as Michaels. Oh, before you go, be sure to measure the inside diameter of the searchlight housing rim — which is .650 inch (or just over 5/8 inch).

Google Eyes (marketed in some stores as Wiggle Eyes), in case you're still trying to figure out what the heck

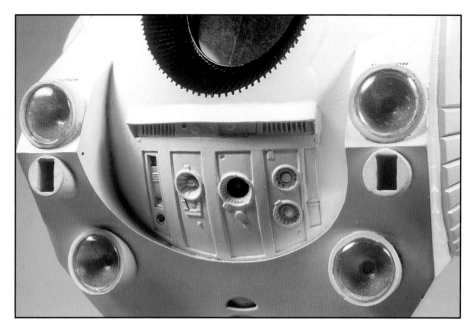

Drop the clear covers into the rims, and all of a sudden you have spotlights.

I'm talking about, are the eyes you see on a lot of stuffed toys and rag dolls such as Raggedy Ann. They actually take their name from the Barney Google comic strip and are nothing more than a round white piece of plastic or cardstock, combined with a flattened clear plastic dome. Trapped inside is a small black disc that is free to move around. They come in all sizes and are dirt cheap in price. In some cases, the diameters are given in metric dimensions. If so, you'll be looking for 17 or 18 mm.

Anyway, buy you a package of Google Eyes that are the right diameter and take four of them apart, saving only the clear covers. Those covers, when cemented into the housing rims, become — drum roll please — the lenses for your searchlights.

THE NEXT TO LAST THING

Since I'd already mounted a threaded bushing in the Pod base, all I did was drill a 5/8-inch hole through the center of a 6 1/2-inch diameter wood craft base. Then the hole was enlarged to 1 1/4 inch on the bottom of the base and half the depth of the base thickness. That allowed me to put the bushing in from the top, add the flat nut on the bottom, and then thread the 1/4-inch nipple into the bushing. The whole thing was sprayed flat black, allowed to dry, and then threaded into

These are Google Eyes. You'll need four 3/8-inch diameter Google Eyes to create the spotlight lenses.

Combine a few plumbing fittings, a craft store wooden base, and some flat black to create a sturdy mount for your Space Pod.

the bushing on the bottom of the Pod.

You couldn't ask for a sturdier base. And, as I said way back in the early part of this chapter, that hollow nipple is a perfect conduit for all your wiring if you choose to light your Pod.

THE LAST THING

Assuming that you've already applied the red stripe decals to the manipulator arms as suggested earlier, go ahead and cement the arms into one end of each arm slide.

Now slide the arms into position on the Pod and your One Man Space Pod is finished. Only one problem remains. Getting HAL to open the door so you can get back inside the ship.

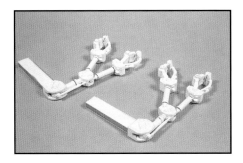

Here are the manipulator arms and slides, ready for installation. If you look close, you can see the red decal stripes.

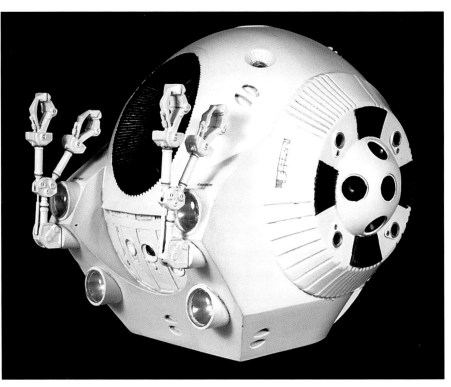

From this angle, you get a good view of the Pod's manipulator arms in their stowed position.

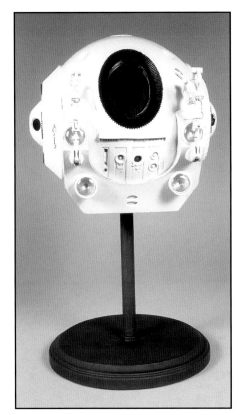

It's finished at last, mounted on its base, and ready for the display case.

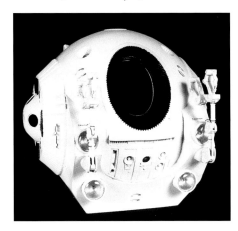

The brow, HAL's eye, and the viewport show clearly in this view.

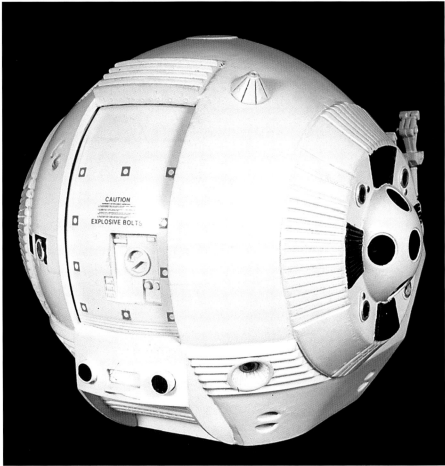

There are more prominent markings on the door, which is on the back of the Pod, than anywhere else on the entire vehicle.

8

How to Build Sci-Fi Model Spacecraft

DISPLAY METHODS

Display methods are as varied as the models themselves. Not only does the specific subject impact how it's displayed, the *type* of model is at least as important, if not more so. Cars, trucks, aircraft, ships, and even missiles are relatively easy. Spacecraft are a whole other story. They tend to require a good deal more creativity, as well as the development of some basic woodworking skills. Why? Read on.

JUST SET IT ON THE COFFEE TABLE, OR BUFFET, OR TV

This is where just about every modeler starts out, no matter what your field of interest. Sitting a finished model on whatever vacant surface is available. Most of the time it's on top of the television (if you have a wood console design) or the coffee table/end table. While convenient and capable of attracting attention from visitors, that isn't all it attracts.

Dust is the first visitor to arrive — lots and lots of dust. Think your house is dust free? Sit a model out in the open, wait a few days, and think again. And models do not take kindly to being dusted. Although dust is the first visitor, it ain't the only one. If you're an animal lover, I don't have to tell you that cats think a beautiful model is the greatest toy ever made. Dogs? That wagging tail attached to an enthusiastic Labrador, German Shepherd, or other medium to large-breed dog will sweep your super-detailed model off the coffee table in nothing flat.

Then there's human nature. It doesn't matter whether a person is living in a homeless shelter or pulling down $5 million a year as a CEO, put them in close proximity to an exposed model and the automatic reaction is to ask "Can I touch it?" — *after* they've already picked it up and broken three small parts that they didn't know were there.

THE BARE — AND OPEN — SHELF

Assuming a reasonably dust-free area, quite a number of modelers, if not the majority, simply line up their finished models side by side on a series of bare wood (sometimes glass or Plexiglas) shelves. The method works for most subjects, but it does have a couple of disadvantages beyond the dust problem. First is that you still can't keep visitors from touching them. Secondly, a large number of spacecraft models have no landing gear — so where's the rationale for sitting them on a shelf? I'll grant you that many manufacturers include support stands, but quite a number of those stands are not as sturdy as they need to be. Beyond that, some spacecraft kits don't come with stands, such as the SMT B-Wing.

VIGNETTES AND DIORAMAS

Build science-fiction models of any kind and it won't be long before

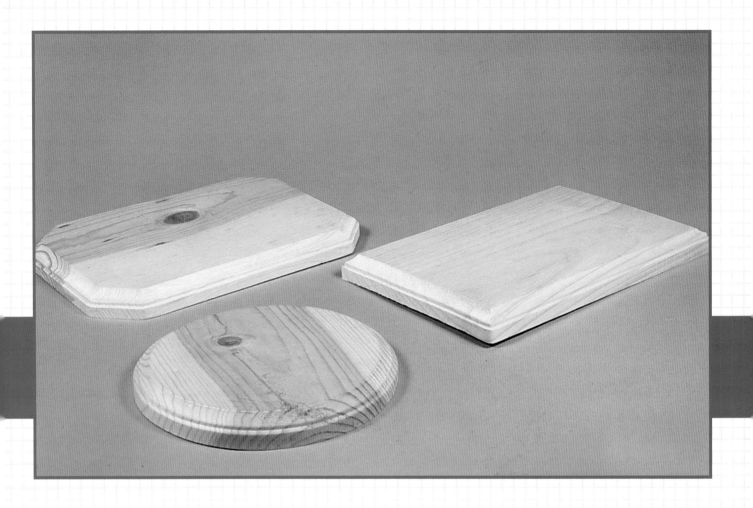

you become familiar with dioramas and vignettes, mostly vignettes. Aside from the fact that they allow you to tell a story or depict a specific scene, their greatest value is permitting a realistic display of the finished model. A beautifully done aircraft model is quite acceptable sitting on a bare wood base, but a spacecraft seems to always beg for more. Of course, if you choose this method, be aware that you absolutely *must* enclose it in a case or dust cover.

Custom Stands

Aircraft modelers have access to a wide variety of custom stands from aftermarket manufacturers. Same for figure enthusiasts where bases are concerned. Science-fiction modelers, more often than not, will have to design and build their own bases and/or stands. Before you faint, let me assure you that it really isn't all that hard. We'll run through a couple or three in this chapter, and you'll see what I'm talking about.

Kit Bases

Kit provided bases range all the way from two or three piece styrene stands to molded diorama bases. Some

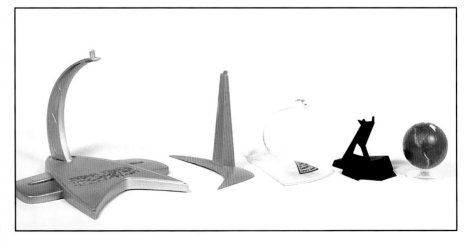

From left to right are five kit-provided bases. They are: AMT Defiant; AMT Klingon Bird of Prey; Aurora/Polar Lights Spindrift; Revell-Monogram Starfury; and Monogram Space Taxi. While the Defiant's stand is the best of the bunch, they all do a decent to good job of supporting the models — except for one. The Bird of Prey stand is virtually useless due to a propensity to tip over with the model in a heartbeat or less.

---

are quite good and require nothing more than a little imagination in the painting department. Others need to be enhanced in one way or the other.

Still others are next to useless, many of them simply being too flimsy for the job. In many cases, the mounted model overbalances the stand. Then you have the ones where the stand actually supports the model — unless the display shelf isn't perfectly level, someone walks across the floor and creates an imperceptible vibration, a light breeze from an air conditioning duct caresses the model, or your dog barks too loudly.

Finally, you have kit-provided bases that are not only totally useless, they're dangerous. The Bird of Prey stand falls in that category. Just *looking* at the two parts that form the stand makes you nervous, and it should. Glue the parts together, mount the BOP on it, and check your watch — the second hand. Unless you permanently bond the model to the stand, and make sure it's perfectly level, it'll take something under three seconds for it to tip over. And that's when the combination is sitting on a level surface!

COMMERCIAL DUST COVERS

They tend to come and go, but kit manufacturers will occasionally put out molded clear styrene dust covers, complete with plastic bases. Most are designed for car models, but I've seen them sized for small aircraft and model locomotives. And the majority of them are stackable. While their size and configuration tend to be somewhat limited, don't ignore them. You never know when one will be exactly what you need.

CASES/CABINETS

This can be anything from adding a couple of wood-framed glass doors to the front of a bookcase to ordering a custom built display cabinet for a price that reaches the far side of four figures ($1,000+). In between, you have surplus glass counters from businesses that have gone belly up, cases being sold for a song by companies that are remodeling, store fixtures being sold — and in some cases, given away —

before a building is demolished, and more. Just keep your eye out for possibilities and don't overlook the classifieds.

One thing that does show up in classified ads is antique candy counters. If you have an old house and are looking for something that won't clash with your house's design, this is a great way to go.

Finally, don't overlook furniture kits. If that's not your style, you can always break out your credit card and visit your nearby department or fine furniture store.

DIY (DO IT YOURSELF) DISPLAYS

If all the options just discussed don't appeal to you, or are simply impractical for one reason or another, why not design and build your own bases and/or dust covers? After all, if you can build complex kits or scratch-build original spacecraft designs, there's no reason why you can't be just as successful where bases and dust covers are concerned. You can also build full-fledged wood-and-glass display cases from scratch, but that's beyond the scope of this book.

TOOLS

The tools you have access to or familiarity with will pretty well determine how complex your bases/stands can be. Just about all of us have a variety of handsaws on hand, everything

from the standard crosscut saw to key-hole saws, coping saws, jeweler's saws, and more. If you don't, spend a little time in your local home-improvement center.

Move up a notch to small power tools and you find such things as jig-saws. And let's not overlook the wide range of power hand tools from Dremel and similar manufacturers. Incidentally, at the top end of the Dremel line is a very nice 16-inch scroll saw.

With this, you can do all kinds of fancy shapes, letters, and fretwork. Thanks to its variable speed control, you can cut a wide variety of materials including clear acrylic.

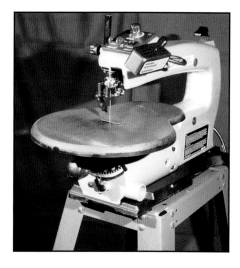

Looking for a way to cut fancy scrollwork, contoured bases, or the like? This variable-speed 16-inch scroll saw from Dremel is something you might want to consider.

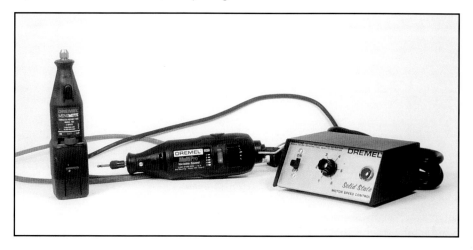

Dremel tools, at least in my mind, are the gold standard for small hobby power tools. Left to right is a rechargable MiniMite; a variable-speed, ball-bearing MultiPro; and for those of you who have a single-speed Dremel — a bench-top speed control.

For the truly ambitious (and hopefully equally knowledgeable), the Shopsmith Mk. V would have to be considered one of the Cadillacs of woodworking equipment. Six feet long and expensive ($1400 the last time I looked), you can build anything with it from custom display cases to sophisticated cabinetry, your own shop, or even an entire house.

For the truly ambitious (which includes building a room addition onto your house — or maybe even the entire house), consider a radial arm saw or a five-in-one system such as the Shopsmith Mk. V. This kind of equipment, combined with the requisite knowledge, gives you the capability of a full-blown commercial woodworking shop.

However, don't get the notion that you *have* to have a shop full of fancy equipment. I used a Mk. V to create some of the stands/bases described in this book simply because I happen to own one, but I could have gotten (and have gotten) the same results with far less in the way of sophisticated tools.

WOOD BASES

The simplest way of all is to browse through the selection of unfinished/prefinished decoupage plaques at your local craft store. They come in all sizes and shapes, frequently being exactly what you're looking for. If there were a disadvantage to them, it would have to be that it can be very difficult to add a dust cover to them. But as long as you have a protected display case to put the finished project in, it's the fastest way to go.

Here are three examples of the kinds of wood bases and plaques that can be found at arts-and-crafts stores. All of these are made from pine.

Of course, creating your own wood base can be almost as simple. At its most basic, just cut a rectangular or square piece of wood, sand it smooth, apply a stain or clear coat, and you're ready to add the model. About the only decisions you have to make are what kind of wood and finish do you want to use, and your local Home Depot or similar store can help you there.

Depending on the model, you might want to get a little more creative where the shape of your base is concerned. For example, if your model is essentially rectangular, repeat its configuration in a rectangular base. A triangular or wedge shaped base would work well with a similarly shaped spacecraft, and so on.

When your base requires more than one piece of wood, things get a little more complicated. But not much.

The Roswell Base

Only slightly more complicated than a flat piece of wood, this base combines *two* flat pieces of wood into a 90-degree angle. There is, of course the question of what kind of wood. Any kind will work, but I happened to have a few pieces of walnut on hand. Besides being available, I'm rather partial to it for use in bases. That walnut is a beautiful wood is reason enough to choose it, but it's also tight grained. It'll sand to a very smooth surface and, being tight grained, doesn't absorb large amounts of clear coats or stain.

These two pieces of 3/4-inch walnut will combine to create the Roswell base.

Anyway, the first thing I did was to cut those two flat pieces from 3/4-inch thick walnut. One piece was 10 3/4 x 7 1/4 inch and the other 10 3/4 x 5 inch. I then drilled three or four pilot holes in the lower edge of the backboard (the narrow one) about 3/8 inch up from the side.

On the lower edge of the upright piece, drill three or four holes more or less equally spaced from left to right. The diameter of the holes should be slightly smaller than the brads (finishing nails) you're planning on using.

Lateral position isn't all that critical, just make sure they'll fall somewhere near the centerline of the base's 3/4-inch thickness. With the holes drilled, tap finishing nails into them until the tips of the nails are just flush with the other side.

Now run a bead of Elmer's Carpenters Wood Glue along the edge of the base, carefully position the backboard along the edge, drive the nails home, and let things dry. While there's really nothing to building this kind of base, if your woodworking skills aren't even this basic, I'd suggest practicing on some scrap pieces of pine first.

Apply a bead of Elmer's Carpenter's Wood Glue along the base edge, position the upright, drive the brads home, and then let things dry.

After the glue has dried, it's time to exhaust a few pieces of sandpaper. For the most part, you can do it by hand, though some would be more comfortable with a sanding block. Either way, sand until you have a nice smooth surface and no glue squeeze-outs are showing.

All that remains is to apply some kind of finish, and that is entirely up to you. You can use stains, MinWax, urethanes, even paint the thing a solid color (though why anyone would want to hide walnut's natural beauty I can't imagine). I happen to be partial to Deft Clear Finish. It's available as gloss, semi-gloss, and satin finish in both spray cans and brush-on. Deft is a coconut alkyd bar top finish that's a superb choice when you want to allow the natural wood grain and color to show through. This stuff is self-leveling, so the application of it is almost impossible to botch, and you can use virtually anything to spread it. Spray cans are easy, of course, but if you prefer a little more hands-on involvement, a conventional brush, roller, or even a

Here is the completed Roswell wood base after it's been sanded and had several coats of Deft Semi-Gloss Clear Wood Finish applied.

folded paper towel does just as well with the brush-on version.

Remember when I said that it's almost impossible to botch? Well, you *can* botch it if you don't apply it heavy enough. And if you do that, just add a little more. It dries in 30 minutes, so it doesn't take long to correct any problems. The only other problem you might encounter is an occasional run, if you put it on *too* heavy. But just like paint runs on a model, all you have to do is let it dry, sand it down, and reapply. Nothing to it. Finally, if you're after one of those satin-smooth, hand-rubbed finishes, 0000 steel wool will do the job.

War of the Worlds

Depending on the kind of wood you're using and the size of the base required, you may find it necessary to edge glue a couple of pieces together to create a sufficiently large, flat base.

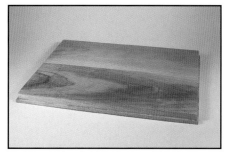

This base is comprised of two edge-joined pieces of walnut intended for the War of the Worlds vignette. A rabbit groove has also been cut around the top edge to accept a dust cover. Don't try this unless you really know what you're doing.

While not all that difficult, it does require more advanced techniques and a pair of large woodworker's bar clamps. I had to do that for my *War of the Worlds* base and wound up using my Mk. V (including its rip fence) and the aforementioned bar clamps. While I was at it, I cut a rabbit around the top edge of the base to allow for eventual installation of a dust cover that would sit down on a lip.

While edge gluing and rabbiting a flat base is still fairly basic, you may need equipment that many don't have. You can hardly justify buying large bar clamps if you're only going to build one wood base in the next five years, never mind a $1400 Mk. V. Either make friends with an experienced woodworker or pay someone to build a base to your specifications.

FRAME IT

Sometimes, as with my Bird of Prey diorama, you're building up terrain or other scenery over the entire base. There's no point in covering up a large piece of walnut (or any other expensive wood) with window screen and Bondo. Instead, you use plywood or wafer wood. When you're done, there's the problem of what to do about those raw edges. Well, it ain't rocket science folks. Put a frame on it — and there's two ways to do it.

Picture Frame Kit

First, if you've used a base dimension that's a standard size, trot down to your local craft store (such as Michaels or Hobby Lobby) and buy a picture frame kit. Bring it home, put it together, lay it face down on the table/counter (it has to be face down to create a recess for your diorama's base), and drop the diorama's base into the recess that you normally find on the back of a picture frame.

Just in case you think there might be something difficult about the process, let's build up the frame I chose. I wound up with two packages of moldings: one pair 18 inches long, and the other 20 inches in length.

Once you get them out of their packages, take one strip of each length, add some Elmer's Carpenter's Wood

These two packages of modular wooden picture-frame strips, which set me back around $15 total, will combine to create a base frame for any diorama. Simply select the correct lengths.

After starting the provided fastener by hand, simply drive it home with a hammer.

Glue to one of the mitered edges, join both miters at a 90-degree angle, start the plastic fitting into its slot, and hammer the thing home until it's flush with the surface.

Repeat the process three more times as you work your way around the perimeter. It won't be more than four or five minutes before you discover a complete picture frame in your hands.

Because the frame will remain permanently face down, you will want to consider that when selecting an appropriate frame. They come in all sizes and shapes, but I'd suggest staying with the smaller, simpler ones. If there's a drawback to this approach, it's that you might have a problem adding a dust cover depending on the outer shape of the molding. Of course, there's nothing like trouble to enhance creativity.

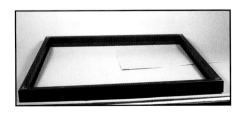

Repeat the process three more times, and you'll have a completed frame waiting for your next diorama.

Custom Framing

Your alternative, and your *only* choice if you've created a diorama with an odd size or shape, is to frame it yourself. In other words, you're going to build your own picture frame, complete with a rabbit to accept a dust cover. For this you'll need major power equipment, such as a power miter saw or Shopsmith Mk. V.

Without a decent amount of woodworking experience *and* the necessary equipment, I'd *strongly* suggest that you find a friend with those qualifications, pay someone to do it, or redesign the size and shape of your diorama. Believe me, if you don't know what you're doing, you can wind up losing a finger or even a hand. Oh, don't be so cocksure that you say it will never happen to you! My oldest uncle (who was a carpenter/builder) lost a finger to a circular saw rather late in life, and an acquaintance of mine nearly lost a hand to a table saw. If you don't already have a very healthy fear of those screaming saw blades, *get one*, or stay as far away from them as you can.

CLEAR ACRYLIC DUST COVERS

Clear acrylic, such as Plexiglas (which is a trade name), comes in every size, shape, and texture you can imagine, as well as a wide variety of colors. It can be sawn, glued, drilled, heat shaped, and more. Prices range from reasonable to "you don't want to know," and it's the material of choice for easily built dust covers (especially if you don't want to run the risk of glass cases shattering).

But clear acrylic also requires some of the same tools and knowledge that you use in woodworking, as well as others that are specific to acrylic material. That doesn't mean you can't create unique base designs and dust covers without power equipment. You can — within limits.

For example, if you know the dimensions you need for a dust cover, most acrylic retailers (the larger wholesale distributors that also have a retail counter in the front of the store) will cut things to size for you — for a fee. If you're willing to pay for it, many will even build the cover for you.

Planning on cutting the parts at home? You don't absolutely have to have a table or radial arm saw, though that's the best way. The thinner acrylic (up to 1/8 inch or so) can be scored with a scriber and snapped. Similar in technique to cutting glass, the method is quickly learned. As a matter of fact, I have no problem scoring and snapping acrylic, yet I've never learned to do the same with window glass.

If you happen to own a scroll saw (such as the one from Dremel), you can easily cut acrylic. Just keep the speed down so the acrylic doesn't overheat and cause the blade to jam. This method works quite well if you're creating a fancy base with curves and cutouts. However, scroll saws aren't the saw of choice for long, straight cuts. I've done it by using the widest scroll blade available and taking a lot of time. Even then, I wound up spending quite a bit of time with a sanding block to clean up, and straighten, the cut edge.

Nothing available but a handsaw? You can still cut acrylic. But don't think you're going to do it with an ordinary carpenter's crosscut or rip saw. Try that and you'll find all kinds of micro-cracks along the cut edge because those kinds of saws will inevitably cause the acrylic to flex as you saw. What you want are very fine-tooth, wide-blade saws, such as a Zona saw. What are ideal are some of these Japanese pull saws that cut on the draw stroke instead of the push stroke. You can generally find them in catalogs and shops that cater to the dedicated woodworker.

IN CLOSING

The various methods and approaches described here that will protect your precious models aren't much more than the tip of the iceberg. Remember, you're limited only by your imagination and construction skills. Imagination and creativity shouldn't be a problem, especially when you build science-fiction subjects. As for skills, they improve with every model, stand, or dust cover we build. If they don't, we're doing something wrong.

How to Build Sci-Fi Model Spacecraft

REFERENCES

Build models of just about anything *other* than science fiction or fantasy and references are pretty much everywhere. Granted, you'll find gaps from time to time, but for the most part, our bookshelves are groaning with books and magazines on the objects of our desire. Shift your focus to science fiction and things change in a hurry. I suspect most science-fiction modelers today build models of spacecraft and vehicles that they've seen on TV or in the movies. Compared to aircraft, cars, trucks, and the like, science-fiction references require a different approach.

BOOKSTORES

Science fiction reference books are out there, but you have to be willing to hunt for them. Mainstream book stores generally have a limited selection, except for the various technical manuals and such that focus on *Star Trek* and *Star Wars*. You'll also find occasional books on the history of real space that will include illustrations and/or artist's concepts of designs that were actually planned for production but were stillborn because they proved impractical or cost too much.

There you have would-be reality becoming science fiction. And don't overlook the remainder bins or bargain tables in those same mainstream bookstores. Quite often you'll be able to find some very interesting books knocked down from $30 or $40 to giveaway prices of $5 or $10.

USED BOOKSTORES

These can be anything from hole in the wall operations that you find in the seedy parts of town to such class operations as Half Price Books. Prices can range all the way from half the publisher's price (MSRP) to as low as 25 cents. It all depends on the subject matter, how long it's been on the shelf,

When it comes to Star Wars or Star Trek references, this is the kind of publication that can be found in virtually any medium to large bookstore.

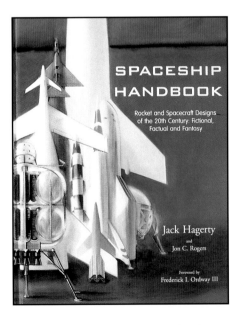

I discovered an ad for this hardcover book in an issue of FineScale Modeler. No matter whether your interest lies in science fiction or science fact, this gem is a treasure trove of rocket and spacecraft design. Pricey? Yes, but a must have. Save your pennies.

condition, and how desperate they are to get rid of it. And depending on the shop, a little haggling might get the price down even lower. You have to develop a feel for when to try that stunt because some stores won't mind at all and others will invite you to leave — immediately.

MAGAZINES, MAGAZINE ADS, AND CATALOGS

When you buy a model magazine, or for that matter, any magazine, get in the habit of scanning the ads. Most of the time there'll be nothing of particular interest, but now and again lightning will strike. And, of course, there are the various mail-order catalogs from book publishers. Some you request but many show up uninvited.

Just because they were uninvited, don't treat them as unwelcome guests. They might contain exactly what you've been looking for.

VIDEOTAPES, DVDS, AND VCRS

This option should be obvious if you build spacecraft that appear in films or on TV. As this is written, the majority of science-fiction films (especially the older ones) are still only available on tape. Newer ones are being released in both tape *and* DVD, though I suspect it won't be long before DVD will be the only format for new releases. But what about the older films? They are probably on videotape and available in the bargain bin for the time being. Eventually, you'll have to resort

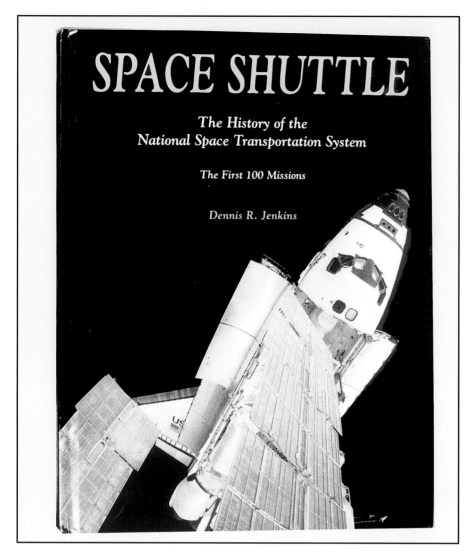

What's a book on the Space Shuttle doing in a science fiction model book? Well, aside from the fact that Dennis Jenkins has produced what must be considered the bible on our Shuttle's first 100 missions, some of the initial Shuttle concepts were futuristic enough (or strange enough) to pique the interest on any science-fiction enthusiast.

to buying used copies. In fact, that's already beginning to occur.

Because videotapes are apparently on their way out, where are you going to find those pre-recorded films that you need for that next model? If you're looking for new copies, the usual places are still where you look. You can check in video stores or electronics stores such as Best Buy, Circuit City, or similar discount operations like Wal-Mart. The trouble is that subject selection is going to become more and more limited as they switch to DVD.

Some of the older or less popular titles will never be found today in the stores. The answer to that problem is two-fold, well actually three. If you're anywhere near a large public library, try checking out the titles you need. Of course, the disadvantage is that you have to return them in two or three days, meaning you can't keep them on hand to refer to while you spend two months building your latest masterpiece. You're a lot better off owning them.

If you're beginning to explore the used videotape market in order to build up a science-fiction reference tape library, absolutely do not overlook Half Price Books. The ones I've been in have a very large selection of used titles. They're usually in excellent condition and sell for, well, half price — generally around $7.98. Sometimes you can find complete sets such as the *Star Wars* trilogy, obviously at a somewhat higher price. Looking for really dirt-cheap titles? Then take a look in a kind of store that most people don't usually consider — your friendly (?) neighborhood pawnshop. That's right, pawnshop. Hey, there's nothing wrong with it. You're buying, not pawning. Believe it or not, I found a special longer edition version of *Star Trek: The Motion Picture* in excellent condition for a paltry $2. This is the place where you'll find titles that'll never show up anywhere else.

If you hate spending even two bucks for a used tape or you're chasing titles that'll never show up anywhere but broadcast, cable, or satellite TV, then lay in a supply of blank tapes and treat your VCR with loving care. Spend a few months with the TV listings and you can amass a creditable tape library. Now when you buy a new model, you'll have the necessary reference tape right at hand.

You'll also need a DVD player if you acquire the newer titles in that format. Of course, the ultimate solution will occur when combination VCR/DVD players/recorders become both widely available and affordable. It may take you a few weeks, or months, but then you'll be able to transfer all your tapes to DVD and your problems will be solved. Until they come up with a new, "superior" format that will make the DVD obsolete.

RAT-HOLE SPARE EQUIPMENT

This may sound a little illogical, but it really isn't. As DVD takes over the pre-recorded market, prices of DVD players *and* VCRs are dropping like an express elevator. Name brand VCRs (such as Sony) with all the bells and whistles that used to cost $400 can now be had for little more than $100 or less. Basic DVD players can be gotten for *under* $100. All that sounds wonderful, but it does raise a few interesting questions if you have a substantial collection of videotapes.

The most obvious is how much longer are you going to be able to find new VCRs in the stores. Then there's the question of repairs when something goes south. Even if repairs are available, the cost will likely be substantially more than buying a new one. Solution? When you find a really good price on one, buy it and stash it in the

How to Build Sci-Fi Model Spacecraft

Videotapes of science-fiction movies and TV series are an essential part of your reference collection. These were all acquired used from either Half Price Books or a local pawnshop. Prices? Anywhere from $7.98 to $2.00.

back of your closet without even opening the box. It will be a VCR for a rainy day as it were.

Another reason for acquiring a spare VCR is the *possibility* that a VCR/DVD player/recorder may never be widely available or affordable. If not, you'll still have a working VCR that can be connected to the DVD recorder in order to copy your old tapes.

Is this scenario likely? Who knows. But like the boy scouts, it doesn't hurt to be prepared.

THE INTERNET

Here is where so many science-fiction modelers have spent, or will spend, so much of their research time, surfing the World Wide Web with Google, Dogpile, and most of the other search engines. Somewhere in that mass of random, un-indexed pages called the internet, is that one site or photo that shows exactly the piece of information that you're looking for. The trick, as they say, is to find it.

Before settling in for an extended session with your favorite search engine, there are a few websites you need to consider automatic starting points. First and foremost is Tony Matteliano's Scale Model Index. Tony has created a massive compendium of some 3500 (at last count) site links to everything from manufacturers to prototype references and personal pages of enthusiasts. Then there's CultTVman's

SF Modeling Page with posted photos and construction articles of various science-fiction models, links to reference sites, and more. Starship Modeler takes a similar approach. Don't overlook the various webzine sites such as Internet Modeler, Hyperscale, and PC Modeler either. Of course, checking the IPMS/USA site is essential as well. Incidentally, if you're not yet an IPMS member, do it now. It's the best $21 (in the U.S.) you'll ever spend. URLs to all the sites I've listed (and many more) can be found in the selected sources appendix in the back of this book.

If you still haven't found the references you're looking for, it's search-engine time. There are as many ways to search, as there are modelers. It all depends on how your mind works. For example, if you're looking for information on *Star Wars* ships, the obvious approach is to type in "*Star Wars*," and you'll be rewarded with several thousand different web pages, most of which have absolutely nothing to do with what you're looking for.

A better approach is to refine your search to something more specific, such as "B-Wing fighter." Still, only a few of the sites will give you what you need but checking out each of the sites will be a lot easier. However, you can refine things even further. If you're looking for photos of the B-Wing, try "B-Wing photos," and things get easier still. The same method can track down sites dealing with "B-Wing models," etc. "SMT B-Wing" will get you both

the SMT manufacturer's site, *and* a kit review that appeared in *Starship Modeler*.

What it all boils down to is logic, common sense, and patience. I'd also suggest that if you grew up in the B.C. (before computers) era using old-fashioned library card catalogs, you're ahead of the game. That's because you had to have a fairly tightly focused idea of what you were looking for before you ever *touched* the catalog, instead of typing in one word and punching a key. In any event, the more general your search term, the greater the number of results returned and the more chaff you have to sort through to find what you're looking for. So, start out by being specific. Then, when you get 9,000 (or 9,000,000) results, get even more specific, and it won't be long before you have the information you need right at your fingertips.

There's one other thing you have to keep in mind during an Internet search: filters. If the computer (actually the browser) you're using for your search happens to have a filter enabled, *disable the beast while you're searching*. Some of these things are so literal that they'd block a web site on the UFO conspiracy, simply because "conspiracy" was on the site or in your search string. You can always reset the filter when you're done.

Finally, and this can't be said too many times where the internet is concerned — websites move, change their names and URLs and/or disappear at a rate approximating the multiplication and mass suicide of Lemmings. If your browser says it can't find the desired page, try a different search method. Maybe you can find the same site by sneaking in the back door. As far as that goes, try a different browser. Sometimes one browser works and another doesn't. And if a URL listed in the appendix doesn't work and you can't find them through any other search method, you still have two options. Either drop them a note by snail mail, or pick up a phone and call them. Just because they've vanished from the web doesn't mean they're not there. If they have a new site or their URL has changed, there's a good chance the search engine robots haven't found it yet.

APPENDIX A

Sci-Fi Model Spacecraft

SOURCE GUIDE

The following list of manufacturers and publishers is provided as an example of what is available. This list is by no means comprehensive. A complete listing would require a book all to itself. However, it does offer a starting point.

All firms listed produce quality products, stand behind their work, and the majority have been around for years. If you have a problem, give them a call, discuss the problem, and give them time to address it.

Do keep one other thing in mind. Most companies on this list have an Internet presence. I have provided the current URLs, but there is no guarantee that these URLs will be working by the time you read this. This is not the fault of the companies listed. Internet service providers change policies, merge, or simply vanish at an astonishing pace. So if one of the listed URL addresses fails to work, don't assume the company has vanished. Find them using an Internet search engine, pick up the phone, or drop a letter into snail mail.

Ambroid Company
61 Katie Lane
Swanzey, NH 03446
800-242-2794
http://www.ambroid.com
(glues and solvents)

Aztek Airbrush
620 Buckbee Street
Rockford, IL 61104
800-962-6654
http://www.testors.com
(airbrushes, compressors, and accessories)

Badger Airbrush
9128 W. Belmont Avenue
Franklin Park, IL 60131
1-800-AIR-BRUSH
http://www.badger-airbrush.com

Barney Robinson Hardwoods
2500 E. Lancaster
Ft. Worth, TX 76103
817-534-8901
(fine hardwoods)

Bob Smith Industries
8060 Morro Road
Atascadero, CA 93422
805-466-1717
http://www.bsiadhesives.com
(cyanoacrylates and epoxies)

Bondo/Mar-Hyde Corporation
4677 Devitt Drive
Cincinatti, OH 45246
513-874-5151
http://www.bondomarhyde.com/
(surfacing putties, fillers, paint, etc.)

Brad' s Stands
1409 Plum Tree Court
O'Fallon, IL 62269
http://www.mystands.com
Email: akbreger@earthlink.net

Custom Replicas
26711 N. Isabella Pkwy. Suite 103
Canyon Country, CA 91351-4889
http://www.customreplicas.com
Email: replicas@pacbell.net
(high-quality custom replicas)

Deft, Inc.
Irvine, CA 92614
Alliance, OH 44601
800-682-4372
http://www.deftfinishes.com
(quality wood finishes)

Donegan Optical Company
P.O. Box 14308
Lenexa, KS 66285-4308
913 492-2500
http://www.doneganoptical.com/
Email (general): info@doneganoptical.com
(Opti-Visor and visual aids)

Dremel
4915 21st Street
Racine, WI 53406
1-800-437-3635
http://www.dremel.com
(small power tools)

Dupli-Color Products Company
Cleveland, OH 44115
http://www.duplicolor.com
(automotive acrylic lacquer paint)

Excel Tools
481 Getty Avenue
Paterson, NJ 07503
800-845-2770
http://www.exceltools.net
(specialty tools)

Federation Models
P.O. Box 725165
Berkley, MI 48072-5165
248-540-7908 or 877-688-8537
http://www.federationmodels.com
Email: pl@federationmodels.com
(sci-fi resin-models and related products)

Floquil
620 Buckbee Street
Rockford, IL 61104
800-962-6654
http://www.testors.com
(paint and paintbrushes)

General Tools
80 White Street
New York, NY 10013-3567
212-431-6100
http://www.generaltools.com
Email: gentools@generaltools.com
(specialty tools)

Glencoe Models
176 Stiles Road
Boylston, MA 01505
1-508-869-6877
(Plastic kit manufacturer)

Half-Price Books
http://www.halfpricebooks.com/
Check your local directory for locations.
(publications of all kinds)

International Plastic Modelers' Society
P.O. Box 2475
North Canton, OH 44720-2475
330-478-3882
http://www.ipmsusa.org

John F. Green, Inc.
P.O. Box 55787
Riverside, CA 92517
909-684-5300 or 800-807-4759
http://www.greenmodels.com
(out-of-production or hard-to-find kits)

Krylon
Division of Sherwin Williams Company
Solon, OH 44139
http://www.krylon.com
(automotive acrylic lacquer paint)

Richard Marmo
416 Chicago
Ft. Worth, Texas 76103
817-536-0128
http://modelbuilding.freeyellow.com
(author/professional model builder)

Model Master
620 Buckbee Street
Rockford, IL 61104
800-962-6654
http://www.testors.com
(paint, tools, and accessories)

Monsters In Motion
181 W. Orangethorpe Avenue, Unit E
Placentia, CA 92870
714-577-8863
http://www.monstersinmotion.com
Email: cservice@monstersinmotion.com
(science-fiction and fantasy models of all kinds)

MyStands.com
1409 Plum Tree Court
O'Fallon, IL 62269
http://www.mystands.com
Email: akbreger@earthlink.net

Ott-Lite Technology
1214 West Cass Street
Tampa, FL 33606
800-842-8848
http://ott-lite.com/
(natural lighting products)

Polar Lights
3618 Grape Road
P.O. Box 388
Mishawaka IN 46545-2770
574-256-0300
http://www.polarlights.com
(plastic science-fiction kits)

ProWeb Fort Worth
P.O. Box 24242
Ft. Worth, TX 76124
817-534-0209
http://www.prowebfortworth.com
Email: proweb@cowtown.net
(electronic publishing and agent for Tony Weddel art)

Revell-Monogram, Inc.
8601 Waukegan Road
Morton Grove, IL 60053-2295
http://www.revell-monogram.com
(styrene model kits)

Rich Airbrushes
Salis International Inc.
4093 North 28th Way
Hollywood, Florida 33020
954-921-697
800-843-8293
http://www.docmartins.com/
(precision airbrushes)

Scale Model Technologies
www.smt.theshoppe.com
Email: smtemail@telusplanet.net
(resin science-fiction kits)

Scale Publications
416 Chicago
Ft. Worth, Texas 76103
817-536-0128
http://scalepublications.freeyellow.com
(how-to CD-ROM publications)

Sherline Tools
170 Navajo Street
San Marcos, CA 92069-3674
http://www.sherline.com
(precision bench-top lathes and accessories)

SilentAire Technology
711 Rutland
Houston, TX 77007
713-864-8994
(silent compressors)

Shopsmith, Inc.
6530 Poe Avenue
Dayton, OH 45414
Corporate phone: 937-898-6070
Sales and Service: 800-543-7586
http://www.shopsmith.com
(woodworking power tools)

Specialty Press
39966 Grand Avenue
North Branch, MN 55056
1-800-551-4754
(publisher of aviation and hobby books)

The Floyd A. Holes Company
Box 254
Ashland, OR 97520
Fax: (815) 425-0951
http://www.hotsplice.com/holes.html
(specialty knife)

The Squadron Shop
1115 Crowley Drive
Carrollton, Texas 75011-5010
972-242-8663
http://www.squadron.com
Email: mailorder@squadron.com
(mail-order hobby shop)

The Testor Corporation
620 Buckbee Street
Rockford, IL 61104
800-962-6654
http://www.testors.com
(styrene model kits, paint, and airbrushes)

The Tool Man
7621 Lake Highland Dr.
Ft. Worth, Texas 76179-2807
817-236-7609
http://www.hobbytools.com
Email: tools@hobbytools.com
Email: badger@hobbytools.com
(specialty tools)

The UFO Store
16235 SW Westwind Drive
Beaverton, Oregon 97007-2050
Fax/Order: 503-591-0980
http://www.theUFOstore.com
Email: randy@theUFOstore.com
(UFO-related products)

Tony Matelliano's Scale Model Index
http://scalemodelindex.com
Email: tonym@buffnet.net

Tony Weddel
May be contacted thru ProWeb Fort Worth or Richard Marmo
(Professional artist)

Woodland Scenics
P.O. Box 98
Linn Creek, MO 65052
(573) 346-5555
http://www.woodlandscenics.com/
sales@woodlandscenics.com
(scale-model scenic materials)

X-Acto
http://www.huntmfg.com/office/xacto/officeframe.html
(hobby knives and specialty tools)

Xuron Tools
60 Industrial Park Road
Saco, ME 04072
207-283-1401
http://www.xuron.com/
(specialty tools)

Zenith Books
P.O. Box 1
Osceola, WI 54020-0001
800-826-6600
http://www.motorbooks.com
(books)

How to Build Sci-Fi Model Spacecraft